100

Cross-curricular

Maths

Lessons

David & Penny Glover

Years 5&6

Scottish Primary 6–7

Authors
David Glover and Penny Glover

Editor
Lyn Imeson

Assistant Editor
David Sandford

Series Designer
Heather C Sanneh

Illustrations
Shirley Walker

Cover photography
© Martyn F Chillmaid

Text © Penny Glover and David Glover
© 2002 Scholastic Ltd

Designed using Adobe Pagemaker

Published by Scholastic Ltd, Villiers House,
Clarendon Avenue, Leamington Spa, Warwickshire CV32 5PR

Visit our website at www.scholastic.co.uk

Printed by Cromwell Press Ltd, Trowbridge

1 2 3 4 5 6 7 8 9 0   2 3 4 5 6 7 8 9 0 1

British Library Cataloguing-in-Publication Data A catalogue
record for this book is available from the British Library.

ISBN 0-439-98346-0

Acknowledgements
Extracts from the National Curriculum for England © Crown copyright
material is reproduced with the permission of the Controller of HMSO
and the Queen's Printer for Scotland.
Extracts from the National Numeracy Strategy *Framework For Teaching
Mathematics* © Crown copyright. Reproduced under the terms of HMSO
Guidance Note 8.

Contents

Year 6

Introduction

Few of us are pure mathematicians. Our mathematical skills are practical, not abstract. We use mathematics to compare prices as we shop, to make measurements for DIY projects and to follow recipes in the kitchen. Often, we are hardly aware of the maths skills we are using. However, children need to have the value and application of their mathematics skills in other school subjects, as well as everyday life, made clear. Such realistic contexts broaden and develop their mathematical understanding and skills. For this reason, the National Numeracy Strategy, National Curriculum, and Scottish National Guidelines on Mathematics 5–14, emphasise the importance of looking for links between mathematics and other curriculum areas.

The *100 Cross-curricular Maths Lessons* series presents lesson plans linking objectives from the National Numeracy Strategy to objectives in other subjects. The lessons are intended to take place during your numeracy time, but the mathematics is set in a cross-curricular context.

Each book in this series provides content for the daily maths lessons of two year groups. This book supports Years 5 and 6. The materials presented here can be used to substitute or supplement your daily maths lessons. The organisation of the mathematical objectives covered by the lesson plans follows the term-by-term sequence of topics set out in the National Numeracy Strategy's *Framework for Teaching Mathematics* (March 1999). Their content is also appropriate for, and adaptable to, the requirements of Primary 6–7 in Scottish schools. In Scotland, and in schools elsewhere that have decided not to adopt the National Numeracy Strategy, it will be necessary to choose activities to match your planning. To help you with this, reference grids listing the lessons' objectives are provided for each year group (see pages 10–2 and 92–4), together with a comprehensive index of maths topics and the cross-curricular content on pages 175 and 176.

These lesson plans offer ideal additional or alternative activities for the main teaching activities given in the lesson plans of *100 Maths Lessons: Year 5* or *Year 6*, also published by Scholastic.

In Year 5/Primary 6, children should be multiplying and dividing integers up to 10 000 by 10 or 100; ordering positive and negative integers; using decimal notation for tenths and hundredths; and relating simple fractions, decimal fractions and percentages. They should be able to do column addition and subtraction; short multiplication and division of a three-digit number by a single-digit number; use the formula for the area of a rectangle; recognise parallel and perpendicular lines and the properties of rectangles; and use all four operations to solve word problems involving quantities and time, explaining methods and reasoning. In Year 6/Primary 7, children should extend their knowledge of multiplication by 10, 100 and 1000 to decimal numbers; reduce a fraction to its simplest form by cancelling factors and use fractions as operators; find percentages of whole number quantities and solve problems involving ratio and proportion; extend their calculation skills to numbers involving decimals; use a protractor to measure angles to the nearest degree; calculate the areas and perimeters of shapes that can be split into rectangles and read and plot coordinates in all four quadrants; and solve problems by extracting and interpreting information presented in tables, charts and graphs.

The lessons in this book are planned to support this progression of mathematical knowledge and skills with activities designed to match the children's developing abilities. Each lesson presents a mathematical challenge in the context of work in another subject, thus developing the child's knowledge and skills in that subject area also.

Using this book

The materials

This book provides 50 cross-curricular maths lessons for Year 5 and 50 for Year 6. Each lesson plan sets out its numeracy objectives and objectives for another curriculum subject or subjects. The intention is that the mathematics is developed in a context that links strongly to another subject area, simultaneously fulfilling the linked subject objectives. Photocopiable activity sheets and assessment activities support the lesson plans for each term.

Organisation

This book follows the Year 5 and Year 6 topic plans given in the National Numeracy Strategy's *Framework for Teaching Mathematics*. Complete planning grids for both years are set out on pages 10–2 for Year 5 and 92–4 for Year 6.

An extract from the planning grid for Year 5 is reproduced opposite. Columns one and two list the National Numeracy Strategy unit numbers and topics. Column three gives the numeracy objective(s) to be met by the lesson plan. The cross-curricular objectives are set out in column four, together with links to relevant units in the QCA's primary schemes of work. The individual lesson titles, with brief descriptions of their content, are listed in column five.

Lesson plans

Each lesson plan contains the following sections:

Objectives

The numeracy and cross-curricular subject objectives are stated, together with links to relevant QCA schemes of work.

Resources

This lists resources required for the lesson.

Vocabulary

The vocabulary sections have drawn on the National Numeracy Strategy's *Mathematical Vocabulary* booklet. New or specific maths vocabulary to be used during the lesson is listed. Use this vocabulary with the whole class so that all the children have a chance to hear it in context and understand it. Encourage children to use the vocabulary orally, when asking or answering questions, so that they develop understanding of its mathematical meaning.

Background

Key maths strategies, skills or operations relevant to the specific lesson are outlined and the cross-curricular context is introduced. This section may provide useful information for the lesson, such as historical facts or science explanations.

Planning Grid

Term 1	Topics	Maths objectives	Cross-curricular objectives	Activities
Unit 1	Place value, ordering, rounding Using a calculator	Read whole numbers in figures and words and know what each digit represents. Order a set of integers less than 1 million. Use the vocabulary of comparing and ordering numbers.	**Geography** To recognise how places fit within a wider geographical context. To use secondary sources of information. Could link to Geography QCA Units 13: A contrasting UK locality and 20: Local traffic.	**p13: Populations** Compare and sequence populations of UK towns and cities
2–3	Understanding × and ÷ Mental calculation strategies (× and ÷) Pencil and paper procedures (× and ÷)	Read and write whole numbers in figures and words and know what each digit represents. Multiply and divide any positive integer up to 10 000 by 10 or 100 and understand the effect. Develop calculator skills and use a calculator effectively.	**ICT** Use a range of ICT tools. Create instructions to make things happen.	**p14: Big numbers** Paired games – enter large numbers on a calculator, round to the nearest 10, 100 or 1000
	Money and 'real-life' problems Making decisions and checking results, including using a calculator	Recognise multiples of 1, 2, 3, 4, 5, 6, 7, 8, 9 and 10, up to the 10th multiple. Identify numbers that are multiples of more than one number.	**ICT** Use a variety of ICT tools. Organise and reorganise text and tables.	**p15: Multiple grids** Use a computer-based 100-square grid to explore multiples of more than one number.
4–5	Fractions, decimals and percentages Ratio and proportion	Know by heart all multiplication facts up to 10 × 10 Derive quickly doubles of all whole numbers 1 to 100. Multiply by 4 by doubling and doubling again. Use units of time.	**Physical education** To be taught how exercise affects the body. **Science** To be taught that the heart acts as a pump to circulate the blood around the body. To be taught about the effect of exercise and rest on pulse rate. Links to QCA Science Unit 5A: Keeping healthy.	**p16: Feel the pulse** Use multiplication to calculate pulse rate from timings over 10s, 15s...
6	Handling data Using a calculator	Use all four operations to solve simple word problems. Solve a problem by interpreting data in a table.	**History** To study changes at that have taken place in Britain since 1930. Links to QCA History Unit 13: How has life in Britain changed since 1948?	**p17: Cost of living** Answer questions based on changes in the cost of living since 1948.
		Use all four operations to solve word problems involving numbers and quantities based on 'real	**English** To talk effectively as members of the group.	**p18: Tell a story** Make up number stories to [...] ents involving four operations.

Preparation
Preparation needed in advance of the lesson is highlighted – for example, assembling materials, making resources and photocopying activity sheets.

Main teaching activity
This explains what the teacher should do in the whole-class teaching session, lasting about 30 minutes. In some lessons, much of the time will be spent in whole-class interactive teaching. In others, the whole-class session will be shorter, with practical or paper-based activities provided for groups, pairs or individuals.

Differentiation
This section suggests adaptations and extensions to the main teaching activity in order to meet the needs of less able and more able children within your class.

Plenary
This is an opportunity to bring the children back together for a concluding whole-class session. It offers opportunities to review and reinforce key ideas, compare strategies and outcomes, develop the cross-curricular links and assess the children's progress.

Planning and organisation
These lesson plans do *not* form a self-contained mathematics course. Rather, they are designed to be integrated into your overall scheme of work for mathematics and, more generally, to be linked to your plans for other subject areas. The planning grids on pages 10–2 and 92–4 are the best starting point for deciding how these lessons can be incorporated into your teaching.

Assessment
Three termly assessment activity sheets, together with supporting notes (including practical assessment opportunities) are included with each year's lesson plans. These can be incorporated into your assessment strategy for mathematics.

The assessment activity sheets are designed to introduce children to the style of questions found in the national tests. They are set in cross-curricular contexts drawn from the preceding term's lessons. Three activities are included on each assessment sheet. It is not essential for the children to have had experience of these particular contexts, but it is important that they are comfortable with using their maths in a variety of less obviously mathematical situations. More able children will probably complete the exercises with minimal guidance. Most children, however, will need considerable support the first few times they tackle this type of activity.

Practical assessment tasks are also of great value in making a judgement of a child's progress, particularly for less able children who find formal paper and pencil activities demanding. A suggestion for a practical assessment task has been included in each assessment lesson. Set selected children to complete the practical task while the rest of the class work on the paper-based activities. Review the answers as a class. Collect the completed activity sheets and make notes on your observations of the practical work to use as an aid to judging individual children's progress and to include in your records.

Resources

Photocopiable sheets

These sheets support individual lessons, and may be freely copied for distribution to your class. Some sheets serve as more general resources that have applications in more than one lesson (for example, ordinal numbers, days of the week, months and seasons). These sheets can be copied onto or backed with thin card before cutting up. They may be laminated to produce more durable resources.

Classroom equipment

All the equipment used in this book will normally be found within any primary school. The following list gives items that will be needed on a regular basis:

- A flipchart and marker pens (and/or a whiteboard or chalkboard)
- Counting apparatus (such as counters, sorting toys, wooden cubes, beads and laces)
- Measuring apparatus, including cm rules, tape measures, measuring jugs, classroom balance and thermometers
- Craft or technology materials and tools – scissors, glue, adhesive tape, card, dowel, modelling clay, construction kits with gears and pulleys and so on
- Shape apparatus, including shape tiles and 3-D shapes
- Safety mirrors
- Art materials
- Coins, real and plastic
- Demonstration analogue and digital clock faces
- Recyclable materials, including card boxes and plastic containers
- PE apparatus, including stop watches, bean bags, hoops and balls
- Wall maps of the World, Europe, UK and the local environment
- A globe
- Musical instruments.

ICT

A number of the activities are computer based. These activities require a computer program with text, table and drawing capabilities such as *Textease* (Softease Ltd) or *Microsoft Word*. There are many equivalent programs in use that allow children to enter and edit text, and to create and manipulate geometrical shapes on the same page. Use a program with which you are familiar, and check that you can produce the desired outcome with confidence before setting children to work on the activity. These activities will be greatly enhanced if the computer is connected to a printer on which the children can print their work for subsequent discussion and display.

100
Cross-curricular
Maths
Lessons

**Lesson plans and
photocopiable
activity pages**

**Year
5**

Term 1	Topics	Maths objectives	Cross-curricular objectives	Activities
Unit 1	Place value, ordering, rounding Using a calculator	Read whole numbers in figures and words and know what each digit represents. Order a set of integers less than 1 million. Use the vocabulary of comparing and ordering numbers.	**Geography** To recognise how places fit within a wider geographical context. To use secondary sources of information. Could link to Geography QCA Units 13: A contrasting UK locality and 20: Local traffic.	**p13: Populations** Compare and sequence populations of UK towns and cities
2–3	Understanding × and ÷ Mental calculation strategies (× and ÷) Pencil and paper procedures (× and ÷)	Read and write whole numbers in figures and words and know what each digit represents. Multiply and divide any positive integer up to 10 000 by 10 or 100 and understand the effect. Develop calculator skills and use a calculator effectively.	**ICT** Use a range of ICT tools. Create instructions to make things happen.	**p14: Big numbers** Paired games – enter large numbers on a calculator, round to the nearest 10, 100 or 1000
	Money and 'real-life' problems Making decisions and checking results, including using a calculator	Recognise multiples of 1, 2, 3, 4, 5, 6, 7, 8, 9 and 10, up to the 10th multiple. Identify numbers that are multiples of more than one number.	**ICT** Use a variety of ICT tools. Organise and reorganise text and tables.	**p15: Multiple grids** Use a computer-based 100-square grid to explore multiples of more than one number.
4–5	Fractions, decimals and percentages Ratio and proportion	Know by heart all multiplication facts up to 10 × 10 Derive quickly doubles of all whole numbers 1 to 100. Multiply by 4 by doubling and doubling again. Use units of time.	**Physical education** To be taught how exercise affects the body. **Science** To be taught that the heart acts as a pump to circulate the blood around the body. To be taught about the effect of exercise and rest on pulse rate. Links to QCA Science Unit 5A: Keeping healthy.	**p16: Feel the pulse** Use multiplication to calculate pulse rate from timings over 10s, 15s...
6	Handling data Using a calculator	Use all four operations to solve simple word problems. Solve a problem by interpreting data in a table.	**History** To study changes that have taken place in Britain since 1930. Links to QCA History Unit 13: How has life in Britain changed since 1948? **English** To talk effectively as members of the group.	**p17: Cost of living** Answer questions based on changes in the cost of living since 1948. **p18: Tell a story** Make up number stories to reflect statements involving all four operations.
		Use all four operations to solve word problems involving numbers and quantities based on 'real life', money and measures. Explain methods and reasoning.		
		Begin to understand percentage as the number of parts in every 100. Solve simple problems using ideas of ratio and proportion.	**Geography** To record and analyse evidence. Links to QCA Geography Unit 20: Local traffic.	**p19: What percentage?** Interpret data from a traffic survey of 100 vehicles.
		Solve a problem by representing and interpreting data in tables. Find the mode and range of a set of data.	**Physical education** To perform actions and skills with increasing control and quality. Links to QCA Physical Education 27: Net/wall games.	**p20: Record scores** Interpret and make calculations based on a table of scores.
		Estimate by approximating then check result. Develop calculator skills and use a calculator effectively. Make simple conversions of pounds to foreign currency.	**Geography** To study a range of places in different parts of the world. Links to QCA Geography Unit 18: Connecting ourselves to the world.	**p21: Holiday money** Use a calculator to make foreign exchange calculations.
7	Assess and review			**See p29.**
8–10	Shape and space Reasoning about shapes Measures, including problems	Make shapes with increasing accuracy. Visualise 3-D shapes from 2-D drawings and identify different nets for an open cube.	**Art and design** To learn about materials and processes used in crafts and design. Links to QCA Art and Design Unit 5B: Containers. **Design and technology** To evaluate a range of familiar products.	**p22: Making boxes** Explore nets for making open boxes.
11	Mental calculation strategies (+ and −) Pencil and paper procedures (+ and −) Money and 'real-life' problems Making decisions and checking results, including using a calculator	Understand and use angle measure in degrees. Identify, estimate and order acute and obtuse angles. Use a protractor to measure and draw acute and obtuse angles to the nearest five degrees. Calculate angles in a straight line.	**History** To study beliefs and achievements in ancient Greece. Links to QCA in History Unit 15: How do we use ancient Greek ideas today?	**p23: Find the angle** Introduce angular measure in the context of Euclid.
		Read the time on a 24-hour digital clock and use 24-hour clock notation, such as 19:53.	**ICT** To learn how to create sequences of instructions to make things happen. Links to QCA ICT Unit 5E: Controlling devices	**p24: Set the timer** Program heating controls, video recorders and other 24-hour timers (worksheet simulation).
12	Properties of numbers Reasoning about numbers	To find differences by counting up through the next multiple of 10 000 or 1000, for example to calculate mentally a difference such as 8006 − 2993. Use all four operations to solve simple word problems involving numbers and quantities. Interpret data in tables.	**Geography** To study water and its effects on people. Links to QCA Geography Unit 11: Water	**p25: Paying for water** Make calculations and estimates based on water bills.
		Find simple percentages of small whole number quantities (eg 25% of £8). Express one half, one quarter, three-quarters, tenths and hundredths as percentages (eg know that $^3/_4$ = 75%).	**Geography** To study characteristics of localities, for example their local high street. Could be linked to QCA Geography Unit 12: Should the high street be closed to traffic?.	**p26: Sale price** Work with percentages in the context of discounts.
		Develop calculator skills and use a calculator effectively. Recognise and extend number sequences formed by counting from any number in steps of constant size, extending beyond zero when counting back. Know squares of numbers to at least 10 × 10.	**ICT** To use a range of ICT tools to create instructions to make things happen.	**p27: Calculator fun** Use a calculator to explore number sequences and other properties.
		Make in words and investigate a general statement about familiar numbers or shapes by finding examples of that satisfy it. Explain a generalised relationship in words.	**English** To write instructional texts and test them out.	**p28: How do you?** Give specific oral examples of general statements about numbers.
13	Assess and review			**p29: Assessment 1**

YEAR 5

Term 2	Topics	Maths objectives	Cross-curricular objectives	Activities
1	Place value, ordering, rounding Using a calculator Understanding × and ÷ Mental calculation strategies (× and ÷)	Use the vocabulary of estimation and approximation; make and justify estimates of large numbers, and estimate simple proportions. Order a set of integers less than 1 million on a number line.	**History** Use dates and vocabulary relating to the passing of time.	**p30: Millennium line** Place events on an undivided millennium time line.
2–3	Pencil and paper procedures (× and ÷) Money and 'real-life' problems	Read and write whole numbers in figures and know what each digit represents. Know and apply tests of divisibility by 2, 4, 5, 10 or 100.	**Literacy** To write instructional texts and test them out.	**p31: Making numbers** Devise and write rules for a place value number game.
		Use the vocabulary of estimation and approximation. Develop calculator skills and use a calculator effectively. Know imperial units (pint, gallon).	**History** To study changes that have taken place in Britain since 1930. Links to QCA History Unit 13: How has life in Britain changed since 1948? Could also be linked to QCA Art and Design Unit 5B: Containers	**p32: How much does it hold?** Estimate – then use a calculator to make calculations based on the capacities of containers. Round appropriately.
	Making decisions and checking results, including using a calculator	Know by heart all multiplication facts up to 10 × 10. Find factors of numbers to 100.	**ICT** Work with others to explore a variety of ICT tools. Links to QCA ICT Unit 5A: Graphical modelling.	**p33: Seating plans** Use object-based computer program to arrange seats in arrays. Relate to factors of numbers to 100.
4 5	Fractions, decimals and percentages Using a calculator	Use all four operations to solve simple word problems involving numbers and quantities using one or more steps. Use and write standard metric units including litres. Know imperial units (mile, gallon).	**English** To talk effectively as members of a group. To consider alternatives and draw others into reaching agreement.	**p34: Petrol prices** Answer story problems based on petrol prices and journeys.
	Shape and space Reasoning about shapes	Solve a problem by representing and interpreting data in tables, including those generated by a computer. Use, read and write standard metric units. Solve simple problems using ideas of ratio and proportion.	**ICT** Work together to explore a variety of ICT tools. Looks forward to QCA ICT Unit 6B: Spreadsheet modelling. **Design and technology** Undertake design and make assignments using materials including food. Links to Design and Technology Units 5B: Bread and 5D: Biscuits.	**p35: Recipe spreadsheets** Program a spreadsheet to calculate costs and quantities for a biscuit recipe.
		Express one half, one quarter, three-quarters, and tenths as percentages. Discuss the chance or likelihood of particular events.	**Geography** To learn to analyse evidence and draw conclusions. To develop decision-making skills. Links to QCA Geography Unit 16: What's in the news?	**p36: Will it rain tomorrow?** Interpret simple weather forecasts in which the chance of rain is given as a percentage probability.
		Measure and draw lines to the nearest mm. Understand, measure and calculate perimeters of rectangles and regular polygons. Complete symmetrical patterns with two lines of symmetry at right angles. Recognise reflective symmetry. Recognise where a shape will be after reflection. Recognise where a shape will be after translation.	**Design and technology** To measure, mark out and assemble components and materials accurately.	**p37: Pinboard** Make a pinboard. Use it to explore shape rotations, translations and reflections.
		Solve mathematical problems or puzzles, recognise and explain patterns and relationships. Make shapes with increasing accuracy. Identify multiples of 5.	**Design and technology** To undertake design and make assignments using a range of materials including sheet materials. Measure and cut materials accurately.	**p38: Pentomino puzzles** Design and make a pentomino puzzle.
6	Assess and review			See p47.
7–8	Measures, including problems Handling data	Relate fractions to their decimal representations. Use division to find fractions of quantities. Develop calculator skills. Measure lengths to the nearest mm.	**History** To study beliefs and achievements in ancient Greece. Links to QCA History Unit 15: How do we use ancient Greek ideas today? **Music** To study how music is produced in different ways. Links to QCA Music Unit 18: Journey into space.	**p39: Musical measures** Measure and investigate the spacing between frets on a guitar to the nearest mm. Discuss Pythagoras.
9–10	Mental calculation strategies (+ and −) Pencil and paper procedures (+ and −)	Solve a problem by interpreting data in line graphs, including those where intermediate points have meaning.	**Science** To learn about the stages in the human life cycle.	**p40: Height graph** Evaluate data for a height against age graph.
	Money and 'real-life' problems Making decisions and checking results, including using a calculator	Solve a problem by interpreting data in tables. Find the mode of a set of data.	**Design and technology** Evaluate a range of familiar products – thinking about how they are used. Looks forward to QCA Design and Technology Unit 6B: Slippers.	**p41: Shoe sizes** Use a shoe size survey to explore range and mode of a data set.
11	Properties of numbers Reasoning about numbers	Add several numbers mentally (strings of single digits or multiples of 10). Solve mathematical problems or puzzles.	**Physical education** Take part in outdoor activity challenges, including following trails in familiar environments. Links to QCA Physical Education 30: Outdoor and adventurous activities.	**p42: Treasure hunt** Take part in an orienteering 'treasure hunt' activity, gaining and losing points by visiting stations and answering questions.
		Use all four operations to solve problems involving numbers and quantities, based on money and measures.	**Geography** Analyse evidence and draw conclusions. Collect and record evidence. Could link to QCA Geography Units 12: Should the high street be closed to traffic? and 20: Local traffic.	**p43: Price wars** Compare prices in different stores.
		Know squares of numbers to at least 10 × 10.	**ICT** Work together to use a variety of ICT tools. Links to QCA ICT Unit 5A: Graphical modelling.	**p44: Square numbers** Use a spreadsheet to generate square numbers. Relate to area of a square.
		Discuss the chance or likelihood of particular events. Solve a problem by interpreting data in tables. When generalising, explain methods and reasoning about numbers orally and in writing.	**Science** To learn about the effects on the human body of tobacco and how these relate to their personal health.	**p45: Smoking kills!** Interpret simple statistics on smoking and health.
		Use informal pencil and paper methods to support, record or explain additions/ subtractions/ multiplications/divisions.	**English** Speak audibly and clearly, using spoken Standard English in formal contexts. Use vocabulary and syntax that enables communication of more complex meanings.	**p46: Explain yourself** Give oral/written explanations of mental calculation strategies.
Unit 12	Assess and review			**p47: Assessment 2**

Planning Grid

Term 3	Topics	Maths objectives	Cross-curricular objectives	Activities
1	Place value, ordering, rounding	Order a set of integers less than one million. Order a given set of positive and negative integers.	**Science** To learn that the Sun, Earth and Moon are approximately spherical. That the Earth orbits the Sun once each year.	**p48: The planets** Interpret data on the planets, sequencing in ascending/descending order.
2–3	Using a calculator		**ICT** To interpret information. Links to QCA ICT Unit 5B: Analysing data and asking questions using complex searches.	
	Understanding × and ÷			
	Mental calculation strategies (× and ÷)	Multiply and divide whole numbers, then decimals, by 10, 100 or 1000.	**Literacy** To collect, define and spell technical words derived from work in other subjects.	**p49: Ten times more** Make patterns of words and numbers using calculator/spreadsheet to explore repeated multiplication by ten.
	Pencil and paper procedures (× and ÷)		**ICT** Work together to use a variety of ICT tools.	
	Money and 'real-life' problems	Know and apply tests of divisibility by 4. Use the vocabulary and units of time.	**Science** Know that the Earth orbits the Sun once each year. Links to QCA Science Unit 5E: Earth, Sun and Moon.	**p50: Leap years** Use division by 4 to check if a year is a leap year.
4–5 6	Making decisions and checking results, including using a calculator	Use the relationship between multiplication and division. Recognise patterns and relationships. Use multiplication and division to solve simple word problems involving numbers and quantities.	**English** To use writing to help their thinking and learning. To write for other children.	**p51: What's the connection?** Write alternative story problems expressing alternative facts derived from $a \times b = c$.
	Fractions, decimals and percentages			
	Ratio and proportion Handling data	Solve mathematical problems and puzzles. Use units of time. Record data in tables.	**Physical education** Take part in and design challenges that call for precision and speed. Pace themselves in challenges and competitions. Links to QCA Physical Education Unit 29: Athletic activities.	**p52: Relay race** Plan and test the best strategy for a relay race: fast short legs, or slower longer ones?
	Using a calculator	Measure lines to nearest mm. Use fraction notation. Use ideas of ratio and proportion.	**History** To study beliefs and achievements in ancient Greece. Links to QCA History Unit 15: How do we use ancient Greek ideas today?	**p53: Golden rectangles** Use a ruler and calculator to investigate the proportions of rectangles including cinema and TV screens and buildings.
		Solve a problem by interpreting data from graphs, including those generated by a computer.	**Science** Make systematic observations and measurement, including the use of ICT.

ICT To use ICT to monitor events and environmental changes. Links to QCA ICT Unit 5F: Monitoring environmental conditions and changes. | **p54: Classroom sensors** Interpret line graphs of temperature, light and sound levels recorded through the day in a classroom. |
		Make and justify estimates of large numbers, and estimate simple proportions such as $\frac{1}{3}$ and $\frac{7}{10}$.	**Science** Make systematic observations and measurements. Identify locally occurring animals. Builds towards QCA Science Unit 6A: Interdependence and adaptation.	**p55: What fraction?** Estimate large numbers and simple proportions.
7	Assess and review			**See p62.**
8–10	Shape and space	Understand area measured in square centimetres (cm²). Understand and use the formula in words 'length × breadth' for the area of a rectangle. Understand, and calculate perimeters of rectangles.	**ICT** Work together to explore a variety of ICT tools. Builds towards QCA ICT Unit 6B: Spreadsheet modelling.	**p56: Area and perimeter** Program a spreadsheet to calculate the area and the perimeter of rectangles of any size.
	Reasoning about shapes			
	Measures, including problems	Visualise 3-D shapes from 2-D drawings.	**Design and technology** Communicate design ideas in different ways.	**p57: Unfinished buildings.** Interpret 2-D diagrams of 3-D shapes.
11	Mental calculation strategies (+ and −)		**Art and design** Be taught about visual elements including form and space.	
	Pencil and paper procedures (+ and −)	Relate fractions to their decimal representations. Use division to find fractions of quantities. Develop calculator skills. Measure lengths to the nearest mm.	**History** To study beliefs and achievements in ancient Greece. Links to QCA History Unit 15 How do we use ancient Greek ideas today?	**p58: Wind chimes** Explore relationship between length and pitch, ratio, concord and discord, in relationship to making simple wind chimes.
	Money and 'real-life' problems			
	Making decisions and checking results, including using a calculator	Suggest suitable measuring equipment, recording estimates and readings from scales to a suitable degree of accuracy.	**Science** To learn how to change the pitch and loudness of sounds made by some vibrating objects. Links to QCA Science Unit 5F Also links to QCA Design and Technology Unit 5A	**p59: Making allowances** Read between divisions on a scale to say how much a reading has changed (temperature, weight etc.).
12	Properties of numbers		**Science** To make systematic observations and measurements.	
	Reasoning about numbers			
		Choose and use appropriate number operations to solve problems. Add several numbers. Develop calculator skills and use a calculator effectively.	**Geography** To use maps at a range of scales. To study localities at a range of scales.	**p60: Missing map** Use a calculator to explore missing number problems set in the context of distance and area recorded on a map.
		Use the vocabulary of estimation and approximation. Make and justify estimates of large numbers. Develop calculator skills and use a calculator effectively.	**Science** To be taught about life processes common to humans and other animals. Could be linked to QCA Science Unit 5A: Keeping healthy.	**p61: Human numbers** Use a calculator to estimate the number of times your heart beats in a day. The number of times you blink in a week. The number of times you stand up and sit down in a year…
13	Assess and review			**p62: Assessment 3**

100 CROSS-CURRICULAR MATHS LESSONS Years 5 & 6/Scottish Primary 6–7

Populations

Objectives

Numeracy
Read whole numbers in figures and words and know what each digit represents.
Order a set of integers less than 1 million.
Use the vocabulary of comparing and ordering numbers.

Geography
To recognise how places fit within a wider geographical context.
To use secondary sources of information.
Could link to Geography QCA Units 13: A contrasting UK locality and 20: Local traffic.

Resources

A copy of photocopiable page 63 for each child; a map of the local environment (this could be a county map showing towns and villages, or a city map showing districts and boroughs); research materials for locating population data, such as county guides or access to the Internet (UK population data can be searched and sequenced at *www.neighbourhood.statistics.gov.uk*).

Vocabulary

hundred thousand
million
greatest, most, biggest
least, fewest, smallest
ascending, descending

Background

The populations of communities in the UK vary from tens or hundreds in small rural hamlets and villages to hundreds of thousands, or even millions, in cities. Reading and comparing population figures for different communities in a region develops children's appreciation of the relative sizes of numbers to one million and beyond. Constructing a table of population data for the local region develops their local geographical knowledge.

Preparation

Make and distribute copies of the worksheet. Assemble research materials for use in the classroom. Display the map.

Main teaching activity

Introduce the lesson with a geographical discussion of the communities in which the children live. Do they live in a village, town or city? Which part of the town or city do they live in? What are the characteristics of these different communities? When does a village become a town, and a town become a city? How many people live in the children's communities? Is it tens, hundreds, thousands, tens of thousands…? Which is the biggest community in the region? Which is the next biggest? What are their populations?

Develop the lesson by setting the children to work through the activities on the worksheet. The population figures listed are for selected communities in the West Midlands. You could produce your own version of the worksheet in advance of the lesson based on your local region, alternatively children can research similar data for the local region once they have completed the worksheet supplied. Children should answer the questions, comparing and sequencing the population data as indicated.

Differentiation

Make sure that less able children can read and translate the population figures into words, for example 76 700 is read as 'seventy-six thousand seven hundred'. Help them to complete the sequencing and comparison activities.

When more able children have completed the basic task, set them to use the research materials to compile a similar table of data for communities in the locality. They should identify population centres on the map and use the research resources to find population figures.

Plenary

Review the worksheet as a class, asking children to take turns to read aloud one population figure and compare it with another. Have the children compiled information about local population centres? Which is the biggest city in the region? What are the names of large towns? Which are the biggest villages? The answers are: **1.** eighty-seven thousand eight hundred, **2.** three hundred and eleven thousand five hundred, **3.** one million thirteen thousand four hundred, **4.** see table.

city/town	population
Redditch	76 700
Bromsgrove	85 200
Rugby	87 800
Lichfield	94 100
Warwick	123 800
Solihull	205 600
Wolverhampton	241 600
Walsall	261 200
Coventry	304 300
Dudley	311 500
Birmingham	1013 400

2 Big numbers

Background

By Year 5/Primary 6, children begin to use calculators to support work in mathematics. As with other ICT tools, using a calculator effectively requires children to key in data and use the function keys carefully and systematically. Children should take time to develop good 'calculator habits', estimating results in advance of performing calculations and checking them by repetition. To develop children's knowledge of ICT tools and resources, you could show them how to use the on-screen calculator available in Windows (in the *Start* menu).

Preparation

Distribute the calculators. Set up the demonstration calculator.

Main teaching activity

In the first part of the lesson, children should each have a calculator with which they can reproduce the keystrokes you make on the demonstration calculator. Start the lesson by discussing the layout of the calculator keys. Identify the number keys, the decimal point, the four principal function keys +, −, ×, ÷ and the clear 'C' key. Ask the children for a number between 1 and 10, enter it and tell them that you are going to use the calculator to multiply by 10. Explain the importance of predicting or estimating answers in advance of making calculations 'in case you press the wrong key by mistake and get a silly answer'. Ask them to predict the answer, then perform the calculation, saying the name of each key as you press it: '5 × 10 = 50'. Ask

the children to reproduce the calculation on their calculators as you talk it through again. Develop the procedure by asking for numbers between 10 and 100 and multiplying them by 10 and then by 100.

Set the children to work in pairs on the following activity. The first person enters a number between 10 and 100, then passes the calculator to their partner. Without showing what they do, the partner multiplies the number by 10, 100 or 1000 and passes the calculator back. The first person reads the new number out loud. Can they say what their partner did to the starting number? They explain how they know. Their partner should say if they are right or wrong. Then the partner enters a starting number.

Differentiation

Less able children should concentrate on entering numbers between 10 and 100 and multiplying them by 10 or 100.

More able children can enter numbers between 1 and 1000 and multiply or divide them by 10, 100 or 1000.

Plenary

Ask selected children to use the demonstration calculator to work quickly through further examples in front of the class. Can they make general statements about the effect of multiplying by 10 and 100 on the number on the calculator display?
● 'Multiplying by 10 shifts all the figures one place to the left and puts a zero in the units column.'
● 'Multiplying by 100 shifts all the figures two places to the left and puts zeros in the units and tens columns.'

Can any children make statements about the effect of division by 10 and 100?

3 Multiple grids

Numeracy
Recognise multiples of 1, 2, 3, 4, 5, 6, 7, 8, 9 and 10, up to the 10th multiple.
Identify numbers that are multiples of more than one number.
ICT
Use a variety of ICT tools.
Organise and reorganise text and tables.

Computers running software with table/ spreadsheet capabilities, for example *Microsoft Word*, *Microsoft Excel* or *Textease*; printers and paper; a large 100-square grid for display.

count
multiple
grid
cell
column
row

Background

A 100-square grid is a valuable resource for identifying and exploring patterns created by multiples of numbers to 10. Grids are readily reproduced by photocopying, however the production of a grid from scratch on the computer is an informative and enjoyable activity in which children can develop ICT skills as they work with numbers.

Preparation

Set up the computers running your chosen software package and check that you can use it confidently to produce a 10 × 10 array of cells. This can be achieved in a number of ways, for example by creating a table with ten rows and ten columns, generating a spreadsheet with ten rows and columns, or by copying and pasting text boxes repeatedly. In *Microsoft Word*, text separated by tab characters can be converted into a table by highlighting it, then selecting 'Convert Text to Table' from the *Table* menu. This is a valuable technique that children could explore in this activity.

Main teaching activity

Introduce the lesson with some times-table practice supported by the enlarged 100-square grid. Point to the numbers on the grid as you recite the tables. Remind the children that the numbers you are identifying are described as multiples of the times-table number you are reciting.

Explain that the children are going to make their own number grids on the computers and use them to identify patterns of multiples. Set the children to work in small groups with the software package to produce their initial grids. Demonstrate how to select a cell and change its background colour. Ask different groups of children to choose a number from 2 to 10 and to select and colour the cells of a grid to identify multiples of their number.

Differentiation

Set less able children the basic task of identifying the multiples of a single integer on one grid and printing it off.

More able children can combine multiples of two numbers on a single grid. They should select different colours for the multiples of the two numbers and a distinct third colour to mark numbers that are multiples of both numbers.

1	2	3	4	5	6	7	8	9	10
11	12	13	14	15	16	17	18	19	20
21	22	23	24	25	26	27	28	29	30
31	32	33	34	35	36	37	38	39	40
41	42	43	44	45	46	47	48	49	50
51	52	53	54	55	56	57	58	59	60
61	62	63	64	65	66	67	68	69	70
71	72	73	74	75	76	77	78	79	80
81	82	83	84	85	86	87	88	89	90
91	92	93	94	95	96	97	98	99	100

	multiples of 4
	multiples of 5
	multiples of 4 and 5

Plenary

As a class, look at the grids children have produced and discuss the ICT techniques they used to generate them. Make a display of the grids that various groups have produced.

Linked to
P E
S c i e n c e

4 Feel the pulse

Objectives

Numeracy
Know by heart all multiplication facts up to
10 × 10.
Derive quickly doubles of all whole numbers
1 to 100.
Multiply by 4 by doubling and doubling again.
Use units of time.
Physical education
To be taught how exercise affects the body.
Science
To be taught that the heart acts as a pump
to circulate the blood around the body. To
be taught about the effect of exercise and
rest on pulse rate.
**Links to QCA Science Unit 5A: Keeping
healthy.**

Resources

A large display clock with a second hand;
notebooks and pencils; the hall/playing field
for PE activities.

Vocabulary

second
minute
multiply
double
mental calculation

Background

As part of their
work in PE and
science, children
should explore
the effect of
exercise and
rest on their
heart rate by
locating and
measuring their
pulse. Pulse rate
is generally
quoted in beats
per minute. It is
measured by
using two fingers
to locate the pulse in
the wrist and counting
the beats in a fixed
time. When you are
taking someone else's
pulse, you should use
fingers rather than a
thumb or you may
mistakenly count your
own pulse. In this
lesson, children
measure and record
their pulse rate during activities in a PE
lesson, making mental multiplications to find
the number of beats in a minute.

the children how
to find their pulse
in their wrists.
Explain how to
record pulse rate
by counting the
number of beats in
one minute. Set
the children to
record their
'resting' pulse rate.
Proceed to
discuss the
advantages and
disadvantages of
counting for a full
minute. A minute
seems a long time to count, but you get an
accurate result. What if your pulse is
changing rapidly during the minute, for
example as you cool down after a race?
Perhaps counting for a shorter time would
be more accurate in this case. Suggest that
the children count their pulse for 15
seconds and multiply the number of beats
by 4. What is a quick way to multiply by 4 in
your head? (Double and double again.) Is
the result the same as counting for a full
minute? Discuss alternative measurement
times. What factors must you multiply by if
you measure for 10, 20 or 30 seconds?

When the children can find their pulse
and measure it by counting for 15 seconds,
set them to investigate how their pulse
changes during various activities. Warm up
gently with some jogging or skipping, then
measure and record pulse rates. Run some
short races. What are the children's pulse
rates immediately after the race? What are
they one minute or two minutes later? Why
do they gradually slow down? (**Safety:**
children should engage only in normal PE
activities; warn them that it is dangerous to
try to work 'extra hard' to raise their pulse
rate beyond normal levels.)

Preparation
Prepare for a PE lesson according to your
normal practice. Set up a clock with a second
hand where children can use it to time pulse
rate during activities.

Main teaching activity
Take the children, with notebooks and
pencils, into the hall or outside for a PE
lesson.

Introduce the lesson by talking about the
heart and exercise. Explain that when you
exercise hard, your heart must beat more
quickly to pump more blood through your
muscles. The blood carries the oxygen and
fuel that supply energy to the muscles. Show

Differentiation
Less able children should concentrate on
finding their pulse and making and recording

a measurement before and after taking exercise.

Challenge more able children to record their pulse rate in a table every minute for five or more minutes after exercising. How does their pulse rate change? Can they use the data to draw a graph?

Plenary

Discuss the techniques the children developed for measuring pulse rate. Did they find that measuring for 15 seconds was accurate? Discuss their observations of pulse rate. By how much did their pulse rate increase during exercise? Did it double?

Linked to
H i s t o r y

Objectives

Numeracy
Use all four operations to solve simple word problems.
Solve a problem by interpreting data in a table.
History
To study changes that have taken place in Britain since 1930.
Links to QCA History Unit 13: How has life in Britain changed since 1948?

Resources

A copy of photocopiable page 64 for each child; calculators.

Vocabulary

money
price
cost
pound
pence
more
less

5 Cost of living

Background

Children will be familiar from family discussions that the 'cost of living' has risen over time. Grandparents will talk about buying a loaf of bread for the equivalent of 10p or a bar of chocolate for 5p. Prices have risen over time, but so have incomes. In this activity, children compare prices and wages in 1948 with those in 2002. How has the cost of living changed? Are we better or worse off than people were in 1948?

Preparation

Copy and distribute the worksheets to groups. This lesson could build on previous history lessons in which you have looked at life in the 1940s, for example by watching the Channel 4 programme *The 1940s House*.

Main teaching activity

Introduce the lesson with a discussion of prices. Are prices always the same in the supermarket? Do they go up or down? How do the prices of food and other commodities in the 1940s compare with those today? What do parents and grandparents say about price changes over the years?

Develop the lesson by showing the children the worksheet. Explain that it lists prices 'then and now' for various items. Prices in 1948 are given in pounds, shillings and pence, with the equivalent decimal pounds and pence. The table also gives average weekly wages.

Set the children to work in pairs or small groups to answer the questions on the worksheet. These should lead them to conclusions about the ways in which the cost of living has changed.

Differentiation

Less able children should concentrate on making the basic calculations to complete the final column of the table.

More able children should write a brief account comparing the relative prices of different items then and now.

Plenary

Discuss the children's answers to the worksheet problems as a class. What is their opinion? How have living costs and standards changed? Things were 'cheaper' 50 years ago, but were they more or less 'affordable' for the average family? The answers are: Chocolate bar 20, Fish and chips 50, Loaf of bread 30, Television set 6, Car 30, House 100, Train journey 100, Weekly wages 50. The answers to the questions will vary, and should be discussed.

Linked to
L i t e r a c y

 Tell a story

Objectives

Numeracy
Use all four operations to solve word problems involving numbers and quantities based on 'real life', money and measures. Explain methods and reasoning.
English
To talk effectively as members of the group.

Resources

A list of calculations for each group. These can be taken from photocopiable page 65 which gives four sets of increasingly difficult problems. Alternatively, you can produce lists of calculations yourself, tailored to the ability of your groups. Pencils, paper and calculators; a pack of 'context' cards for each group, listing settings for their story problems. These could include: money, length, containers, weight.

Vocabulary

story problem
addition
subtraction
multiplication
division
answer
calculation

Background

In this activity, children write and answer 'real-life' story problems using all four operations. They collaborate in small groups to write story problems set in a variety of contexts to illustrate a list of calculations. They should use their speaking and listening skills to agree a format for each problem. Groups then exchange and answer problems, and mark each other's solutions.

Preparation

Copy and distribute photocopiable page 65 and the calculators, pencils and paper on tables in preparation for group work. Make a set of context cards for each group.

Main teaching activity

Introduce the activity to the class by writing an example on the board, such as
$24.9 \div 3 = 8.3$

Explain that the challenge is to write a story problem to illustrate the calculation, but the story must be set in the context stated on the card you draw from the pack of context cards. Draw a card from the pack and ask the children to help you compose a suitable story. Repeat for some alternative contexts, for example:

Money – Three children made a train journey. Altogether their tickets cost £24.90. What was the price of each ticket?

Length – Shane cut a 24.9cm length of string into three equal parts. How long was each part?

Containers – Laura needed three buckets of water to fill a fish tank. The tank held 24.9 litres. What was the capacity of the bucket?

Set the children to work in groups on the composition exercise. They should pick a context card at random for each calculation, and suggest and discuss alternative story problems. Explain that they should consider whether or not their suggested stories are realistic. For example, it would not be realistic to write problems in which a pencil costs £10 or a person weighs 2kg. When the group has agreed on a realistic problem, they should record it in writing. Finally, groups should exchange problems and solve each others' problems.

Differentiation

Less able children should be given simpler calculations to work with, for example a problem from the worksheet.

Challenge more able children to create story problems with two or more steps, for example to illustrate the problems in Set 4 on the worksheet.

Plenary

Ask representatives from groups to read out problems that they particularly enjoyed solving. Discuss whether all the problems are realistic, or if some of them give answers that could not be true in the real world? The answers are:
Set 1: 21, 16, 56, 5
Set 2: 96, 40, 72, 3
Set 3: 6773, 212, 494, 80.5
Set 4: 149.4, 31.8, 290.4, 16.826

Linked to
Geography

7 What percentage?

Objectives

Numeracy
Begin to understand percentage as the number of parts in every 100.
Solve simple problems using ideas of ratio and proportion.
Geography
To record and analyse evidence.
Links to QCA Geography Unit 20: Local traffic.

Resources

A copy of photocopiable page 66 for each child; a blank 10 × 10 grid for each child; felt-tipped pens; flip chart or board.

Vocabulary

percentage
fraction

Background

Percentage is a widely used method of representing proportions and fractional quantities. Per cent means 'per hundred', thus 1 per cent is a proportion of 1 per hundred or a fraction of $^1/_{100}$. For example, when we say that 1% of the tickets in a lottery are prize-winners, we mean that a proportion of 1 in every 100 tickets wins a prize. When we say that 25% of a wall has been painted, we mean that a fraction of $^{25}/_{100} = ^1/_4$ of the painting is complete. The results of surveys are frequently quoted in percentage terms, but take care: '25% of respondents liked' could mean 1 person out of the 4 an advertiser bothered to ask! In this lesson, children interpret the table of data from a traffic survey of 100 vehicles to develop their understanding of percentages. The activity could be linked to work in geography on doing a local traffic survey.

Preparation

Copy and distribute page 66 and the blank grid. Draw a 10 × 10 grid on the flip chart.

Main teaching activity

Introduce the lesson with a discussion of the meaning of percentage. Use the grid on the flip chart to explain that per cent means 'per hundred'. Ask how many grid squares there are in the grid (100). Colour 1 square and ask what fraction of the grid is coloured ($^1/_{100}$). Introduce the percentage notation and vocabulary, colouring squares as you do so: $^1/_{100} = 1\%$, $^2/_{100} = 2\%$ and so on.

Ask the children to colour various percentages of their grids in different ways, for example: 10% red, 25% green, 50% blue. Use their completed grids to introduce the link between percentages and fractions:
10% red = $^{10}/_{100} = ^1/_{10}$
25% green = $^{25}/_{100} = ^1/_4$
50% blue = $^{50}/_{100} = ^1/_2$

When the children have completed the grid activity, set them to work in pairs or small groups on the worksheet.

Differentiation

Less able children should concentrate on the first survey, which requires them to calculate percentages of 100.

More able children should complete the remaining tables, which require them to calculate percentages of 200 and 50. Explain that 1% of 200 = 2, since 1 per 100 is equivalent to 2 per 200. In other words, $^1/_{100} = ^2/_{200}$. What is 10% of 50?

Plenary

Review the worksheet answers with the whole class. Explain how to check calculations by confirming that the figures in the percentage column add to 100%. Conclude with some rapid questions in which children must state 1%, 10%, 25% and 50% of small whole-number quantities. For example: *What is 1%, 10%, 50% of £1? What is 50% of 4m?*
The answers are:

Town survey

vehicle type	number	percentage
car	40	40%
lorry	15	15%
bus	5	5%
bicycle	20	20%
motorcycle	19	19%
tractor	1	1%

City survey

vehicle type	number	percentage
car	100	50%
lorry	20	10%
bus	10	5%
bicycle	50	25%
motorcycle	20	10%
tractor	0	0%

Village survey

vehicle type	number	percentage
car	20	40%
lorry	5	10%
bus	2	4%
bicycle	10	20%
motorcycle	8	16%
tractor	5	10%

Linked to

P E

8 Record scores

Objectives

Numeracy
Solve a problem by representing and interpreting data in tables.
Find the mode and range of a set of data.

Physical education
To perform actions and skills with increasing control and quality.

Links to QCA Physical Education 27: Net/wall games.

Resources

Bats and balls, paper and pencils; a copy of the class list of children's names for each child.

Vocabulary

data
mode
range
table

Background

The mode is the most frequent or common number in a data set, it is one measure of the 'average' or typical value for the data. The range is the difference between the highest and lowest value. This tells us about the spread or distribution of the data. If the range is small, the data are consistent, having similar values. If the range is large then there is a considerable difference between the highest and lowest value. In this lesson, children collect data in a PE activity in which they count their 'record' for bouncing a ball on a bat or striking a ball against a wall. These activities help develop the hand–eye co-ordination required for 'striking' games.

name	ball bouncing best scores
Bhumika	9
Simon	12
Laura	14
Pran	9
Shane	8
Chloe	12
Ali	9
Zoe	8

Preparation

Prepare for a PE lesson according to your normal practice. Set out bats and balls for children to use. Copy and distribute the class lists on tables in preparation for the second part of the lesson.

Main teaching activity

Take the children into the hall or outside for a PE activity. Demonstrate how to keep a ball aloft by bouncing it repeatedly on a bat, and how to play 'tennis' against a wall. Give the children several minutes to practise each activity. They should count the number of repetitions they achieve and write down their 'record' scores.

Return to the classroom for the second part of the lesson. Ask the children to report their best scores and, as they do so, compile a table for the whole class similar to the sample above.

When the tables are complete, ask the children to find the most common score for ball bouncing. Explain that this is called the mode. What is the mode for wall tennis? By comparing your best score to the mode you can judge if you need to practise to improve your skills to the level of others in the class.

Ask the children to find the highest and lowest scores for each activity. What is the difference between highest and lowest? Explain that this difference is called the range. What is the range of the bouncing scores? What is the range of the wall tennis scores? The range tells you the difference between the most and least skilled in the class. If the range is small, children have similar skills. If it is large, some children have better skills in this activity than others.

Differentiation

Less able children should concentrate on the basic activities of identifying the mode and range of the scores.

More able children could transfer the data from the tables to the computer and plot bar charts. How can they identify the mode and the range from their charts?

Plenary

Conclude the lesson with a discussion of other investigations the children might undertake to investigate mode and range, for example shoe sizes, pocket money, or distance travelled to school. Children could carry out some of these investigations in a follow-up lesson.

9 Holiday money

Objectives

Numeracy
Estimate by approximating then check result.
Develop calculator skills and use a calculator effectively.
Make simple conversions of pounds to foreign currency.

Geography
To study a range of places in different parts of the world.
Links to QCA Geography Unit 18: Connecting ourselves to the world.

Resources

Flip chart or board, calculators, pencils and paper; examples of foreign currency, if available.

Vocabulary

exchange
estimate
check

Background

Many children make overseas trips for holidays or to visit relatives. On a trip abroad, they will become aware that they purchase things using a different currency. When we shop abroad, we are constantly making mental calculations as we exchange money and compare prices with prices at home. In this lesson, children take the first step towards proficiency with foreign exchange calculations. They convert pounds into euros or rupees, first estimating mentally the amount of currency they should receive for their offered number of pounds, then confirming the calculation with a calculator. The activity links to geographical discussions of the children's experiences of visiting locations around the world.

Preparation

Set out calculators, paper and pencils in preparation for group work. If possible, collect some examples of foreign currency from colleagues/parents for the class to look at.

Main teaching activity

Introduce the lesson with a discussion of overseas trips the children have made. Where have they been on holiday? Where have they been to visit relatives? What were the currencies in the countries visited? How did they change their spending money into the local currency? What was the exchange rate? How did prices compare with prices at home? Did they have a quick method of estimating relative prices – for example, 70 rupees are about a pound so 7 rupees are 10 pence?

Develop the lesson by explaining that children are to make some foreign exchange calculations for trips to Spain and India. Write a table of exchange rates similar to the one below on the board. Explain that the children must imagine they are going into a bank or travel agent to exchange their spending money. Before they hand over the money, they should estimate how much currency they should receive in exchange. Discuss how to make estimates by rounding appropriately. For example, £22 exchanged for euros can be estimated as shown here, since £1 = €1.6, £10 = €16 and £20 =

currency	£1 buys
Euro	€1.63
Indian rupee	69.4Rs
US dollar	$1.44

€32, so £22 = €32 + €3.2 = €35.2. The calculator shows that the exact amount at the current exchange rate is €35.86.

Write a list of exchange calculations on the board, such as: £10 into euros, £10 into rupees, £100 into euros, £15 into euros, £20 into rupees. Set the children to work in pairs or small groups to make the calculations.

Differentiation

Less able children should concentrate on estimating exchanges involving whole numbers of pounds. Emphasise how the exchange for £10 or £100 can be made easily by shifting the decimal point appropriately in the exchange rate.

More able children can make more complicated exchanges involving pounds and pence. Discuss with them the significance of the bank/agent's commission. Suggest that they include a 2% commission in their calculations. How does this affect the money they receive?

Plenary

Review the children's answers to the questions you set. Conclude the lesson with some rapid mental exchange calculations. Check the responses with a calculator.

10 Making boxes

Objectives

Numeracy
Make shapes with increasing accuracy.
Visualise 3-D shapes from 2-D drawings and identify different nets for an open cube.
Art and design
To learn about materials and processes used in crafts and design.
Links to QCA Art and Design Unit 5B: Containers.
Design and technology
To evaluate a range of familiar products.

Resources

Cardboard boxes to take apart with the children; sheets of card, adhesive tape, square templates, scissors; a flip chart or board.

Vocabulary

cube
net
plane
solid
2-D
3-D

Background

In surveys of the most significant inventions in history, two prime candidates for the number one spot are the wheel and the pot or container. Ancient civilisations have flourished without the wheel, notably in Africa and the Americas, but no civilisation has managed without pots and other containers. Arguably therefore the container should be top of the list. Containers make an excellent subject for projects in design and art, where children can look at both function and aesthetic qualities in terms of materials and design.

The cardboard box is the ubiquitous modern container. It is manufactured by folding a flat sheet, and a study of the shapes, or 'nets', that will or will not fold to make an open box makes a good practical maths lesson.

Preparation

Assemble the craft materials and set them out on tables in preparation for practical work.

Main teaching activity

Introduce the lesson by taking apart some cardboard boxes in front of the class to see how they are constructed. Show how an open box is folded from a single flat sheet divided into five separate panels – the base and the four sides. Additional flaps and panels give the completed box strength, but do not form part of its basic shape.

Explain that the children's challenge is to make a single sheet that will fold into an open cube with a base and four sides. Sketch two nets on the board from those shown below. Explain that the first net will fold into a cube, but the second will not. Can the children discover any other nets that make cubes?

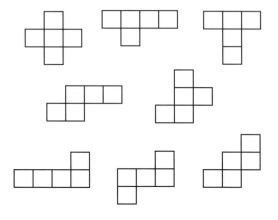

These nets fold to make open cubes.

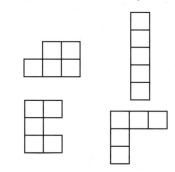

These nets do not fold to make open cubes.

Set the children to work in pairs or small groups to sketch nets using the square templates. They should then cut out their nets to see if they will make cubes by folding and taping along the joins.

Differentiation

Less able children can reproduce the nets you've drawn on the board and perhaps find one other net.

Challenge more able children to find the eight different nets that make a cube (all of which are shown above).

Plenary

Ask the children to sketch the nets they have discovered on the board and to demonstrate the folded cubes. Have they discovered all the possible nets?

Linked to
History

11 Find the angle

Objectives

Numeracy
Understand and use angles measured in degrees.
Identify, estimate and order acute and obtuse angles.
Use a protractor to measure and draw acute and obtuse angles to the nearest five degrees.
Calculate angles in a straight line.

History
To study beliefs and achievements in ancient Greece.
Links to QCA History Unit 15: How do we use ancient Greek ideas today?

Resources

A copy of photocopiable page 67 for each child; protractors and pencils, a large demonstration protractor, a flip chart or board.

Vocabulary

angle
degree
protractor
acute
obtuse

Background

The Greek philosopher and mathematician Euclid (c 300BC) discovered and taught the mathematics of angles, lines and triangles that we learn in schools today. Euclid can be introduced to children in the context of historical work on ideas and discoveries. Some of Euclid's ideas that will stimulate children's thinking about mathematics include: the definition of a line as something which has length but no width; a point as the crossing of two lines which has a location but no size; parallel lines as lines which only meet at infinity. In this lesson, children use a protractor to measure the angles between lines that cross. They identify acute and obtuse angles, and measure the angle (180°) on a straight line.

Preparation

Copy and distribute the worksheets with pencils and protractors.

Main teaching activity

Introduce the lesson by talking about Euclid and his work. Explain that Euclid was a great philosopher and mathematician who lived in ancient Greece. He discovered the principles of geometry: the maths of lines, angles and shapes. His discoveries are still important today, for example in architecture, navigation and astronomy. In today's maths lessons, we learn the same ideas about angles and triangles taught by Euclid to his pupils more than 2000 years ago.

Develop the lesson by drawing a straight line and discussing Euclid's definition of a line. Draw a second line at an angle to the first and say that the lines meet at a point. Mark and discuss the angle between them. Remind the children that angle is a measure of turn: if they imagine the two lines as the hands of a clock, the angle between them is a measure of how much one hand must turn to point in the same direction as the other. Introduce the protractor and show how it is used to measure an angle in degrees.

Develop the vocabulary of acute and obtuse angles with examples. Finally, consider the angles on a straight line – see below. Explain that the angles on a straight line always add to 180°.

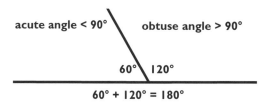

acute angle < 90°   obtuse angle > 90°

60°   120°

60° + 120° = 180°

Set the children to work in pairs or small groups on the worksheet. They should measure the angles, label them as acute or obtuse and confirm that they total 180°.

Differentiation

Less able children should work on the first three examples, which involve angle pairs.

More able children can progress to the final example in which they measure three angles. If time allows you could set them some examples involving angles in a circle. They should recognise that angles in a circle total 360°.

90° 90°
120° 60°

90° + 90° + 60° +
120° = 360°

Plenary

Review the children's answers to the worksheet. Finish with some rapid mental calculations using addition and subtraction to find unknown angles. The answers are: 60° (acute), 120° (obtuse); 135° (obtuse), 45° (acute); 30° (acute), 150° (obtuse); 30° (acute), 60° (acute), 90° (right angle).

12 Set the timer

Objectives

Numeracy
Read the time on a 24-hour digital clock and use 24-hour clock notation, such as 19:53.

ICT
To learn how to create sequences of instructions to make things happen.
Links to QCA ICT Unit 5E: Controlling devices.

Resources

An example of a programmable device (for example, a digital alarm clock, a programmable 13-amp plug timer); a copy of photocopiable page 68 for each child; a demonstration 24-hour digital clock.

Vocabulary

12-hour clock
24-hour clock
digital
hour
minute
am
pm

Background

Programmable devices such as central heating systems, video cassette recorders, alarm clock radios, microwave ovens and security lamps are increasingly common. Many of these devices make use of the 24-hour clock to program time settings on a digital display. Successful programming of such devices requires users to key in commands and numbers in the correct sequence, checking that the information on the display confirms their intentions. This is essentially the same process as programming a computer to control a robot or similar device. This activity develops these basic ICT skills and understanding of 24-hour clock notation.

Preparation

Copy and distribute the worksheets. Make sure that you can program your demonstration devices confidently!

Main teaching activity

Use the 24-hour digital clock to introduce the 24-hour clock to the children. Ask them for examples of places where they have seen this type of display, for example on railway departure and arrival boards. Discuss the reasons for using the 24-hour clock (it avoids confusion between morning and afternoon times). Proceed to discuss conversions between 24-hour and 12-hour clock times. With examples, lead the children to spot the pattern that the 24-hour clock time after noon is the 12-hour clock time plus 12. For

example, 5:00pm = 17:00; 19:30 = 7:30pm.

Develop the lesson by demonstrating your programmable devices. Discuss how they use the 24-hour clock to turn off and on automatically at times you have programmed. Ask children about devices in their homes that can be programmed.

Set the children to work in pairs or small groups on the worksheet activity. They should fill in the 24-hour clock times where indicated to 'program' the devices to turn on or off at appropriate times.

Differentiation

Less able children should concentrate on the basic activity. Help them to decide at what times of day the different devices should operate.

Challenge more able children to program the demonstration devices you have provided. Can they set the alarm clock to go off at the end of the lesson?

Plenary

Review the children's answers to the worksheet problems. Are their time settings appropriate? Conclude the lesson with some rapid mental 24-hour to 12-hour clock conversions and vice versa.

Linked to
Geography

13 Paying for water

Background

Our use of gas, water and electricity is metered and charged for by the utility company. We need to apply our mathematical skills to check bills and compare our consumption from one quarter to the next. Interpreting a water bill, for example, involves finding the difference between the current meter reading and the previous reading; multiplying this figure by the cost per cubic metre of the water supplied and adding the standing charges to find the total charged for the period. In this lesson, children discuss and interpret water bills for various households.

Preparation

Copy and distribute the worksheets together with the calculators. The lesson should build on previous lessons in which you have developed mental strategies for finding differences such as 8006 – 2993. Children should also be able to use calculators to multiply.

Main teaching activity

Introduce the lesson with a discussion of water supply. Where does our water come from? What happens to it when it goes down the drain? Is the water from the tap free? Some children may not be aware that their parents must pay regular bills for water. Discuss the reasons why water companies must charge for water – they must maintain the supply pipes and treat water from reservoirs and rivers to make sure it is safe

to drink; they must also treat sewage at sewage works before returning water to the rivers.

Develop the lesson by showing the children some sample water bills. Explain that water is metered as it is supplied to most of our homes (if possible, show the children the school water meter). All new homes now have water meters installed; some older homes may not have water meters, and will be charged a fixed rate for water depending on the size of the house. Discuss how water is measured and charged for. The meter measures the water used in cubic metres. Use a metre stick to demonstrate the size of a cubic metre; explain that one cubic metre is equal to 1000 litres. The standing charge is a fixed charge for being connected to the water supply, which is independent of the quantity of water used.

Set the children to work in pairs to complete the water bills on the worksheet. They should start by estimating the bills mentally, then use calculators to fill in the missing numbers to find an accurate total. How good are their estimates?

Differentiation

Less able children may find the initial estimates difficult. They could concentrate on the calculator activity.

Challenge more able children to use the figures to draw conclusions about the different households' use of water. How much water does each household use per day? How many bathfuls of water is this equivalent to?

Plenary

Review the worksheet answers as a class. Discuss water conservation. Why should we not be wasteful with water? What can we do to 'save' water?

The answers are: **House 2** – cubic metres used 300; amount £150.00; total bill £385; **House 3** – cubic metres used 50; amount £25.00; total bill £72.50.

14 Sale price

Objectives

Numeracy
Find simple percentages of small whole-number quantities (for example, 25% of £8). Express one half, one quarter, three-quarters, tenths and hundredths as percentages (for example, know that $^3/_4$ = 75%).

Geography
To study characteristics of localities, for example their local high street.

Could be linked to QCA Geography Unit 12: Should the high street be closed to traffic?

Resources

A copy of photocopiable page 70 for each child, calculators.

Vocabulary

percentage
discount
fraction

Background

Seasonal sales are a feature of the shops in most high streets. New year sales, spring, summer and winter sales are marketing tactics to dispose of the remaining season's stock in preparation for new fashions for the coming season. Closing down sales and old stock sales are also frequently seen. Sale prices are usually advertised in terms of a percentage reduction on the original price, reduced by 10%, 20%, 25%, 50%, 75% and so on. But how much are you saving? In this lesson, children talk about the cycle of high street sales in relation to the types of shop in the local high street. They develop their knowledge of percentages by making some sale price calculations.

Preparation

Copy and distribute the worksheets.

Main teaching activity

Introduce the lesson with a discussion of the different types of shop in the local high street. What goods do they sell? Which shops are doing well? Which seem to do less well? Which shops hold sales? Are there special sales at different times of year?

Develop the lesson by discussing sale prices. How are prices normally advertised in a sale? Remind the children about percentages, and write a table similar to the one below on the board.

reduction	new price
10%	$^9/_{10}$ of original price
20%	$^4/_5$ of original price
25%	$^3/_4$ of original price
50%	half price
75%	$^1/_4$ of original price

Set the children to work in pairs or small groups on the worksheet activity. With the help of their calculators they should fill in the missing original and sale prices, and the percentage reductions.

Differentiation

Less able children should concentrate on the missing sale price problems.

More able children can progress to the missing original price and percentage problems. Challenge them to calculate prices for all the items in the sale given a final 'everything must go' reduction of 75%.

Plenary

Review the worksheet answers as a class. Conclude the lesson with some rapid percentage reduction calculations, for example £20 reduced by 25%.

The answers are: £5, £15, £10, £40, 50%, 20%, £4, £35, £100.

Linked to
I C T

15 Calculator fun

Objectives

Numeracy
Develop calculator skills and use a calculator effectively.
Recognise and extend number sequences formed by counting from any number in steps of constant size, extending beyond zero when counting back.
Know squares of numbers to at least 10 × 10.
ICT
To use a range of ICT tools to create instructions to make things happen.

Resources

Calculators with memory functions (memory in MIN and memory recall MR buttons); pencils and paper, a demonstration calculator.

Vocabulary

sequence
calculator
memory function

Background

The calculator is a powerful tool for exploring number sequences. By using the memory function, sequences generated by repeated addition, subtraction, multiplication or division can be explored rapidly and accurately. Other ICT devices, including floor robots and computers, store numbers in 'memory' locations in the same way. Using the memory function of the calculator introduces children to the process of storing and recalling data.

Preparation

Set out pencils, paper and calculators in preparation for paired work.

Main teaching activity

Introduce the lesson by using the demonstration calculator to show how to store a number in memory then recall it to the display. Enter a number on the keypad and press the MIN key. Clear the display and press the MR key. The number will be recalled from memory. Let the children practise this sequence for themselves.

Develop the lesson by explaining that you are going to use the memory button to explore number sequences.

Enter a number in the calculator's memory as above, for example 10.
Display shows 10
Clear the display.
Display shows 0
Enter a starting number, for example 25.
Display shows 25
*Press the + key.

*Press MR.
*Display shows
10*
*Press =.
*Display shows
35*

Repeat the starred steps to generate the sequence 25, 35, 45, 55...

Let the children practise this procedure with the same starting numbers, then proceed to experiment with different starting numbers, operations and step sizes to generate sequences such as:
8, 5, 2, –1, –4...
2.6, 2.8, 3.0, 3.2,...
190, 160, 130...

When the children can generate number sequences confidently using the calculator, set them to work in pairs on a calculator game. They should take it in turns to use the calculator to generate a number sequence, writing down the result. Their partner should then try to reproduce the sequence on their calculator.

Differentiation

Less able children should concentrate on working with sequences generated by addition and subtraction of a constant factor.

Challenge more able children to investigate what happens when they repeatedly multiply or divide by a constant factor. Does it make a difference if the constant is less than or more than 1?

Plenary

Conclude the lesson with a discussion of some of the number sequences the children have discovered. What happens when you generate a sequence by subtraction and the numbers become less than zero? What happens if you generate a number too big to fit on the calculator display?

16 How do you?

Objectives

Numeracy
Make in words and investigate a general statement about familiar numbers or shapes by finding examples that satisfy it. Explain a generalised relationship in words.
English
To write instructional texts and test them out.

Resources

A copy of photocopiable page 71 for each child; paper and pencils.

Vocabulary

calculate
problem
solution
method
strategy
how did you work it out?

Background

In real-life mathematics, we often decide how to make a calculation by recalling examples of similar calculations we have made at some point in the past. We generalise the process so that it can be applied to the new situation. For example, when presented with a shop sign saying '25% off' we recall that 25% is $1/4$ and generalise the calculation of the new price as follows: divide the original price by 4 to find $1/4$, subtract the result from the original price to find the new price. In this lesson, children use their developing language skills to make and explain generalised calculation procedures for a variety of real-life problems. In Year 6/Primary 7, they will begin to use symbols to express a generalised relationship.

Preparation

Copy the worksheet and distribute it with paper and pencils in preparation for group work.

Main teaching activity

Introduce the lesson with some simple 'how do you?' mathematical questions. For example: *How do you find the area of a rectangle; how do you calculate a 50% discount; how do you calculate the number of hours in any number of days?* Encourage selected children to answer questions clearly, checking that the other members of the class understand. Ask for specific examples of each of the calculations.

Explain that the children's task for the lesson is to write simple instructions saying how to make a variety of mathematical

calculations. The required calculations are listed on the worksheet. Set the children to work in groups on the task.

Differentiation

Less able children should concentrate on problems 1 to 4. Encourage them first to talk through their 'how to' methods until they all agree that they understand the procedure and that it is correct. They should then write out their methods with examples.

Challenge more able children to complete all the problems. The last three are particularly challenging.

Plenary

Ask representatives of the groups to read out their 'how to' suggestions. Ask the class to offer specific examples to illustrate each of the methods.

17 Assessment 1

Objectives

The assessment activities in this book are designed to introduce Key Stage 2 children to SAT-style questions. They are set in cross-curricular contexts based on the preceding term's lessons. The questions in Assessment 1 test the children's progress in: sequencing numbers to 1 million; recognising a percentage as the 'number per hundred'; measuring lengths to the nearest millimetre and angles to the nearest degree.

Resources

A copy of photocopiable page 71 for each child; pencils, rulers, protractors; three demonstration analogue clock faces.

Preparation

Make copies of the assessment sheet. If you feel that the sheet is too 'busy', the three activities could be separated and enlarged on individual sheets.

Lesson introduction

Begin the assessment lesson by reviewing the relevant cross-curricular topics covered during the term. Remind the children of some of the projects and investigations they have undertaken, and ask them to recall and recount their work. Emphasise the mathematical content, for example: *Do you remember how we compared the populations of nearby towns and cities?*

Main assessment activity

Distribute the worksheets and ask the children to work on them individually. Guide the whole class through the questions one at a time, reading the text with them and prompting them to work out and fill in their answers. Try to make the whole activity enjoyable!

Practical activity

Ask the children to set an acute angle, an obtuse angle and an angle of 180° between the hands on the clock face. Can they estimate the acute and obtuse angles with the help of a protractor?

Plenary

Review the answers to the questions as a class. Collect the completed question sheets to use as an aid to judging individual children's progress, and to include in your records. The answers are:

1.

city/town	population
Newcastle-upon-Tyne	292 300
Sunderland	276 100
Gateshead	198 900
Middlesbrough	145 100
Darlington	101 400
Durham	90 300
Sedgefield	89 300
Alnwick	31 400

2.

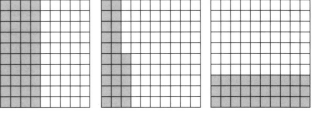

3. 100mm, 80mm, 60mm, 90°, 53°, 37°

Linked to
History

18 Millennium line

Background

Estimating the position of a number on an undivided number line requires children to develop mental strategies for subdividing the line. For example, to mark 1750 on an undivided 1000 to 2000 line, you must recognise that 1750 is three-quarters of the way from 1000 to 2000. The line can then mentally be divided into quarters and the position of 1750 located. To estimate the position of an arrow on the line, you might mentally divide the line into 10 equal parts and judge the position of the arrow against these subdivisions. In this lesson, children talk about these and similar strategies they use for positioning or estimating the location of numbers on an undivided line. They then apply the strategies to estimating the years of significant events in the past millennium from an unlabelled timeline.

Preparation

Copy and distribute the worksheets. Make a collection of suitable history reference materials for researching dates in the millennium AD1000 to AD2000.

Main teaching activity

Introduce the lesson by drawing an undivided 1000 to 2000 number line on the board. Mark an arrow one quarter of the way along the line and ask the children to estimate the number it points to (1250).

Ask the children to describe the strategies they used to make their estimate. Did they see the two portions of the line as fractions? Did they mentally subdivide the line into quarters or tenths? Continue the process by marking several more arrows for the children to estimate. Develop the lesson by asking individual children to come out and mark given numbers on the line. Do the rest of the class think they are correct?

Set the children to work in small groups on the worksheet activity. They should use estimation skills to deduce the years of the significant events marked on the timeline. Once they have made their estimates, they should check them using the history reference materials provided and make corrections where necessary.

Differentiation

Less able children could be given an undivided 1 to 100 number line and some simple estimation problems based on it, to begin to develop their estimation skills.

Challenge more able children to create a worksheet similar to the one provided for the millennium 1000BC to 1BC or AD1 to AD1000 for their friends to solve.

Plenary

Review the worksheet answers. Ask the children to discuss which years they found it easy to estimate. Which years are more difficult to locate? The answers are: 1066, 1215, 1349, 1415, 1588, 1605, 1666, 1837, 1940.

Linked to
Literacy

19 Making numbers

Objectives

Numeracy
Read and write whole numbers in figures and know what each digit represents. Know and apply tests of divisibility by 2, 4, 5, 10 or 100.
Literacy
To write instructional texts and test them out.

Resources

Packs of single-digit number cards 0 to 9; packs of plain cards for writing instructions, pens and paper, a flip chart or board.

Vocabulary

place value
largest
smallest
divisible
divisibility

Background

By Year 5/Primary 6, children's concept of place value should be well established. They should be able to read a number such as 3 528 631 as 'three million, five hundred and twenty-eight thousand, six hundred and thirty-one' and explain that the value of the digits increases by ×10 as you move one place from right to left. In this lesson, children use their understanding of place value and their language skills to devise and write instructions or rules for simple number games. The games may also include tests of the children's knowledge of other number properties, for example divisibility by 2, 4, 5, 10 or 100.

Preparation

Distribute the number cards and other materials in preparation for group work. Prepare instruction cards, of the form 'make the largest possible number', 'make the smallest possible number', 'make the largest number divisible by 4' and so on. Each instruction card carries a number of points.

Main teaching activity

Start with some 'make a number' problems. For example, use the digits 3, 0, 5, 9, 2, 0, 8 to make the largest possible 7-figure number, the smallest possible 7-figure number, the largest number divisible by 100, the smallest number divisible by 5, and so on. You may need to remind the children about tests of divisibility by 2, 4, 5, 10 or 100:
● A number is divisible by 2 if the last digit is even.
● A number is divisible by 4 if the last two digits are divisible by 4.
● A number is divisible by 5 if the last digit is zero or five.
● A number is divisible by 10 if the last digit is zero.
● A number is divisible by 100 if the last two digits are 00.

Explain that the children are going to devise a new version of a number game based on 'make a number' problems. Outline the rules of your game as follows.
1. Play in pairs. Shuffle a pack of number cards and deal out five cards each.
2. Player 1 picks a card from the top of a set of 'make a number' instruction cards (which you have prepared).
3. Player 1 sets out their cards according to the instruction. Player 2 checks the number. If it fits the instruction correctly, player 1 scores a point. If Player 2 can rearrange the cards, for example to make a bigger number, they score a point instead.
4. If a player has to pass, because he or she has no 0 or 5 to make a number divisible by 5 for example, no points are scored and the player may change his or her cards.
5. Players take turns to select and follow instruction cards until one player reaches an agreed winning points total.

Let the children play this game together a few times in pairs. Then ask them to devise their own version of the game and write instruction cards. They should ask other pairs to test their game to make sure the rules work and are clearly expressed.

Differentiation

Less able children should make and play a version of the basic game outlined above.

Encourage more able children to use their imagination to develop the game, perhaps by selecting more number cards and including a wider range of instructions.

Plenary

Ask selected pairs to describe and demonstrate the games they have devised. They should read their rules to the class. Are they clearly expressed and easy to follow?

Linked to
History

20 How much does it hold?

Objectives

Numeracy
Use the vocabulary of estimation and approximation.
Develop calculator skills and use a calculator effectively.
Know imperial units (pint, gallon).
History
To study changes that have taken place in Britain since 1930.
Links to QCA History Unit 13: How has life in Britain changed since 1948?
Could also be linked to QCA Art and Design Unit 5B: Containers.

Resources

If possible, make a collection of vintage containers for demonstration (for example, pint milk bottles, a gallon petrol can, a quart jug). Alternatively, find pictures in fiction and non-fiction texts with historical settings, showing petrol pumps, grocery shops and other locations where liquids were sold in imperial units. You will also need a 1-litre measuring jug or cylinder, calculators, paper and pencils, a copy of photocopiable page 74 for each child, a water bowl.

Vocabulary

capacity
litre
pint
gallon
conversion

Background

Petrol, cooking oil, milk in cartons and other liquids are now sold in metric units – by the litre. However, pints and gallons are still in use, for example the pint milk bottle and pint and half-pint drinks in bars. Children will frequently encounter imperial units in fiction and non-fiction texts concerned with the past, for example petrol was sold by the gallon until the 1980s. They should know the rough equivalents of pints, gallons and litres. These conversions can be used as the basis for some estimation and calculator activities. In this lesson, they are introduced in a historical context in relation to 'old' measures.

Preparation

Collect together resources for demonstration. Copy and distribute the worksheet with calculators, pencils and paper in preparation for group work.

Main teaching activity

Introduce the lesson with a brief discussion of historical measures. What measures do we use today for length, weight and capacity? Do the children know what measures were used 50 years ago when their grandparents were children? Mention the imperial units yards, feet, inches, pounds, ounces, pints and gallons. Ask the children to give examples where these units are still commonly used,

for example pint milk bottles and the birth weight of babies. Explain that in today's lesson you are going to focus on pints and gallons and try to answer the questions: *How big is a pint, How big is a gallon,* and *How do they compare to a litre?*

If possible, show the children pint and gallon containers. Compare them to the 1-litre measuring jug. Ask the children to estimate how many pints make a litre and how many litres make a gallon. Pour water between the containers to check the children's estimates.

By class experiment, establish the following equivalents:

1 pint is just over ½ litre (0.5l)
1 litre is about 1¾ pints
1 gallon is about 4½ litres (4.5l)
1 gallon = 8 pints

In the second part of the lesson, set the children to answer the questions on the worksheet. They should first make and write down estimates as indicated, then make an accurate calculation with the help of a calculator.

Differentiation

Less able children will probably need help initially to make the conversions with a calculator. Show them how to enter a capacity in imperial units and multiply or divide by the appropriate factor to find the equivalent capacity in litres.

Challenge more able children to create conversion charts from pints and gallons to litres. Some children may have spotted similar charts on petrol pumps.

Plenary

Review the worksheet answers with the children. Did their estimates improve with practice? Suggest that they discuss imperial units with their grandparents when they have the chance. Do their grandparents find that they still think in feet, inches, pints and gallons?

21 Seating plans

Background
Theatre seating plans show seats grouped in regular blocks, or arrays, in different parts of the theatre. Individual seats are identified by row letters and seat numbers. Investigating ways of arranging a fixed number of seats in different ways is an opportunity to explore the mathematics of arrays and factors. For example, a 50-seat block can be arranged alternatively as 1 × 50, 2 × 25 or 5 × 10, since the factors of 50 are 1, 2, 5, 10, 25 and 50. Seating plans can be designed using an object-based computer drawing package, developing ICT skills of graphical modelling.

Preparation
Copy and print out a theatre seating plan and distribute it in preparation for the initial discussion. Make sure that you can use your chosen computer software confidently to create, copy, format and move objects, for example squares to represent rows of seats in a seating plan.

Main teaching activity
Introduce the lesson by discussing the theatre seating plan. How many seats are there in different parts of the theatre? How are the seats identified? Why are different seats sold for different prices?

Develop the lesson by explaining that the children are to design a seating plan for a production in the school hall. Initially they must design a plan for 48 seats. Discuss how the seats might be set out. What are the problems of setting them all out in a single block? (It's difficult to access the seats in the middle.) How many blocks should the seats be set in? How many rows in each block? How many seats in a row? How do you calculate the total number of seats in a block? (number in a row × number of rows) How can you find quickly the different ways of arranging seats in blocks of different sizes? Talk about factors and arrays, for example to find the various arrangements of a 24-seat block as illustrated below.

Set the children to work at the computers to design their seating plans. Show them how to draw an object to represent a seat, for example a square, then how to copy and paste it repeatedly to create an array. Children should proceed to work in pairs or small groups on their seating plan designs. If there are insufficient computers for all the children to work simultaneously, some groups can plan their work initially with pencil and paper.

A [1 | 2 | 3 | 4 | 5 | 6 | 7 | 8 | 9 | 10 | 11 | 12 | 13 | 14 | 15 | 16 | 17 | 18 | 19 | 20 | 21 | 22 | 23 | 24] 24×1

A [1 | 2 | 3 | 4 | 5 | 6 | 7 | 8 | 9 | 10 | 11 | 12]
B [1 | 2 | 3 | 4 | 5 | 6 | 7 | 8 | 9 | 10 | 11 | 12] 12×2

A [1 | 2 | 3 | 4 | 5 | 6]
B [1 | 2 | 3 | 4 | 5 | 6]
C [1 | 2 | 3 | 4 | 5 | 6] 6×4
D [1 | 2 | 3 | 4 | 5 | 6]

A [1 | 2 | 3 | 4 | 5 | 6 | 7 | 8]
B [1 | 2 | 3 | 4 | 5 | 6 | 7 | 8] 8×3
C [1 | 2 | 3 | 4 | 5 | 6 | 7 | 8]

Differentiation

Less able children should concentrate on investigating ways of arranging a single block of 16 or 24 seats.

More able children can produce a more sophisticated seating plan similar to those from actual theatres. Their plans could include row and seat numbers and colour-coding of seats according to price.

Plenary

Ask selected children to show and describe the features of their final plans. Make a display of printouts of the children's designs.

22 Petrol prices

Objectives

Numeracy
Use all four operations to solve simple word problems involving numbers and quantities using one or more steps.
Use and write standard metric units including litres.
Know imperial units (mile, gallon).
English
To talk effectively as members of a group.
To consider alternatives and draw others into reaching agreement.

Resources

A copy of photocopiable page 75 for each group; calculators, pens and paper; a litre bottle of water.

Vocabulary

litre
gallon
price
pounds
pence
kilometre
mile
total
amount

Background

In this lesson, children tackle story problems set in the context of purchasing petrol at a garage and estimating the cost of journeys. They work together in small groups to solve a range of problems of increasing complexity, discussing the calculations required and the methods they should use. Reaching a collective conclusion requires both mathematical work on the numbers involved, and language skills to argue and explain their reasoning.

Preparation

Copy and distribute the worksheets with the calculators, pens and paper.

Main teaching activity

Introduce the activity to the class by talking about purchasing petrol at a garage. Most children will have experience of this on journeys in family cars. Ask the children to describe how petrol is dispensed and purchased. Discuss the different grades of fuel. How are they priced? Fuel is normally sold by the litre. Show the children a litre bottle of water. Ask how many litres are required to 'fill up' a typical family car

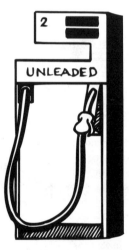

(30–40). Discuss gallons. Petrol was formerly sold in gallons and many adults still think in gallon measures. What is the connection between a gallon and a litre? (1 gallon = 4.5 litres.) How far will a small car travel on 1 gallon of petrol? (About 45 miles.) How far will 1 litre of petrol take the same car? (About 10 miles.) Summarise the key facts on the board:

cost of unleaded petrol per litre = 70p
1 gallon = 4.5 litres
typical small car travels 45 miles on 1 gallon, or 10 miles on 1 litre of petrol.

Set the children to work in groups on the worksheet problems. They should make notes and jottings to record their ideas and answers.

Differentiation

The first three problems are straightforward and all children should solve them. The other problems are more challenging.

Plenary

Ask representatives from the groups to give their solutions to the problems and to explain their calculations. The answers are:
1. 4 star, **2.** £21.00, **3.** 20 litres, **4.** 300 miles, **5.** 100 miles, **6.** 5p, 15 miles

Linked to
I C T
D & T

23 ~~doubling~~ Recipe spreadsheets

Objectives

Numeracy
Solve a problem by representing and interpreting data in tables, including those generated by a computer.
Use, read and write standard metric units.
Solve simple problems using ideas of ratio and proportion.

ICT
Work together to explore a variety of ICT tools.
Looks forward to QCA ICT Unit 6B: Spreadsheet modelling.

Design and technology
Undertake design and make assignments using materials including food.
Links to QCA Design and Technology Units 5B: Bread and 5D: Biscuits.

Resources
Computers running spreadsheet software, for example *Microsoft Excel* or *Textease*; printers and paper, flip chart or board; ingredients for the basic biscuit recipe below.

Vocabulary
quantity
cost
grid
cell
column
row
formula
spreadsheet

Background
Working with recipes requires a range of mathematical ideas, including measurement, ratio and proportion. A biscuit recipe might require 1 tsp of ginger for every 250g of flour to produce 20 biscuits. What quantities are required for 100 biscuits? The measures needed can be explored with the help of a spreadsheet.

Preparation
Write this recipe on the board:

> ### Quantities for 20 biscuits
> Plain flour 250g
> Sugar 120g
> Margarine 120g
> Baking powder 10g
> Ground ginger 10g
>
> ### Instructions
> Wash your hands. Mix the flour, sugar, ginger and baking powder in a bowl. Rub in the margarine with your fingers until the mixture looks like crumbs.
> Add a little water and press the mixture into a ball. Divide the ball into 20 pieces. Roll each piece into a ball and press it flat on a greased baking tray. Bake in a hot oven (180°C) for 20 minutes.

Set up the computers running your chosen software package. Check that you can use it confidently to program a recipe spreadsheet. The example below was produced in *Excel* as follows. The number of biscuits required is entered in cell B2. The 'new' recipe quantities are calculated by multiplying the original quantities by the appropriate factor (number of biscuits required ÷ original biscuit number) using the formulae below:

B5 = 250 * B2/20
B6 = 120 * B2/20
B7 = 120 * B2/20
B8 = 10 * B2/20
B9 = 10 * B2/20

Main teaching activity
Introduce the lesson by discussing the biscuit recipe. In preparation for cooking, the children must calculate the quantities of ingredients required for every child in the class to make six biscuits. To do this they are going to use a spreadsheet on the computer.

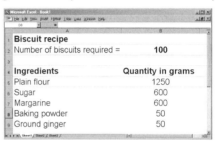

Set the children to work in groups. Show them how to set up the spreadsheet and enter the appropriate formulae into the cells to calculate the new quantities when the number of biscuits is changed. Demonstrate how, when a number in a cell to which the formulae refer is changed, the spreadsheet updates the values in the other cells.

Let children explore the link between the number of biscuits and the ingredient quantities. How many biscuits must be made in total to produce 6 each? What are the total quantities of ingredients for this number of biscuits?

Differentiation
Less able children may find the process of programming a spreadsheet too demanding. Let them work with a spreadsheet you have programmed in advance of the lesson.

Challenge more able children to include a column showing ingredient costs in their spreadsheet model.

Plenary
As a class, look at the children's grids. Discuss the ICT techniques they used to create them. What formulae did they use? In a follow-up lesson, the children should bake biscuits, measuring out quantities according to their spreadsheet calculations.

24 Will it rain tomorrow?

Objectives

Numeracy
Express one half, one quarter, three-quarters, and tenths as percentages.
Discuss the chance or likelihood of particular events.

Geography
To learn to analyse evidence and draw conclusions.
To develop decision-making skills.
Links to QCA Geography Unit 16: What's in the news?

Resources

A copy of photocopiable page 76 for each child; flip chart or board.

Vocabulary

probability
chance
good chance
poor chance
likely
unlikely
likelihood
percentage
equally likely
certain

Background

The concept of chance or probability relates to events that may or may not happen, such as tossing heads with a coin, throwing two sixes with a pair of dice, or rain falling on school sports day. We can predict from experience that some events are more or less likely than others, for example it is more likely to snow in January than in August.

Chances or probabilities can be expressed as numbers and compared on a probability line. Something that has no chance of happening (pigs flying, for example) has a probability of 0 or 0%. Something that is certain (the Sun rising tomorrow) has a probability of 1 or 100%. Something that is equally likely to happen or not happen has a probability of ½ or 50%.

The weather is not completely predictable and therefore ideas of chance or probability are important when making weather forecasts and decisions based on them. National weather forecasts use data from weather stations and records of weather patterns to make forecasts that include statements such as 'There is a 70% chance of rain on Tuesday, falling to 30% by Wednesday.' In this lesson, children discuss the chance or likelihood of different events and use the vocabulary they develop to interpret simple forecasts.

Preparation

Copy and distribute the worksheets.

Main teaching activity

Introduce the lesson with a general discussion of the chance or likelihood of different events. Start by using the vocabulary: *certain to happen*, *very likely*, *equally likely to happen or not*, *very unlikely*, *certain not to happen*. Rank a range of examples similar to those below using this vocabulary:

● the Sun rising tomorrow
● seeing someone you know on the way to school
● tossing heads with a coin
● David Beckham visiting the school
● a pig flying past the window.

Introduce the idea of a probability line. Draw a line on the board from 0 (0%) to 1 (100%) and decide where the various events you have discussed should be located on the line.

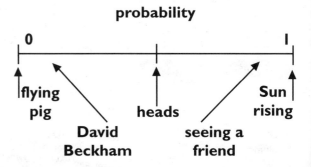

Develop the lesson by explaining that you are going to apply probability ideas to weather forecasting. Have the children heard weather forecasters making statements such as 'there is a 20% probability of rain'? Does this mean that rain is likely or unlikely? Set the children to complete the activities on the worksheet. They should look at the weather forecast for the week ahead in local or national newspapers and answer the associated questions.

Differentiation

Less able children should concentrate on completing the basic activity.

Challenge more able children to compile a table linking alternative expressions such as *very unlikely, a high probability* or *a fair chance* to probability percentages.

Plenary

Review the answers to the worksheet as a class. Discuss in particular the correspondence between the vocabulary of chance and probability and the assignment of values for probabilities on the line. Encourage children to use the vocabulary of probability when they discuss their own predictions for the weather and other events. The answers are:
1. Saturday afternoon
2. Thursday morning and Sunday afternoon
3. Thursday
4. Saturday
5. See table below:

day	probability of rain in the morning	probability of rain in the afternoon
Monday	very unlikely	likely
Tuesday	even	even
Wednesday	unlikely	very unlikely
Thursday	very unlikely	unlikely
Friday	unlikely	likely
Saturday	likely	very likely
Sunday	even	very unlikely

Linked to
D & T

25 Pinboard

Objectives

Numeracy
Measure and draw lines to the nearest mm.
Understand, measure and calculate perimeters of rectangles and regular polygons.
Complete symmetrical patterns with two lines of symmetry at right angles.
Recognise reflective symmetry.
Recognise where a shape will be after reflection.
Recognise where a shape will be after translation.
Design and technology
To measure, mark out and assemble components and materials accurately.

Resources

A copy of photocopiable page 77 for each child. 20cm squares of plywood (a local DIY store may be willing to supply these as off-cuts), panel pins, hammers, rulers, pencils, coloured elastic bands, coloured thread.

Vocabulary

array
grid
shape
perimeter
symmetry
reflection
translation

Background

A pinboard is a valuable tool for making and exploring the properties of shapes. In this practical lesson, children use their measurement and craft skills to set out and construct their own pinboards. They then challenge each other to create and manipulate shapes on the board using rubber bands or coloured threads.

Preparation

Copy and distribute the worksheets. Collect the craft materials and tools and distribute them in preparation for practical work. Make a sample pinboard to show the class.

Main teaching activity

Introduce the lesson by explaining that the children are going to make pinboards to explore shapes and patterns. Show the class the sample pinboard and discuss how it consists of a regular array of panel pins tapped into a wooden base. Discuss the procedure for making a board. A square grid must be ruled onto the board and panel pins tapped in at the intersections of the lines.

Set children to work in pairs to make their own boards. They should start by deciding how many squares they want in their grid (5 × 5 or 10 × 10?) and then plan how to measure and rule the grid to make best use of the space available on their board. Once the grids have been measured and ruled, the children should tap panel pins into the wood. Remind the children of the need to be careful with tools and to work safely.

Completed pinboards can be used in conjunction with the worksheet to investigate shapes and symmetry. Can children reproduce the shapes and patterns on the worksheet and answer the challenges? Can they make up some similar challenges?

Differentiation

Less able children could make 5 × 5 boards.
More able children can make and work with 10 × 10 and larger boards.

Plenary

Ask selected children to show their pinboard and the designs they have created on them to the rest of the class. Make a class display with the finished boards.

26 Pentomino puzzles

Objectives

Numeracy
Solve mathematical problems or puzzles, recognise and explain patterns and relationships.
Make shapes with increasing accuracy.
Identify multiples of 5.
Design and technology
To undertake design and make assignments using a range of materials including sheet materials.
Measure and cut materials accurately.

Resources
Squared paper, felt-tipped pens, card, rulers, scissors, pencils; flip chart or board.

Vocabulary
pentomino
puzzle
square
grid
multiple of 5
pattern

Background
A pentomino is a shape made by linking 5 squares. There are just 12 distinct pentominoes, as shown below.

A pentomino puzzle can be created by dividing a rectangular grid of squares into a number of distinct pentominoes and cutting them out. To make an exact number of pentominoes, the number of squares in the grid must be a multiple of 5. Thus, for example, a 5 × 4 grid can be divided into pentominoes but a 6 × 4 grid cannot. The puzzle is to rearrange the pentominoes into the original rectangle. Usually there is more than one way of solving the puzzle. Examples are illustrated below. In this lesson, children investigate the different pentomino shapes and use their craft and design skills to make their own pentomino puzzles.

There are many good pentomino and puzzle resources on the Internet. The sites below are good starting points.

http://www.benfold.com/will/applets/pent/pent.html

http://kaminari.scitec.kobe-u.ac.jp/PrologCafe/Pentomino.html

http://home.planetinternet.be/~odettedm/

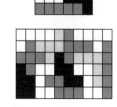

Preparation
Set out the craft materials in preparation for group work.

Main teaching activity
Introduce the lesson by drawing examples of the pentominoes on the board. Explain how they are made by linking 5 squares together. Ask: *How many different pentominoes are there?* Set the children to work in pairs or small groups, investigating this question by colouring pentominoes on squared paper. How many distinct pentominoes can they find? When groups feel they have discovered all the pentominoes, review their findings and sketch the 12 pentominoes on the board.

Develop the lesson by explaining pentomino puzzles. On the board divide a 3 × 5 grid into pentominoes and describe how the pentominoes could be cut out to make a puzzle. Discuss the sizes of grids that could be made into puzzles in this way. Through discussion, establish that the total number of squares in the grid must be a multiple of 5. Discuss how puzzles could be made more appealing (and easier to solve) by colouring grid squares to make a regular pattern prior to cutting out the pentominoes.

Set the children to work in pairs or groups, making their own pentomino puzzles.

Differentiation
Less able children should make puzzles based on smaller grids, for example 3 × 5 or 4 × 5.

More able children can make larger puzzles. Challenge them to make a 10 × 6 puzzle that uses each of the 12 pentominoes just once. Can they find alternative ways to solve the puzzle?

Plenary
Ask representatives to show the puzzles they have created. Exchange puzzles between groups to see how hard they are to solve. Finally, use the children's puzzles to create a pentomino display.

27 Musical measures

Background

The ancient Greek mathematician Pythagoras believed that numbers could explain the mysteries of music, beauty and truth. In the case of music, he discovered that the musical scale can be explained with the help of simple ratios or fractions.

The frets on a guitar divide the length of a string into fractions. When the string is held down at the 12th fret, it is divided in half. The note played by the half-length string is one octave higher in pitch than the note of the full-length string. This is the interval *doh* to *doh'* on the scale. The seventh fret divides the string into parts that are $^1/_3$ and $^2/_3$ the original length. The $^2/_3$ length string sounds the note *soh* on the scale. The fifth fret divides the string into $^1/_4$ and $^3/_4$. The $^3/_4$ length string makes the note *fah*. The fourth fret divides the string into $^1/_5$ and $^4/_5$. The $^4/_5$ length string makes the note *me*. The other notes can also be positioned with fractions, but in a more complex way.

Preparation

Collect and set out the resources.

Main teaching activity

Introduce the lesson by singing the musical scale with the class: *doh, ray, me, fah, soh, lah, te, doh'*. Show the children how the scale is played on a single string of the guitar by holding down the string successively at frets 2, 4, 5, 7, 9, 11 and 12. Introduce Pythagoras' ideas about music and numbers. Explain that Pythagoras discovered that different notes are related by simple fractions, for example the 12th fret on a guitar divides the string into halves.

Set the children to measure the full length of the guitar string (*doh*) to the nearest mm, and the distances from frets 4, 5, 7 and 12 (*me, fah, soh, doh'*) to the bridge. Results can be recorded in a table like the one below.

Ask the children to use calculators to convert their measured lengths into decimal fractions of the full string length. Can they identify the nearest simple fraction in each case? (These are included in the table below for your reference.)

fret number	length in mm	length ÷ full string length	nearest simple fraction
full string	650	650 ÷ 650 = 1	1
4	520	520 ÷ 650 = 0.8	$^4/_5$
5	488	488 ÷ 650 = 0.751	$^3/_4$
7	434	434 ÷ 650 = 0.668	$^2/_3$
12	324	324 ÷ 650 = 0.498	$^1/_2$

Differentiation

Less able children should concentrate on the measurement exercise.

More able children can explore the relationship between the lengths and fractions with their calculator.

Plenary

Review the children's findings. What fractions of the original length do the notes *me, fah, soh, doh'* correspond to? Explain that the positions of the other frets are also fixed by fractions, but in a more complicated way. You may like to go on to (or plan to cover) Lesson 46 in this section of the book.

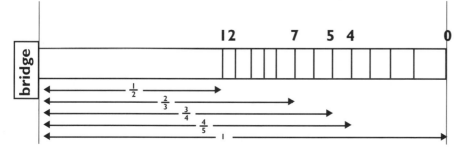

28 Height graph

Objectives

Numeracy
Solve a problem by interpreting data in line graphs, including those where intermediate points have meaning.
Science
To learn about the stages in the human life cycle.

Resources

A copy of photocopiable page 78 for each child; rulers and pencils.

Vocabulary

line graph
axis
point
line
plot

Background

When do children grow most quickly? Do teenagers grow more quickly than ten-year-olds? How old are you when you stop growing? Height versus age data plotted on a line graph reveals the answers to these questions for boys and girls. Growth is most rapid in the first two years of life. Growth in childhood is steady until the teenage years, then there is a growth spurt – this usually comes at an earlier age for girls than for boys, but after a year or two boys catch up with girls, and eventually overtake them in average height. In this lesson, children practise plotting line graphs from tables of data. They see that line graphs give a better visual picture of changes and trends than the basic numerical data listed in columns.

Preparation

Copy and distribute the worksheets with squared paper, rulers and pencils.

Main teaching activity

Introduce the lesson with a discussion of growth. At which stage in their lives do the children think they grow most quickly – as babies, teenagers or adults? When do they think they will stop growing? Do boys and girls grow at the same rate?

Set the children to work in pairs or small groups on the graph-plotting activity on the worksheet. Show them how to plot the points listed on the table with vertical crosses using the axes on the worksheet.

For this graph, intermediate values have meaning since the children's heights must increase smoothly between successive

points. It is therefore appropriate to connect the points with a smooth line as illustrated below.

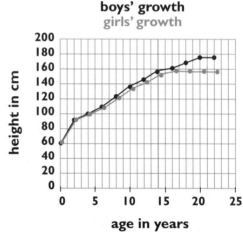

Children's heights

boys' growth
girls' growth

Differentiation

Less able children will require considerable assistance to draw satisfactory graphs. Help them to locate each of the points relative to the axes.

More able children could complete the graph-plotting activity on the computer. Can they use their graphs to estimate children's heights at intermediate ages, for example at 9.5 years?

Plenary

Discuss the children's graphs as a class. Emphasise particularly how the line graphs give a good visual impression of the height change with time. The line is steep when growth is rapid, but levels off as growth slows down. Relate this to stages in the life cycle, including baby–toddler and the pubertal growth spurt.

Linked to

D & T

29 Shoe sizes

Objectives

Numeracy
Solve a problem by interpreting data in tables. Find the mode of a set of data.
Design and technology
Evaluate a range of familiar products – thinking about how they are used.
Looks forward to QCA Design and Technology Unit 6B: Slippers.

Resources

The children's gym shoes; pencils and paper, flip chart or board.

Vocabulary

survey
frequency table
mode
bar chart

Background

The mode is the most frequent or common value in a set of numerical data. For example, seven of the 12 months have 31 days. Therefore 31 is the mode for the number of days in a month. In this lesson, children learn about the mode as one measure of average. They do so in the context of shoe and clothing sizes. The activity can be linked to work on the design and evaluation of familiar products in Design and technology.

Preparation

Ask the children to bring their gym shoes to school for this lesson, or arrange the lesson on a day when you know they will have their gym shoes with them.

Main teaching activity

Ask the children to imagine setting up their own shoe shop. One of the things they must do is to order stock in preparation for their opening day. What sizes should they order? Should they order the same number of each size, or are some sizes more common than others?

Explain that the children are going to conduct a survey of shoe sizes in the class. Ask the children to bring their gym shoes in turn to the front of the class and place them in size order. Group and count the number of different-sized shoes, then discuss ways of interpreting and presenting the data. Suggestions might include plotting a bar chart showing the frequency of different shoe sizes, or using pictograms to represent the data.

Set the children to work in groups to choose and use a method of data display.

Some groups may wish to work at the computer to produce bar charts, pictograms or pie charts.

Review the children's progress and introduce the concept of the mode. The mode is the most frequent size in the data set and will thus appear as the highest bar, the biggest segment of pie or the most pictograms on the charts. What is the mode for the shoe sizes in the class?

Differentiation

Less able children should concentrate on the basic survey, perhaps recording the data in a frequency table. Make sure they know that the mode corresponds to the highest number that appears in their table.

More able children could broaden the survey to include other classes. How does the modal shoe size change with age?

Plenary

Ask representatives of the groups to show and explain their methods for displaying the data. Make sure they have clearly understood what is meant by the mode of a data set. Have a final discussion of the selection of shoe sizes for stocking a shop. Why might knowledge of the mode be important?

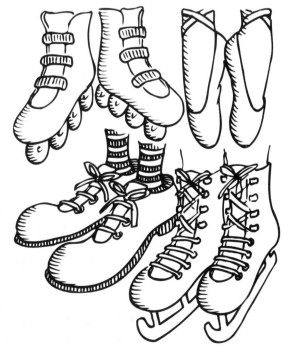

30 Treasure hunt

Objectives

Numeracy
Add several numbers mentally (strings of single digits or multiples of 10).
Solve mathematical problems or puzzles.
Physical education
Take part in outdoor activity challenges, including following trails in familiar environments.
Links to QCA Physical Education 30: Outdoor and adventurous activities.

Resources

Photocopied treasure maps and question lists.

Vocabulary

add
strategy
problem
subtract

Background

A 'treasure hunt' around the school grounds can take some time to plan and organise, but once it has been prepared it can be used year after year. A good format for such a hunt is as follows. Produce a map of the school grounds (or another safe area around which children can wander in pairs to hunt for clues). Mark various numbered 'stations' on the map, which the children must visit to find the answers to a series of questions. For example, station 1 might be the plaque unveiled when the school was opened. The question might be 'Who opened the school?' Station 2 might be a climbing frame in the playground with the question 'Which company manufactured the climbing frame?' Try to mark at least ten stations on the map at a range of distances from the starting point. Assign a number of points for each correct answer. Answers to questions at more distant stations should be worth more points than those for nearby stations.

To make the treasure hunt more mathematically challenging, you could devise problems to be solved at each station, for example 'The number of rungs on the climbing frame ladder + the number of paving stones around the play area.' You could label the distances between stations in metres, then prompt children to calculate the total distance travelled. Who found the shortest route?

Preparation

Prepare the map and questions. Time yourself as you walk around the stations at a steady pace to establish a reasonable target time for the children to visit all the stations and to find the answers to the questions.

Main teaching activity

Distribute the treasure maps and questions and explain the treasure hunt to the whole class. Set the target time for visiting all the stations. Explain that you will blow a whistle at 5-minute intervals so that the children know how much time remains. You will blow a final whistle 1 minute before the time expires and the children must then return to the start. They will lose 1 point for each second they are late returning.

Children should work in pairs or threes and can visit the stations in any order. Before they start they will have 5 minutes to plan their strategy. Should they visit the nearby stations first or head for the more distant stations? They should note that the answers to questions at the more distant stations carry more points.

Differentiation

Prompt less able children to visit nearby stations first to ensure that they score at least some points.

More able children may opt to adopt the riskier but potentially more rewarding strategy of heading for the most difficult stations first.

Plenary

When the children have all returned, discuss the answers to the questions. Were they all easy to find, or were some more difficult than others? Children should add their scores mentally, deduct any penalties for late return, and report their totals.

Linked to
Geography

31 Price wars

Background

Shopping price comparisons and surveys combine work with money with work on measures. Discussion of relative prices in convenience stores, small high street shops and out-of-town superstores links with work on the geography of the local area, including discussion of transport issues. Ask questions such as: *Why can large superstores charge lower prices for their goods? Why may this be a problem for smaller local stores? Who could be disadvantaged by high prices in convenience shops or the closure of smaller shops due to competition?* (People without cars, for example the elderly.) In this lesson, children compare prices for goods bought in three hypothetical stores. They then plan their own survey of prices in local shops as part of exploring the local area.

Preparation

Make copies of the worksheet and distribute them.

Main teaching activity

Introduce the lesson with a discussion of local food shopping facilities. Where are the nearby superstores? Where do the children's parents prefer to shop? Are there any convenience stores nearby? Are there any food stores in the local high street? Is there a local street market? How do prices compare between stores?

Set the children to work in pairs or small groups on the worksheet activity. The imaginary bills shown are for items purchased in three different stores. The children must interpret the bills to answer the questions and make comparisons.

Review the worksheet problems and the children's answers. Are the superstore prices always less than the corner shop or street market? What issues other than price might cause you to shop at one store rather than another?

In the final part of the lesson, ask the groups to plan a price survey which they would like to undertake. Suggestions might include the price of bread, the price of fruit and vegetables, or the price of drinks and crisps.

Differentiation

Suggest that less able children make a simple price comparison of identical items such as well-known soft drinks when they visit the supermarket and other outlets with their parents.

More able children can make a more extensive survey of price variations between alternative outlets. A possible extension activity is to use the Internet to compare prices for home delivery of books or DVDs from sites such as www.tesco.com, www.amazon.co.uk and www.bookshop.co.uk.

Plenary

Conclude the lesson with some mental arithmetic based on the worksheet shopping lists. How much would 3kg of potatoes cost at the market? How much more would they cost at the superstore? The answers are:
1. £7.20, £5.15, £6.80
2. superstore, corner shop
3.

item	superstore	corner shop	market
baked beans	1	3	2
bread	1	3	2
Cola	1	2	3
apples	2	3	1
cornflakes	2	3	1
dog food	2	3	1

Linked to
I C T

32 Square numbers

Background

The square of a number is the number multiplied by itself, for example 'two squared' = $2^2 = 2 \times 2 = 4$. The squares of numbers are readily visualised with the help of square grids as shown below. The area of a square is found by 'squaring' its side length. Creating a sequence of square grids to illustrate square numbers is a useful exercise to perform on the computer. The process develops both knowledge of the squares of numbers and the link between squaring and area.

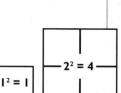
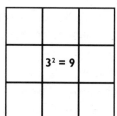
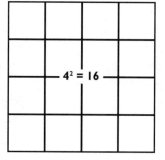

$1^2 = 1$ $2^2 = 4$ $3^2 = 9$ $4^2 = 16$

Preparation

Set up the computers running your chosen software package and check that you can use it confidently to draw square arrays. For example, in *Microsoft Word* click the rectangle icon on the drawing toolbar, hold down the SHIFT key and drag the mouse to produce a square. Select the square you have drawn by clicking on it, then reproduce it by copying and pasting. Drag the copied squares into position to create an array. (Lining up shapes is made easier by selecting the 'Grid' menu item from the *Draw* drop-down menu, then checking 'Snap to shapes'.)

Main teaching activity

Introduce the lesson by talking about squaring a number. Define squaring as multiplying a number by itself and develop the vocabulary '2 squared = 2 times 2 = 4; 3 squared = 3 times 3 = 9…' Write a table of squares to 10 on the board as follows:

$1^2 = 1 \times 1 = 1$
$2^2 = 2 \times 2 = 4$
$3^2 = 3 \times 3 = 9$
$4^2 = 4 \times 4 = 16$
and so on.

Demonstrate the link between squaring and the area of a square. Sketch square grids to illustrate 1^2, 2^2, 3^2 and so on. Explain that the children are to use computers to continue the sequence up to 10^2. Set them to work in pairs or threes at the computers and demonstrate how to draw and copy a square to create a square grid. Children should proceed to design a page of grids to illustrate the squares of numbers up to 10.

Differentiation

Less able children should create grids to illustrate squares of numbers to 5.

More able children could extend the sequence beyond 10. Can they find efficient ways of copying and pasting their square grids as the numbers increase?

Plenary

Select children to show printouts of their work to the rest of the class. This could be used to create a class display. Conclude the lesson by asking some rapid mental squaring problems to reinforce children's knowledge of squares to 10 × 10.

33 Smoking kills!

Objectives

Numeracy
Discuss the chance or likelihood of particular events.
Solve a problem by interpreting data in tables.
Science
To learn about the effects on the human body of tobacco and how these relate to their personal health.

Resources

A copy of photocopiable page 80 for each child.

Vocabulary

chance
likelihood
probability

Background

Statistics show unequivocally that smoking is linked to ill health and increases the probability or likelihood of an early death. Defenders of smoking often argue that 'I knew someone who smoked 40 a day and lived to 90 – so it didn't do him any harm!' The only response to this is that the 90-year-old was extremely lucky. Smoking increases the likelihood of a premature death more than any other activity we undertake, including riding a motorbike, going rock climbing or joining the armed forces. In this lesson, children interpret some simple statistics on smoking and health, making numerical comparisons and developing the vocabulary of chance or likelihood.

Preparation

Copy and distribute the worksheets.

Main teaching activity

Introduce the lesson with a discussion of smoking and health. This may be a sensitive issue due to parents or siblings smoking. *Why do people smoke? What pleasure do they say it gives them? What problems does smoking create? Why do people want to give up? Why do many people find it so hard to give up?*

Set the children to work in groups to answer the worksheet questions. Questions 1 to 3 are fairly straightforward and require the children to extract figures from the tables and make simple calculations. Questions 4 and 5 are more open ended, involving the concept of chance and probability.

Differentiation

Less able children should concentrate on questions 1 to 3.

More able children should complete all the questions. Suggest that they design an anti-smoking poster using some of the statistics they have derived from the table on the worksheet.

Plenary

Review the answers to the worksheet questions. Reinforce the use of the vocabulary of probability. Smoking greatly increases your chance of developing lung cancer. If you smoke you are much more likely to suffer from asthma. Smokers have a higher probability of dying young. Use any posters that children have designed to create a display about the hazards of smoking. The answers are: **1.** smoking, accidents at work or home, alcohol and drugs, road accidents, drowning, murder, lightning strike, **2.** 2666, **3.** 2000, **4.** dying through smoking, **5.** don't smoke.

34 Explain yourself

Objectives

Numeracy
When generalising, explain methods and reasoning about numbers orally and in writing.
Use informal pencil and paper methods to support, record or explain additions/subtractions/multiplications/divisions.
English
Speak audibly and clearly, using spoken Standard English in formal contexts.
Use vocabulary and syntax that enables communication of more complex meanings.

Resources

A copy of photocopiable page 81 for each child, pencils and paper, flip chart or board.

Vocabulary

addition
subtraction
multiplication
division
calculate
method
jotting
answer
how did you work it out?

Background

In this lesson, children practise and explain mental calculation strategies. They perform mental calculations, explain them to a partner using the appropriate vocabulary, and record them using conventional notation. Each pair compares the strategies they use and, in the plenary session, present an oral report contrasting the alternative approaches.

Preparation

Copy and distribute the worksheets.

Main teaching activity

Introduce the lesson by writing some calculations to be solved mentally on the board. For example:

6002 − 5997	39 × 40
25 × 12	123 ÷ 31
350 × 40	$^1/_8$ of 288

Ask for solutions to each problem in turn, and for explanations of the methods used. Summarise the calculations using the appropriate notation. Discuss alternative methods where they are suggested. For example:

6002 − 5997
5997 + 3 = 6000, add 2 more is 6002.
Answer: 5

25 × 12
This is 25 × 4 × 3 = 100 × 3 = 300.
Alternatively, this is (25 × 10) + (25 × 2) = 250 + 50 = 300

350 × 40
This is the same as 3500 × 4 = 14 000
Alternatively, this is 35 × 4 × 10 × 10 = 140 × 100 = 14 000

39 × 40
This is the same as 40 × 40 = 1600, subtract 40 gives 1560

123 ÷ 31
31 × 4 = 124, subtract 1 is 123.
Answer: $3^{30}/_{31}$

$^1/_8$ of 288
$^1/_2$ of 288 = 144, $^1/_2$ of 144 = 72, $^1/_2$ of 72 = 36, so $^1/_8$ of 288 = 36

Set the children to work in pairs on the worksheet problems. They should each volunteer the answer to a problem and an oral explanation of how the answer was calculated. When they have agreed an answer they should record the method or methods used.

Differentiation

Less able children should concentrate on problems 1 to 5, which are fairly straightforward.
More able children can move onto problems 6, 7 and 8 which are more challenging.

Plenary

Ask pairs to choose a problem for which both members of the pair found the correct answer, but used alternative strategies. Challenge one member of the pair to explain both strategies to the whole class. The answers are:
1. 5, **2.** 60, **3.** 1500, **4.** 2070, **5.** $9^{20}/_{21}$, **6.** 14, **7.** 3028, **8.** 300

35 Assessment 2

Objectives

The assessment activities in this book are designed to introduce Key Stage 2 children to SAT-style questions. They are set in cross-curricular contexts based on the preceding term's lessons. The questions in Assessment 2 test the children's progress in: recognising equivalent simple fractions, decimal fractions and percentages; placing whole numbers and decimal fractions on an undivided number line; multiplying decimal numbers by 10, 100 and 1000 and making simple currency conversions. The practical activity tests their understanding of reflection symmetry and translations.

Resources

A copy of photocopiable page 82 for each child, pencils, pinboards and rubber bands.

Preparation

Make copies of the assessment sheet. If you feel that the sheet is too 'busy', the three activities could be separated and enlarged on individual sheets.

Lesson introduction

Begin the assessment lesson by reviewing the relevant cross-curricular topics covered during the term. Remind the children of some of the projects and investigations they have undertaken, and ask them to recall and recount their work. Emphasise the mathematical content, for example: *Do you remember how we investigated fractions on the guitar fingerboard?*

Main assessment activity

Distribute the worksheets and ask the children to work on them individually. Guide the whole class through the questions one at a time, reading the text with them, and prompting them to work out and fill in their answers. Try to make the whole activity enjoyable!

Practical activity

Use a rubber band to make a triangle on a pinboard. Mark a line with a second band. Ask the children to make the reflection of the triangle in the line. Ask them to translate a shape a fixed number of spaces horizontally and vertically.

Plenary

Review the answers to the questions as a class. Collect the completed question sheets to use as an aid to judging individual children's progress, and to include in your records. The answers are:

1.
fraction	decimal	percentage
$1/2$	0.5	50%
$1/4$	0.25	25%
$1/5$	0.2	20%
$3/4$	0.75	75%
$1/3$	0.33	33%
$7/10$	0.7	70%

2. 1500, 1750; 10.3, 10.9, **3.** 16.3 euros, 6940 rupees, 1440 dollars

Linked to

S c i e n c e
I C T

36 The planets

Objectives

Numeracy
Order a set of integers less than one million.
Order a given set of positive and negative integers.
Science
To learn that the Sun, Earth and Moon are approximately spherical.
To learn that the Earth orbits the Sun once each year.
ICT
To interpret information.
Links to QCA ICT Unit 5B: Analysing data and asking questions using complex searches.

Resources

A copy of photocopiable page 83 for each child, pencils and paper; reference materials, including books and CD-ROMs, for researching information about the Solar System.

Vocabulary

data
table
sequence
bigger
smaller
positive
negative

Background

The majority of Year 5/ Primary 6 children will know the basic features of the Solar System. Knowledge of the planets is a requirement in Scotland, but not in England and Wales (although, as a result of children's interest in this subject, the planets are frequently studied). The Sun, a star, sits at the centre of the Solar System. The nine planets, their moons and many smaller objects including asteroids and comets, orbit the Sun at various distances. In this lesson, children interpret a table of data about the planets in the Solar System. They sequence the planets by size, distance from the Sun and surface temperature, developing their knowledge of the relative size of positive and negative numbers to one million and beyond.

Preparation

Copy and distribute the worksheets. Make a collection of suitable reference materials for follow-up work on the Solar System.

Main teaching activity

Introduce the lesson by asking the children if they know the names of the planets. *Can anyone name them in the correct sequence starting from the Sun?* (Mercury, Venus, Earth, Mars, Jupiter, Saturn, Uranus, Neptune, Pluto.) Which is the largest planet? (Jupiter) *Which is the smallest planet?* (Pluto.)

Continue the lesson by showing the

children the worksheet. In the data table at the top, the planets are listed in alphabetical order. The children's task is to complete the other tables, sequencing the planets by distance from the Sun, size and surface temperature.

Differentiation

Less able children should concentrate on the first activity. They may need help, in particular, with sequencing positive and negative temperatures.

Challenge more able children to use the reference materials to research more data about the planets and to compile additional tables, for example tables of day and year length.

Plenary

Review the completed tables as a class. Discuss how the reorganised data tables are easier to interpret and compare. For example, can the children use the tables to describe the relationship between a planet's distance from the Sun and its surface temperature? Use the tables as the basis for some questions comparing planetary statistics. For example, how much hotter is it on Mercury than on Earth? How many times bigger is Jupiter than Mars? You could use the children's work as the basis for a class display on the planets. The answers are:
Distance order (ascending): Mercury, Venus, Earth, Mars, Jupiter, Saturn, Uranus, Neptune, Pluto.
Size order (descending): Jupiter, Saturn, Uranus, Neptune, Earth, Venus, Mars, Mercury, Pluto.
Temperature order (descending): Venus, Mercury, Earth, Mars, Saturn, Jupiter, Neptune, Uranus, Pluto.

Linked to
L i t e r a c y
I C T

37 Ten times more

Background

In this lesson, children develop their knowledge of place value and the vocabulary of numbers and place value. In the decimal number system, multiplication by 10 moves each digit in a number one place to the left. Division by 10 moves digits one place to the right. This process is illustrated by the pattern below. The associated number words are also written down.

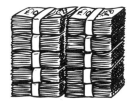

Multiplication by 10

three hundred thousand	300 000
thirty thousand	30 000
three thousand	3000
three hundred	300
thirty	30
three	3
nought point three	0.3
nought point nought three	0.03

Division by 10

Patterns such as these can be created with various starting numbers, both single- and multi-digit. Children can write them out by hand, or generate them on the computer. They will need to experiment with tab characters and fonts to get digits to line up in columns. With a proportional font, such as *Arial* or *Times*, the character spacing varies and alignment is difficult. If *Courier* is selected, however, the spacing between every character is the same and alignment is straightforward.

Preparation

Set out paper, pencils and calculators in preparation for group work.

Main teaching activity

Start the lesson by writing a single-digit number in the centre of the board. Explain that you are going to explore the effect of multiplying the number by 10 over and over again. Perform the multiplication and create a pattern of numbers similar to the illustration below. Ask the children to say each of the numbers in words and write the words next to the digits. Discuss how multiplying by 10 moves the original digits one 'place' to the left at each step.

Discuss division by 10 as the 'inverse' of multiplication. Start from the top of the pattern and demonstrate how division by 10 moves the digit one 'place' to the right. Continue beyond the original digit to the first two places of decimals.

Repeat the exercise with a two-digit starting number, for example 57.

Set the children to work in groups to generate their own number patterns in the same way. Some groups could work with pencil and paper, while others work at the computer.

Differentiation

Give less able children a single-digit starting number for their pattern.

More able children could start with two digits then progress to three-digit numbers and beyond.

Plenary

Ask representatives of the groups to display and describe their number and word patterns to the class. Have they written the number words correctly? Groups that used the computer should describe the ICT techniques they used to set out their number and word patterns.

Conclude by making a list of the vocabulary on the board and asking children to define each term with reference to the number patterns they have created.

38 Leap years

Objectives

Numeracy
Know and apply tests of divisibility by 4.
Use the vocabulary and units of time.
Science
Know that the Earth orbits the Sun once each year.
Links to QCA Science Unit 5E: Earth, Sun and Moon.

Resources

Paper and pencils, calculators; flip chart or board.

Vocabulary

day
year
calendar
leap year
multiple
divisible

Background

A year is the time taken for the Earth to complete one orbit of the Sun. This time is approximately 365$\frac{1}{4}$ days. The extra $\frac{1}{4}$ day creates a problem for the calendar. If we included just 365 days in every calendar year, the seasons would gradually move out of step with the months. After four years, Midsummer's Day would have moved on by one day; after 40 years it would be 10 days later, and after 400 years summer would be in November! To avoid this problem we save up the quarter days and add an extra day to the year every fourth year. A leap year has 366 days. The extra day is February 29th. Leap years occur in years that are multiples of 4, for example 1996 and 2008. However, there are some exceptions. To allow for the fact that a year is just less than 365$\frac{1}{4}$ days, the last year of a century is not a leap year unless it is divisible by 400. The year 2000 was a leap year, but 2100 will not be!

Preparation

Distribute the resources in preparation for group work.

Main teaching activity

Introduce the lesson by talking about the number of days in a year. How is the length of a year determined? Do the children know that every fourth year is a leap year? What is special about a leap year? Do the children know anyone who was born on February 29th? What do they do about celebrating birthdays? Do the children know any folklore associated with leap years?

Discuss the rules for establishing whether a year is a leap year or not. To be a leap year the year must be a multiple of 4. *How can we decide if a number is divisible by 4?* (The rule is that a number is divisible by 4 if its last two digits are divisible by 4.) Write some example years between 0 and 3000 on the board for the children to test using the divisibility rule:
Are these leap years?
456, 1860, 1932 and so on.

Differentiation

Suggest that less able children write out the four times table up to 4 × 25 to help them check if a year is a leap year or not.

Discuss the end-of-century exceptions with more able children. Can they suggest why these exceptions are made?

Plenary

Conclude the lesson with some quick-fire 'leap year or not?' questions.

39 What's the connection?

Objectives

Numeracy
Use the relationship between multiplication and division.
Recognise patterns and relationships.
Use multiplication and division to solve simple word problems involving numbers and quantities.

English
To use writing to help their thinking and learning.
To write for other children.

Resources
Computers running word-processing software, for example *Microsoft Word* or *Textease*; flip chart or board; a list of numbers connected by the relationship $a \times b = c$. Select appropriate numbers for the abilities of your children.

Vocabulary
multiplication
division
number sentence
story problem
relationship

Background
What is the connection between the numbers 360, 72 and 5? Mathematically the relationship can be expressed in four ways:

$72 \times 5 = 360$
$5 \times 72 = 360$
$360 \div 5 = 72$
$360 \div 72 = 5$

Children should recognise that if they know one of these relationships they also know the other three. In this lesson, the children write sets of story problems based on three connected numbers to illustrate the relationships above. For example:
1. There are 72 biscuits in a pack. How many biscuits are there in 5 packs?
2. A girl buys 5 pens. Each pen costs 72p. How much does she spend altogether?
3. A pie is cut into 5 equal slices. What is the angle of each slice?
4. 360 daffodils are made into 72 bunches. How many daffodils are there in each bunch?

The children should use their writing skills to set out creative problems and challenge other children to solve them.

Preparation
Set up the computers running your chosen word-processing software.

Main teaching activity
Introduce the lesson with an example similar to the one outlined in 'Background'. Ask the children to make the connections between the three numbers – lead them to suggest the four alternative mathematical statements linking the numbers.

Develop the lesson by writing a story problem for each expression.

Set the children to work in groups to write their own story problems based on sets of three numbers that you give them 'secretly'. Emphasise that their story problems must be realistic – for example it would not be realistic to have cars costing £12 each or pencils costing £57!

Differentiation
Differentiate ability groups by the numbers you give them to work with. For example, less able children could be given 20, 5, 4; more able children could be given 448, 56, 8.

Some children could work at the computer using word-processing software and the on-screen calculator to develop and present their story problems. Less able children could work with the support of an adult scribe; more able children should work independently.

Plenary
Ask representatives from the groups to read their story problems for the rest of the class to solve mentally. The other class members should try to spot the three connected numbers. Can they identify them from the first problem and hence solve the other problems more easily?

40 Relay race

Objectives

Numeracy
Solve mathematical problems and puzzles.
Use units of time.
Record data in tables.
Physical education
Take part in and design challenges that call for precision and speed.
Pace themselves in challenges and competitions.
Links to QCA Physical education 29: Athletic activities.

Resources

Flip chart or board; paper and pencils, stopwatches, relay batons.

Vocabulary

strategy
time
problem
puzzle
distance
speed

Background

What is the best strategy for four runners to carry a baton as fast as possible around four laps of a rectangular course? Should the runners complete a whole lap each, or should they run shorter legs, perhaps a side at a time? In this lesson, children consider alternative strategies for such a relay and test them in a PE lesson.

Preparation

Prepare for a PE lesson focusing on athletics in the school hall or on the playground, according to your normal practice.

Main teaching activity

Introduce the lesson in the classroom by explaining the relay activity. The children will be divided into groups of four. Each group must run four laps of the hall/playground as a team, passing the baton from child to child. Individual team members can run in any order and for any distance. The goal is simply to get the baton around the course four times as quickly as possible.

Explain that the teams' task is to devise alternative strategies for the relay and then to test them to see which is better. Use the flip chart to consider alternative approaches. The team members could simply take it in turns to run one complete lap. Alternatively, the team could space itself out around the course so that team members run several part-laps. What are the advantages and disadvantages of the two strategies? What is the best way of spacing the team out?

Set the children to work in their teams to devise two strategies that they wish to test.

Take the class to the hall/playground and ask them to compare their strategies by timing with a stopwatch. The teams should record their times for the alternative methods. Make sure that teams have time to recover between one run and the next so that the test is 'fair'.

Differentiation

Less able groups could concentrate on the timing activity without worrying too much about comparing strategies.

Stretch more able groups by suggesting they consider strategies for a similar relay race with just two runners. This might involve one runner carrying the baton while the other walks across the course to shorten the distance before the start of the next leg.

Plenary

Return to the classroom. Ask the groups to report their findings on the effectiveness of the different strategies. Which strategy produced the fastest time?

Linked to
History

 Golden rectangles

Objectives

Numeracy
Measure lines to the nearest millimetre.
Use fraction notation.
Use ideas of ratio and proportion.
History
To study beliefs and achievements in ancient Greece.
Links to QCA History Unit 15: How do we use ancient Greek ideas today?

Resources

A copy of photocopiable page 84 for each child; rulers and pencils; flip chart or board.

Vocabulary

ratio
proportion
rectangle
breadth
width

Background

The proportions of a rectangle are the ratio of its breadth to its height. For example, the rectangular house fronts below have proportions 1 to 1, 1.5 to 1 and 2 to 1. These proportions affect the appearance of the building, whether it is long and low or nearly square. The proportions of rectangles play a significant role in the design of buildings and other rectangular structures. The ancient Greeks considered that the ideal proportions for a building were those of the 'golden ratio' – 1.618 to 1. This ratio crops up again and again in classical architecture.

Many children will be familiar with the idea of describing rectangles with ratios from the settings on their television sets and DVD players at home. A conventional TV has proportions 4:3 (1.33:1), a widescreen TV has proportions 16:9 (1.78:1), a cinema screen is 20:9 (2.22:1). In this lesson, children measure the sides of a series of rectangles and find their proportions. They can relate the activity both to the modern context of television and cinema, and to classical architecture.

Preparation

Copy and distribute the worksheets with the rulers and pencils.

Main teaching activity

Introduce the lesson by drawing some rectangular 'houses' with different proportions on the board. Discuss the ideal proportions for a good-looking building.

Should it be low and long, or tall and narrow? Develop the idea of the proportions of a rectangle. Show how the proportions can be represented as a ratio. Demonstrate how the ratio can be determined by measuring the lengths of perpendicular sides, dividing one into the other, and expressing the result as a proportion such as 2 to 1 or 1.5 to 1. Use the appropriate vocabulary to help explain the concept of ratio: 'three times as wide as it is tall', '1.5 metres of width for every metre of height.'

Set the children to work in groups to measure the widths and heights of the buildings on the worksheet. They should make and record measurements to the nearest millimetre. The proportions should be calculated from the measurements.

Differentiation

Less able children should concentrate on the measurement. Ask them to compare the heights and widths of the buildings orally: *How many times wider is this house than it is high?*

1.618:1
golden
rectangle

More able children should calculate the proportions of the buildings as numerical ratios in the form 1.5 to 1 or 1.5:1. House 4 has the ideal golden ratio 1.618:1. Do they think it is the most well-proportioned house – that it 'looks right'? Challenge children who have completed the activity to find the proportions of rectangles in the classroom, such as desktops and computer screens.

Plenary

Review the answers to the worksheet. What proportions do the children think look best for a house? Link this to the golden ratio. Explain that the designs of many ancient Greek buildings, notably the Parthenon, were based on this ratio. Look for examples of the golden ratio in architecture and design. The answers are: 1. 60mm × 60mm; 1 to 1 2. 110mm × 55mm; 2 to 1 3. 80mm × 60mm; 1.340 to 1 4. 81mm × 50mm; 1.630 to 1.

42 Classroom sensors

Objectives

Numeracy
Solve a problem by interpreting data from graphs, including those generated by a computer.
Science
Make systematic observations and measurement, including the use of ICT.
ICT
To use ICT to monitor events and environmental changes.
Links to QCA ICT Unit 5F: Monitoring environmental conditions and changes.

Resources

Datalogging sensors and software running on a computer in the classroom, for example *DataHarvest*; a copy of photocopiable page 85 for each child.

Vocabulary

line graph
axes
plot
change
rise
fall

Background

Simple computer sensors and data-logging equipment can be used to monitor temperature, light and sound levels in the classroom. The software displays the values of the monitored quantities as line graphs. The quantity is plotted on the vertical axis against time along the horizontal axis. Sudden changes, for example a rapid decrease in light level when the lights are switched off, appear as steep steps in the graphs. More gradual changes, for example the room cooling down at the end of the day, appear as slopes. In this lesson, the children set up equipment to monitor their classroom over a 24-hour period. They interpret graphs from a typical classroom in preparation for discussion of their own results.

Preparation

Set up the datalogging equipment and ensure that you can set the software to monitor the output of the temperature, light and sound sensors over a 24-hour period. Copy and distribute the worksheets.

Main teaching activity

Introduce the lesson by showing the children the datalogging equipment. Set the software to plot the sensor output over a short interval (say, 1 minute). Explain the function of each of the sensors and demonstrate how the output graphs change as the temperature changes (for example, by holding the temperature sensor in your hand) and as the light and sound levels change. Explain that you are going to monitor temperature, light and sound in the classroom over a 24-hour period, then commence monitoring.

As a class, make predictions of the shapes the graphs might make during this period. When will the light, temperature and sound levels be greatest? When will they be lowest? Which do the children think will change most rapidly at the end of the day? Which will change least rapidly?

Set the children to complete the worksheet activity in pairs or small groups. They should interpret the graphs, answering the questions listed.

Differentiation

Less able children should tackle questions 1–5.

More able children can proceed to question 6, describing the events they think may have occurred.

Plenary

Review the children's answers to the worksheet questions as a class. Ask for their imaginative interpretations of the events recorded by the rises and falls of the sound, light and temperature lines. In a follow-up lesson, interpret the actual graphs recorded for the children's classroom in a similar way. The answers are: **1.** 19°C, **2.** 22°C, **3.** between 13:15 and 13:30, **4.** 9:15, **5a)** 10:55 to 11:10, **b)** 12:00 to 13:00, **c)** 14:40 to 14:55, **d)** 15:30, **6.** The teacher left the classroom and turned off the light at 17:45. The cleaner looked into the classroom at 18:10, then came in and used the vacuum cleaner between 18:15 and 18:30.

 # What fraction?

Builds towards QCA Science Unit 6A:

Objectives

Numeracy
Make and justify estimates of large numbers, and estimate simple proportions such as $1/3$ and $7/10$.

Science
Make systematic observations and measurements.
Identify locally occurring animals.
Builds towards QCA Science Unit 6A: Interdependence and adaptation.

Resources

A copy of photocopiable page 86 for each child; plastic minibeasts or similar small items, for example plastic bricks; a large tray; photographs/book illustrations of large flocks of birds, shoals of fish or insect swarms.

Vocabulary

estimate
count
fraction
proportion

Background

How many birds are there in a flock? What proportion of birds have black heads? Making rapid estimates of quantities such as these is a valuable fieldwork skill in science investigations. Counting each individual in a rapidly moving flock is not possible, therefore sensible estimation strategies must be employed. One possibility is to see the whole flock as an array, make simpler estimates of the number of individuals along the length and width of the array, and multiply to find the total in the group. Proportions of different individual types can be estimated by focusing on a sample of the total, then counting to determine the proportions in the sample and hence the whole group. If the types are distributed randomly this technique will work – count a selection of samples to check. However, if the types are grouped, then an alternative technique must be applied, for example, visualising the groups as wholes and estimating the proportion of the whole flock occupied by the group.

Preparation

Copy and distribute the worksheets. Set out a regular array of minibeasts/bricks on a tray.

Main teaching activity

Introduce the lesson by showing the children photographs of large groupings of animals. Discuss the problem of estimating numbers in a moving flock in circumstances where it is impossible to count every individual. One technique might be progressive grouping – counting 10, judging the size of a group of 10, estimating the size of ten groups of 10, estimating the size of ten groups of 100 and so on. Another technique is to see the flock/swarm as an array (see Background). Demonstrate this with the array you have prepared on a tray. Remind the children how to calculate the number by multiplying the numbers along the length and the width. Perform this calculation for the regular array, then apply the technique with minibeasts or bricks scattered randomly over the tray.

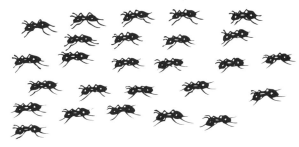

Develop the lesson by considering the estimation of proportions. Set up some examples using the items on the tray, for example 200 bricks: $7/10$ red, $2/10$ white and $1/10$ yellow.

Set the children to practise their estimation skills in pairs or small groups by solving the worksheet problems.

Differentiation

Less able children should concentrate on problems 1 and 2.

More able children who complete the problems satisfactorily could challenge each other with some practical estimation problems using minibeasts/bricks on trays. Alternatively they could make estimates of animal numbers in photographs of flocks, swarms and herds.

Plenary

Conclude the lesson by reviewing the worksheet problems. What techniques did the children use to make their estimates? Did anyone count to check the answers? Ask any children who have made estimates from photographs to describe their findings. The answers are: **1.** $1/2$, **2.** $1/3$, **3.** $1/4$.

44 Area and perimeter

Objectives

Numeracy
Understand area measured in square centimetres (cm^2). Understand in words and use the formula 'length × breadth' for the area of a rectangle. Understand and calculate perimeters of rectangles.
ICT
Work together to explore a variety of ICT tools.
Builds towards QCA ICT Unit 6B: Spreadsheet modelling.

Resources

A computer running software with spreadsheet capabilities, for example *Microsoft Excel* or *Textease*; printers and paper, flip chart or board.

Vocabulary

rectangle
area
perimeter
length
breadth
formula
grid
cell
column
row

Background

A formula is a generalised mathematical relationship or rule that describes how to calculate a quantity that is determined by the values of one or more other quantities. The concept of a formula is best introduced with examples of 'rules' for making calculations in practical situations. For example, the rule for calculating the total cost of a number of identical items is 'total cost = number × cost of one item'. The rule for sharing a number of sweets between a number of children is 'number of sweets each = total number of sweets ÷ number of children'. In this lesson, children explore the rules for calculating the area and perimeter of a rectangle. These rules may be written as word formulae as follows:
area = length × breadth
perimeter = length + length + breadth + breadth = (2 × length) + (2 × breadth).

A spreadsheet is a good tool with which to explore rules and the effect of substituting specific values into general formulae.

Preparation

Set up the computer running your chosen software package. Check that you can use it confidently to calculate the perimeter and area of a rectangle. A sample spreadsheet is shown opposite. This was produced in *Excel* by entering the following formulae in cells C2 and D2.

C2=A2*B2
D2=A2+A2+B2+B2
When length and breadth values are entered in cells A2 and B2, the spreadsheet calculates the area and perimeter values using the formulae.

Main teaching activity

Introduce the lesson by reminding the children about areas and perimeters of rectangles with some examples on the board. Introduce the idea of a formula or rule, and through discussion arrive at formulae for the area and perimeter of any rectangle.

Tell the children they are going to use a spreadsheet on the computer to explore the formulae. Set the children to work in small groups at the computer. Show them how to set up the spreadsheets and enter the appropriate formulae into the cells. Demonstrate how, when a number in a cell to which the formulae refer is changed, the spreadsheet updates the values in the other cells.

Let the children explore the effect of changing the length and breadth values. They should print sample results for discussion in the plenary session.

Differentiation

Less able children may find the process of programming a spreadsheet too demanding. Let them work with a spreadsheet you have programmed in advance of the lesson.

Challenge more able children to use their spreadsheet to investigate the following questions:
● *How does doubling both the length and breadth of a rectangle change the area? What effect does it have on the perimeter?*

● *How does trebling the length and breadth of a rectangle change the area? What effect does it have on the perimeter?*

● *Can you predict how multiplying the length and the breadth of a rectangle by 5 will change its area and perimeter? Test your prediction.*

Plenary

Look at the spreadsheets the children have produced. Discuss the ICT techniques they used. Have any of the children used their spreadsheets to make the suggested investigations? What have they found out?

45 Unfinished buildings

Linked to
D & T
Art & Design

Objectives

Numeracy
Visualise 3-D shapes from 2-D drawings.
Design and technology
Communicate design ideas in different ways.
Art and design
To explore visual elements including form and space.

Resources

A copy of photocopiable page 87 for each child; sets of wooden building cubes.

Vocabulary

cube
cuboid
pyramid
two-dimensional
three-dimensional

Background

Anyone who has attempted to follow the instructions to assemble flat-pack furniture will be familiar with the problem of visualising a three-dimensional structure from a two-dimensional drawing! Once the structure is put together successfully, the drawing becomes obvious, but it can be a considerable struggle to reach this stage. Practical experience is the best way of developing understanding of the visual conventions linking a 3-D object to its 2-D representation. As the flat-pack example demonstrates, this is an important skill in design and technology projects. In this lesson, children solve problems based on 2-D drawings of 3-D structures, for example working out how many more blocks are required to complete a wall. They then use building blocks to check their conclusions.

Preparation

Copy and distribute the worksheets on tables together with the building blocks.

Main teaching activity

Introduce the lesson by building a structure like the one illustrated using the wooden blocks. Ask the children to predict how many

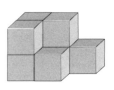

more blocks are required to turn the shape into a cuboid. Check the children's predictions by completing the cuboid.

Develop the lesson by showing the children the worksheet. Discuss how the drawings represent unfinished or decayed ancient buildings. Explain that the children's task is to answer the questions by interpreting the diagrams. They may then wish to check their answers by reproducing the structures using actual cubes. Set the children to work in small groups on the task.

Differentiation

Less able children may struggle to solve problems visually from the 2-D diagrams. Suggest that they use building blocks to help from the outset.

Challenge more able children to attempt to generate their own similar problems. They should make a partially completed structure and then try to sketch it (or perhaps draw it using the 3-D shape tools in a software package such as *Microsoft Word*). They could imagine their structure as a decayed ancient temple discovered in the jungle. Can their friends interpret the drawings and say what the shape of the original structure might have been?

Plenary

Review the answers to the worksheet problems. Have any children created problems of their own? If so, solve them as a class. The answers are: **1.** 3, **2.** 4, **3.** 8, **4.** 7, **5.** 22, **6.** 7.

Linked to
H i s t o r y
S c i e n c e

 **Wind chimes**

Objectives

Numeracy
Relate fractions to their decimal representations.
Use division to find fractions of quantities.
Develop calculator skills.
Measure lengths to the nearest mm.
History
To study beliefs and achievements in ancient Greece.
Links to QCA History Unit 15: How do we use ancient Greek ideas today?
Science
To learn how to change the pitch and loudness of sounds made by some vibrating objects.
Links to QCA Science Unit 5F: Changing sounds.
Also links to QCA Design and Technology Unit 5A: Musical instruments.

Resources

A collection of wind chimes (you could ask children to bring chimes from home for this lesson); rulers, craft materials for making wind chimes (for example, aluminium, wood, plastic and card tubes and rods, thread, wire, large wooden beads, tape, junior hacksaws and hand drills); calculators.

Vocabulary

measure
millimetre
fraction
length
ratio

Background

This lesson builds on Lesson 27, 'Musical measures'. Pythagoras' discoveries about the relationship between the musical scale and numbers can be exploited to produce harmonious sounding wind chimes. When two notes are sounded together, the pitches may combine to produce a pleasing harmonious effect (concord) or an unpleasant clash (discord). Pythagoras found that the notes produced by tapping two rods or bars that are identical in every way but length are harmonious if the ratio of the lengths of the bars is a simple fraction such as $\frac{1}{2}$, $\frac{2}{3}$, $\frac{3}{4}$ or $\frac{4}{5}$. In this lesson, children measure the lengths of wind chime bars to see if Pythagoras' rule is obeyed. They use their design and technology skills to make wind chimes of their own.

Preparation

Make a collection of wind chimes and set them out with the craft resources.

Main teaching activity

Introduce the lesson by listening to the sounds of different wind chimes. Which ones play harmonious combinations of notes? Are there any that sound discordant? Ask children the question: *How does the wind chime maker know how long to make the wind chime bars?* Describe Pythagoras' discoveries

about scales, harmony and numbers.

Set the children to work in small groups to investigate the various wind chimes you have collected. They should measure and record the lengths of the wind chime bars in a table like the one below. They should then calculate the ratios of the lengths of the different bars. Are the ratios simple fractions as Pythagoras suggested? Develop the lesson by challenging the

length of chime bar in cm	ratio to longest bar	nearest simple fraction
30	$^{30}/_{30} = 1$	1
24	$^{24}/_{30} = 0.8$	$\frac{4}{5}$
20	$^{20}/_{30} = 0.67$	$\frac{2}{3}$
15	$^{15}/_{30} = 0.5$	$\frac{1}{2}$

children to work in groups to design and make their own wind chimes. They should investigate the different materials for the chime bars and select the material they wish to use. Which materials make ringing sounds, and which make dull sounds? How long should the bars be? Can they use Pythagoras' ideas to make a harmonious chime? To complete the chimes they must measure and cut the bars to length (or ask an adult to do this for them), and devise a method of suspending them, perhaps with wire and threads, so they can swing and clash in the wind.

Differentiation

Help less able children to make a simple chime with three bars with lengths in the ratio 1 to $\frac{4}{5}$ to $\frac{2}{3}$ (*doh, me, soh*). So if the longest bar is 15cm, the other bars are 12cm and 10cm.
More able children can explore more complex combinations of bar lengths.

Plenary

Ask representatives of the groups to describe and demonstrate their wind chime designs.

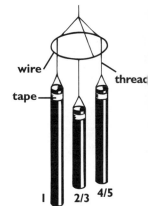

Activities

Linked to
Science

47 Making allowances

Objectives

Numeracy
Suggest suitable measuring equipment, recording estimates and readings from scales to a suitable degree of accuracy.
Science
To make systematic observations and measurements.

Resources

Kitchen scales, measuring cylinders; flip chart or board; a copy of photocopiable page 88 for each child.

Vocabulary

measurement
scale
initial reading
final reading
difference
m
litre
kg
°C

Background

In a number of practical measurement situations it is necessary to find the desired quantity by taking the difference between two separate scale readings. For example, when weighing a quantity of liquid the weight of the container must be 'allowed for'. When finding a temperature change, the initial temperature must be subtracted from the final temperature. When finding the height by which a plant has grown in a set period, the initial height must be subtracted from the final height. In this lesson, children develop their measuring skills by reading scales between divisions, for example to find a weight, length or temperature change.

Preparation

Copy and distribute the worksheets. Set out the measuring resources in preparation for practical work.

Main teaching activity

Introduce the lesson by setting the children the problem of weighing water. How much does half a litre of water weigh? Set the children to work in groups to devise a method for weighing water. Discuss the procedure with each group before they make their measurements. Children should recognise that they must make allowance for the weight of the water container in their measurement:
weight of water = weight of water in container – weight of container

Review the children's results, checking that they have allowed for the container weight correctly.

Continue the lesson by setting the children to solve the worksheet problems in their groups. Make the link between the water-measuring activity and the examples on the worksheet. In each case, the difference between two scale readings must be found to determine the required quantity.

Differentiation

Less able children should concentrate on the basic worksheet activity.

Challenge more able children to extend the water-weighing exercise to other materials. Can they compare the weights of half a litre of sand, half a litre of sugar and half a litre of soap powder? How do the weights compare with the same volume of water?

Plenary

Review the answers to the worksheet problems as a whole class. Conclude the lesson with some rapid mental calculations based on finding differences between pairs of scale readings. The answers are:
1. 1.25m
2. 600ml
3. 60°
4. 3.1kg

Linked to
Geography

48 Missing map

Objectives

Numeracy
Choose and use appropriate number operations to solve problems.
Add several numbers mentally.
Develop calculator skills and use a calculator effectively.
Geography
To use maps at a range of scales.
To study localities at a range of scales.

Resources

Michelin maps of locations of interest to the class; a copy of photocopiable page 89 for each child; calculators, pencils and paper; flip chart or board.

Vocabulary

map
calculator
addition
subtraction

Background

Many road maps, particularly continental maps such as those produced by Michelin, show distances along main routes with 'flags' linked to population centres. These flags indicate journey distances at different levels. For example, the distance between two large towns, indicated with large open-circle flags, is subdivided into distances between smaller towns and villages, indicated with smaller closed-circle flags as shown below.

below on the board. Explain the distance marking system and ask the children to check mentally that the distances between the smaller flags add up to the distance between the larger flags, then to confirm their calculations with a calculator. Remind them how to check a calculation by performing it in a different sequence.

Set the children to complete the worksheet activity in pairs or small groups. Explain that coffee has been spilled on the map, obscuring some of the distance markings. Their task is to use the information that remains, together with their calculators, to restore the original numbers.

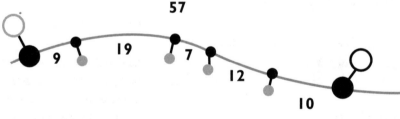

At first the system may seem confusing, but it is easy to use once you understand it. In this lesson, children practise using the system on a hypothetical section of map reproduced on the worksheet. They then use a real Michelin map of France (or another European location they are studying), to ask and answer questions about road distances.

Preparation

Make a collection of appropriate maps. Copy the worksheets and distribute them with calculators, pencils and paper.

Main teaching activity

Introduce the lesson by sketching a portion of a road map similar to the illustration

Differentiation

Less able children should concentrate on the basic activity. Help them to plan the calculations that must be made to find the numbers that have been blotted out.

More able children can proceed to look at some actual Michelin maps. Set them the task of comparing the length of alternative routes between two destinations using the data on the map.

Plenary

Review the worksheet answers with the whole class. Ask children to double-check the calculations with their calculators. Ask any children who have made route comparisons with the Michelin maps to explain their findings. The answers are (clockwise from the top): 10, 34, 21, 26.

49 Human numbers

Objectives

Numeracy
Use the vocabulary of estimation and approximation.
Make and justify estimates of large numbers.
Develop calculator skills and use a calculator effectively.
Science
Learn about life processes common to humans and other animals.
Could be linked to QCA Science Unit 5A: Keeping healthy.

Resources

Books, CD-ROMs and other reference materials on the human body; calculators.

Vocabulary

estimate
calculate
count
measure
round
approximately
multiple of 10

Background

There are some large numbers associated with the human body. For example:
● we have about 100 000 hairs on our heads
● we take 100 000 breaths a week
● our heart beats 30 000 000 times a month.

Estimating such quantities requires children to research the basic scientific facts and make calculations involving large numbers. In this lesson, children use their research and calculator skills to complete a chart of 'natural numbers'.

Preparation

Assemble the research materials and set them out with the calculators.

Main teaching activity

Introduce the lesson by asking the children how many times they take a breath in a day. Ask for some initial guesses, then discuss the process of making a more scientific estimate. Time the number of breaths taken by a child in a minute and use a calculator to find the number in a day.

number of breaths in a day = number of breaths in a minute × 60 × 24

Discuss rounding the results obtained to an appropriate degree of accuracy.

Set the children to work in pairs or small groups on the following questions. They should make estimates of each of the quantities, using the research materials or simple measurements to establish the data for their calculations.

1. The number of times you are born. (1)
2. The number of litres of blood in a human body. (5)
3. The number of breaths you take in an hour. (600)
4. The number of times you blink in a minute. (20)
5. The number of times your heart beats in a minute. (70)
6. The number of times you stand up and sit down in a day. (around 100; depending on what you're doing that day)
7. The number of breaths you take in a day. (14 000)
8. The number of times your heart beats in day. (100 000)
9. The number of hours you spend asleep in a year. (3000)
10. The number of hairs on your head. (100 000)
11. The mass of food you eat in a year. (350kg)
12. The number of litres of water you drink in a year. (700 l)

Differentiation

Less able children may need considerable help to plan their calculations. Help them to decide what data they need and what calculation must be made.

Challenge more able children to make a number chart like the one shown below. Can they identify a quantity for each power of 10 associated with the human body?

Human numbers

1 head
10 fingers
100 loops in a thumb print
1000 breaths an hour
10 000…

Plenary

Ask the groups to report their estimates to the class. Do the groups agree on the numbers? How were their estimates made? Have any children managed to complete a table of human numbers?

50 Assessment 3

Preparation

Make copies of the assessment sheet. If you feel that the sheet is too 'busy', the three activities could be separated and enlarged on individual sheets.

Lesson introduction

Begin the assessment lesson by reviewing the relevant cross-curricular topics covered during the term. Remind the children of some of the projects and investigations they have undertaken, and ask them to recall and recount their work. Emphasise the mathematical content, for example: *Do you remember how we investigated temperature changes in the classroom over 24 hours?*

Main assessment activity

Distribute the worksheets and ask the children to work on them individually. Guide the whole class through the questions one at a time, reading the text with them, and prompting them to work out and fill in their answers. Try to make the whole activity enjoyable!

Practical activity

Ask the children to find the mass of 500ml of water. They should take two readings: the mass of the empty measuring cylinder and the mass of the cylinder plus water. Check that they read the balance and the measuring cylinder scale with appropriate accuracy. Children should recognise that the mass of the water is the difference between the two readings.

Plenary

Review the answers to the questions as a class. Collect the completed question sheets to use as an aid to judging individual children's progress, and to include in your records. The answers are:
1. –5°C, 45°C, 50°C
2. £12.28, 50p, Vegieburger, £3.60
3. See diagram below.

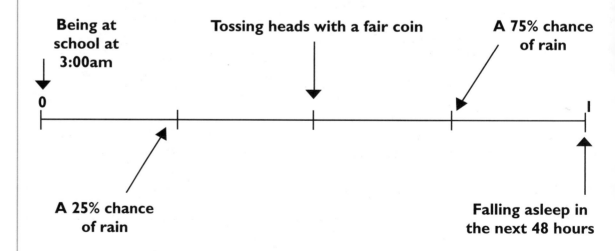

Being at school at 3:00am — 0

Tossing heads with a fair coin

A 75% chance of rain

A 25% chance of rain

Falling asleep in the next 48 hours

Populations

● This table gives the populations of towns and cities in the Midlands

city/town	population
Birmingham	1 013 400
Bromsgrove	85 200
Coventry	304 300
Dudley	311 500
Lichfield	94 100
Redditch	76 700
Rugby	87 800
Solihull	205 600
Walsall	261 200
Warwick	123 800
Wolverhampton	241 600

1. Write the population of Rugby in words.

_____

_____

_____

2. Write the population of Dudley in words.

_____

_____

_____

3. Write the population of Birmingham in words.

_____

_____

_____

4. Put the towns and cities in order according to their population. Write them in ascending order (smallest first).

city/town	population

Cost of living

Prices have increased since 1948. But by how much?
● Divide the present day price by the 1948 price to find how many times more things cost now. Use your calculator to check your results.

item	1948 price £ s d	1948 price £.p	present day price £.p	present day price ÷ 1948 price
Pair of shoes	£1 0s 0d	£1	£25	25
Chocolate bar	2d	1p	20p	
Fish and chips	1s 0d	5p	£2.50	
Loaf of bread	6d	2.5p	75p	
Television set	£50 0s 0d	£50	£300	
Car	£300 0s 0d	£300	£9000	
House	£800 0s 0d	£800	£80 000	
Train journey	2s 0d	10p	£10	
Weekly wages	£8 0s 0d	£8	£400	

1. Which items have increased most in price since 1948?
Can you think why?

2. Which items have increased least in price since 1948?
Can you think why?

3. Look at the change in weekly wages. Which items are easier to afford now? Which items were easier to afford in 1948?

Tell a story

● Write story problems for these calculations.

set 1
9 + 12 =
32 − 16 =
8 × 7 =
25 ÷ 5 =

set 2
37 + 59 =
120 − 80 =
18 × 4 =
150 ÷ 50 =

set 3
2563 + 4210 =
392 − 180 =
26 × 19 =
483 ÷ 6 =

set 4
121.5 + 27.9 =
53.6 − 21.8 =
26.4 × 11 =
38.7 ÷ 2.3 =

● Use your calculator to help.

■ SCHOLASTIC

What percentage?

The tables below give the results of traffic surveys in different places.

● Fill in the missing numbers and percentages.

Town survey
Total number of vehicles = 100

vehicle type	number	percentage
car	40	40%
lorry	15	
bus		5%
bicycle	20	
motorcycle	19	
tractor		1%

City survey
Total number of vehicles = 200

vehicle type	number	percentage
car	100	
lorry		10%
bus		5%
bicycle	50	
motorcycle	20	
tractor	0	

Village survey
Total number of vehicles = 50

vehicle type	number	percentage
car	20	
lorry	5	
bus	2	
bicycle		20%
motorcycle	8	
tractor		10%

Find the angle

- Use your protractor to measure these angles.
- Label each angle **acute** or **obtuse**.

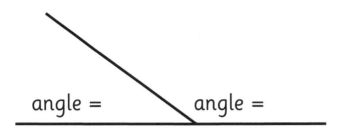

angle =   angle =

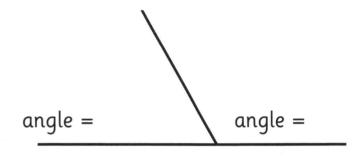

angle =   angle =

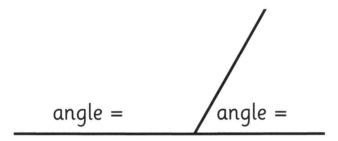

angle =   angle =

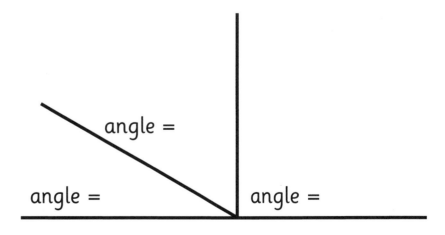

angle =

angle =   angle =

- Check your results.

The angles on a straight line should add to 180°.

Set the timer

● Programme the heating to come on 30 minutes before you get up, and go off when you go to bed.

Heating controller

Heating on | : |

Heating off | : |

● Programme the cooker so that your dinner is ready when you get home from school. It takes 45 minutes to cook.

Cooker

Oven on | : |

Oven off | : |

● Programme the video to record your favourite TV programme the next time it's on.

Video

Start | : |

Stop | : |

Channel | |

Date | / / |

Paying for water

● Check the bill for House 1. Is it correct? Fill in the gaps in the other bills.

House 1

Meter readings				
Last time	This time	Cubic metres used	Price per cubic metre (pence)	Amount (£)
900	1020	120	50	60.00
			Standing charges	10.00
			Sewage charge	90.00
			Total bill	160.00

House 2

Meter readings				
Last time	This time	Cubic metres used	Price per cubic metre (pence)	Amount (£)
1905	2205		50	
			Standing charges	10.00
			Sewage charge	225.00
			Total bill	

House 3

Meter readings				
Last time	This time	Cubic metres used	Price per cubic metre (pence)	Amount (£)
8962	9012		50	
			Standing charges	10.00
			Sewage charge	37.50
			Total bill	

Sale price

● Fill in the missing prices and percentages.

Original price = £10	Original price = £20	Original price = £40
50% reduction!	**25% reduction!**	**75% reduction!**
Sale price =	Sale price =	Sale price =
Original price = £50	Original price = £30	Original price = £100
20% reduction!	**% reduction!**	**% reduction!**
Sale price =	Sale price = £15	Sale price = £80
Original price =	Original price =	Original price =
25% reduction!	**50 % reduction!**	**75% reduction!**
Sale price = £3	Sale price = £17.50	Sale price = £25

How do you?

Work with a partner.
● Write instructions and give examples to explain how to:

1. Find the number of biscuits in 10 packets.

_____

2. Find the number of days in a number of weeks.

_____

3. Share 100 sweets between a number of children.

_____

4. Find the number of stamps on a sheet.

_____

5. Calculate the cost of a sheet of stamps.

_____

6. Find the perimeter of a square.

_____

7. Square a number.

_____

8. Estimate the number of words in a book.

_____

9. Calculate a sale price with a 20% reduction.

_____

10. Multiply a 3-digit number by a 2-digit number.

_____

Name

1. Put these places in order by population – greatest first.

city/town	population	city/town	population
Alnwick	31 400		
Darlington	101 400		
Durham	90 300		
Gateshead	198 900		
Middlesbrough	145 100		
Newcastle upon Tyne	276 100		
Sedgefield	89 300		
Sunderland	292 300		

2. Shade these percentages of the grids.

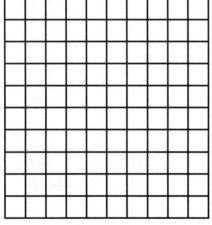

50%

25%

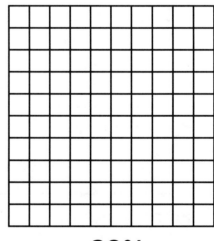

30%

3. Use a ruler to measure the sides of this triangle to the nearest millimetre.

Use a protractor to measure the angles to the nearest degree.

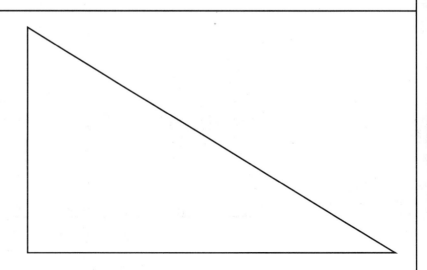

Millennium line

Estimate the dates of these events in the last millennium from the timeline.

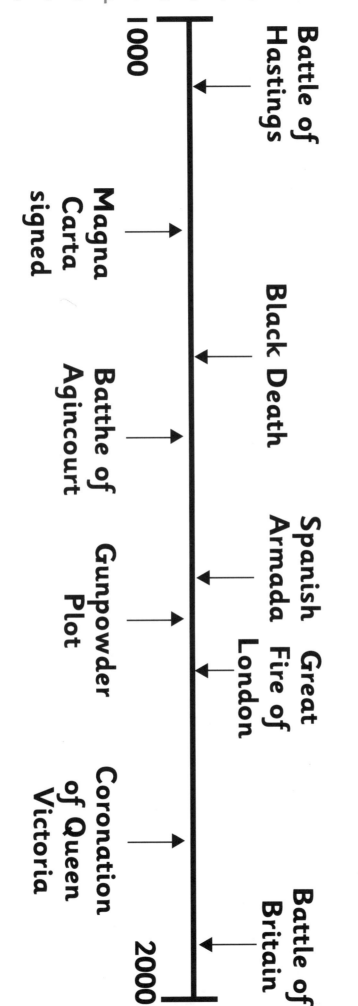

Battle of Hastings

1000

Magna Carta signed

Black Death

Batthe of Agincourt

Spanish Armada

Great Fire of London

Gunpowder Plot

Coronation of Queen Victoria

Battle of Britain

2000

Use history reference materials to check your estimates of the dates.

How much does it hold?

● Estimate the capacities of these containers in litres.

Petrol prices

Fuel prices per litre		
unleaded 70p	diesel 75p	4 star 80p

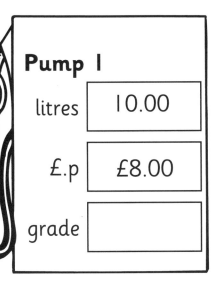

Pump 1

litres	10.00
£.p	£8.00
grade	

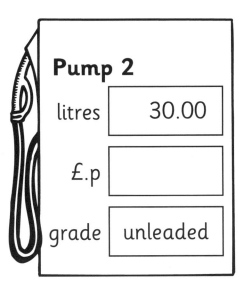

Pump 2

litres	30.00
£.p	
grade	unleaded

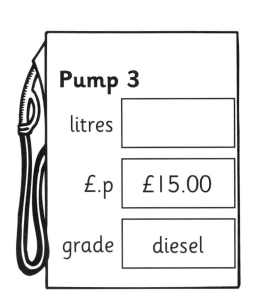

Pump 3

litres	
£.p	£15.00
grade	diesel

1. What grade of fuel was served at pump 1? _____

2. How much did the fuel at pump 2 cost? _____

3. How much fuel was served at pump 3? _____

4. The car that filled up at pump 2 does 10 miles to the litre.

How far can it travel with the petrol purchased? _____

5. The car that filled up at pump 1 does 45 miles to the gallon.

How far can it travel for £8.00? _____

6. The car that filled up at pump 3 uses all the fuel to travel 300 miles.

How much did the fuel for each mile cost? _____

How far does the car travel per litre? _____

Will it rain tomorrow?

Rain forecast for the coming week

day	probability of rain in the morning	probability of rain in the afternoon
Monday	10%	70%
Tuesday	50%	50%
Wednesday	20%	10%
Thursday	5%	30%
Friday	40%	60%
Saturday	70%	90%
Sunday	50%	5%

1. When is it most likely to rain? _____

2. When is it least likely to rain? _____

3. Which is the best day to plan to mow the lawn? _____

4. Which is the best day to plan to do jobs indoors? _____

5. Use these words instead of percentages in the forecast.
   very unlikely, unlikely, even, likely, very likely

day	probability of rain in the morning	probability of rain in the afternoon
Monday		
Tuesday		
Wednesday		
Thursday		
Friday		
Saturday		
Sunday		

Pinboard

● Use rubber bands to make these shapes on your pinboard.
Solve the challenges by making more shapes.

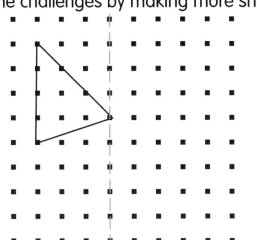

Reflect the triangle in
the dotted line.

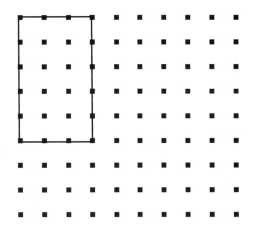

Make shapes with the same area.

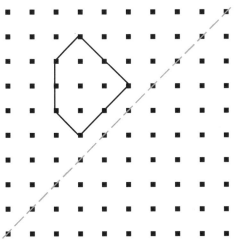

Reflect this shape in the dotted line.

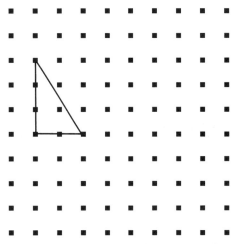

Translate this shape 5 spaces
to the right.

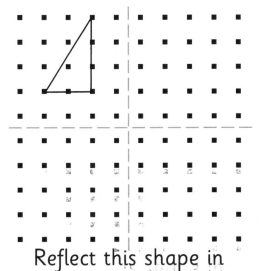

Reflect this shape in
the dotted lines.

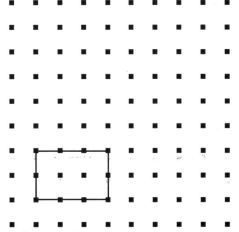

Translate this shape 4 spaces to
the right and 5 spaces up.

Height graph

● Plot this data on the graph.

age in years	girls' heights in cm	boys' heights in cm
0	55	55
2	90	89
4	100	100
6	109	109
8	124	124
10	137	135
12	151	145
14	157	159
16	162	163
18	163	171
20	163	174
22	163	174

Growth graph

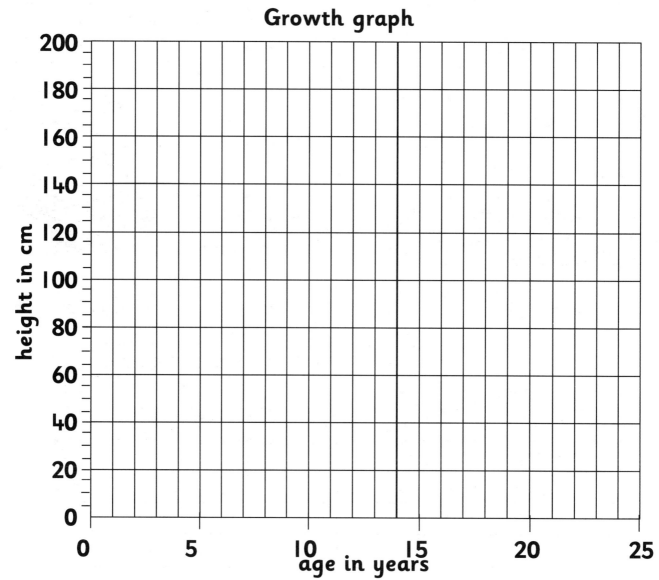

Price wars

Superstore	£.p
baked beans 400g	0.45
bread large sliced	0.65
Cola 6 pack	1.20
apples 2kg	1.60
cornflakes 750 g	1.80
dog food 2kg	1.50
Total	

Corner shop	£.p
baked beans 200g	0.30
bread large sliced	0.95
Cola 1 can	0.35
apples 1kg	1.20
cornflakes 500 g	1.40
dog food 1kg	0.95
Total	

Market	£.p
baked beans 400g	0.50
bread large sliced	0.80
Cola 1 can	0.50
apples 2kg	1.00
cornflakes 500g	1.00
dog food 5kg	3.00
Total	

1. Calculate the total for each bill.

2. Where is bread cheapest? Where is it most expensive?

3. Compare the value for money for the other items.
- Complete the table below.

1 = best value   2 = mid-value   3 = worst value

item	superstore	corner shop	market
baked beans			
bread	1	3	2
Cola			
apples			
cornflakes			
dog food			

Smoking kills!

Everybody eventually gets old and dies.
Some people die at a younger age than expected because
they have accidents or do not look after themselves.

The table below compares the number of people each year
who die early for different reasons.
The numbers are for a typical large city.

cause of early death	number	rank
Alcohol and drugs	250	
Road accidents	100	
Smoking	2000	
Murder	5	
Drowning	10	
Accidents at work or home	300	
Lightning strike	1	
Total		

1. Rank the causes of death in order – greatest first.

2. Calculate the total number of people who die early as a result of all these causes in the
city each year.

3. How many lives could be saved each year if nobody smoked?

4. Which is more likely – being murdered, dying in an accident, or dying through smoking?

5. What is the best advice you could give to young people to avoid dying early?

Explain yourself

● Can you do these calculations in your head? How do you think them through? Write an explanation of your method.

1. 3004 – 2999 _____

_____

2. 15 × 4 _____

_____

3. 250 × 6 _____

_____

4. 69 × 30 _____

_____

5. 209 ÷ 21 _____

_____

6. $\frac{1}{8}$ of 112 _____

_____

7. 6014 – 2986 _____

_____

8. $\frac{1}{16}$ of 4800 _____

_____

Name

1. Fill in the gaps in this table of fractions and percentages.

fraction	decimal	percentage
$\frac{1}{2}$	0.5	
$\frac{1}{4}$		25%
	0.2	
		75%
	0.33	
$\frac{7}{10}$		

2. Estimate the positions of the arrows on these lines.

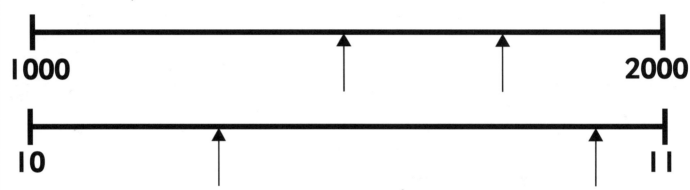

1000   2000

10   11

3. Use the currency table to calculate:

currency	£1 buys
euro	€1.63
Indian rupee	69.4 R
US dollar	$1.44

The number of euros you can buy for £10.

_____

The number of rupees you can buy for £100.

_____

The number of dollars you can buy for £1000.

_____

The planets

Sequence the planets in the blank tables.

planets in alphabetical order	distance from Sun in millions of km	size in km	surface temperature in °C (maximum)
Earth	149.6	12 756	55
Jupiter	778.3	142 800	−160
Mars	227.9	6794	25
Mercury	59.9	4878	430
Neptune	4496.7	49 500	−213
Pluto	5900	2284	−230
Saturn	1427.0	120 000	−150
Uranus	2869.6	51 800	−220
Venus	108.2	12 104	480

planets in distance order (ascending)	distance from Sun in millions of km

planets in temperature order (descending)	temperature in °C

planets in order of size	size (km)

Golden rectangles

- Measure the height and width of these houses. (Do not include the roof.)
- Calculate the proportions of each building.
- Which do you think looks best?

1.

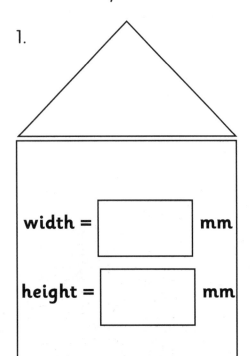

width = [ ] mm

height = [ ] mm

proportions _____ to _____

2.

width = [ ] mm

height = [ ] mm

proportions _____ to _____

3.

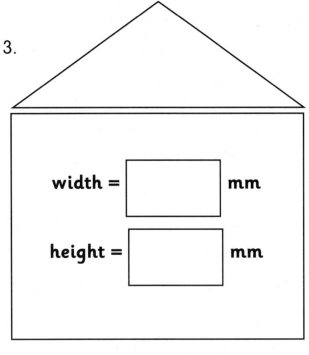

width = [ ] mm

height = [ ] mm

proportions _____ to _____

4.

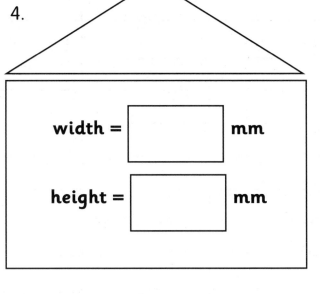

width = [ ] mm

height = [ ] mm

proportions _____ to _____

Classroom sensors

Year 5 set up light, temperature and sound sensors in their classroom.
Their teacher started recording the data on the computer at 8:15, then started to take the register at 9:00.

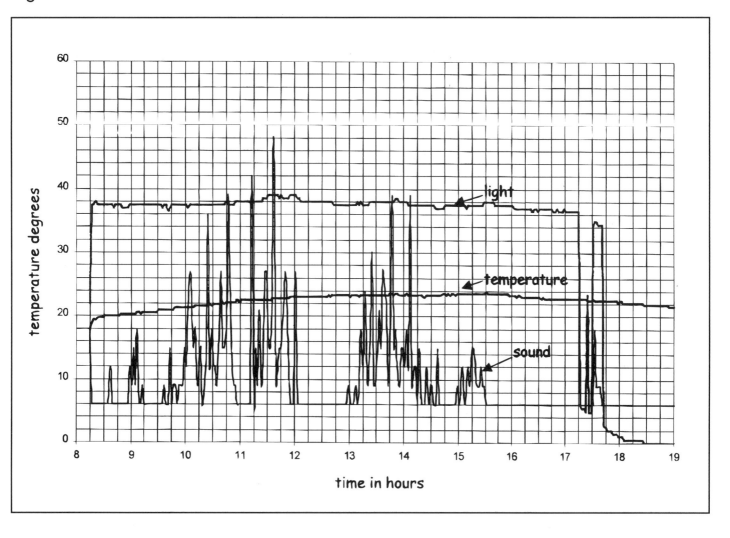

1. What was the temperature in the room at 8:30? _____

2. What was the temperature at 15:30? _____

3. At what time was there most noise in the classroom? _____

4. At what time did the class leave the room to go to assembly?

_____

5. Estimate the times of:

a) morning break   b) lunch   c) afternoon break   d) home time

_____   _____   _____   _____

6. Can you suggest what happened between 17:00 and 19:00?

_____

What fraction?

● Estimate the number of fish in these shoals.
What fraction of each shoal is black?

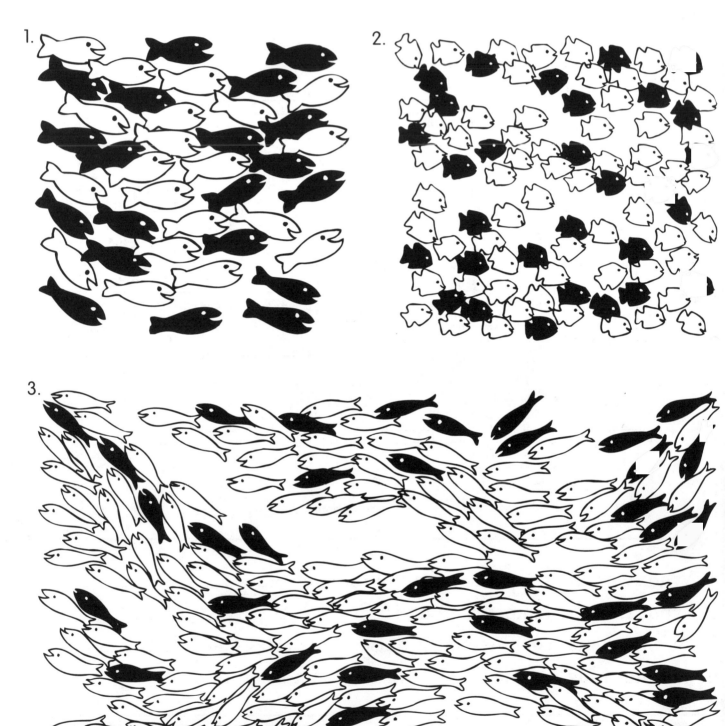

Unfinished buildings

● How many blocks are missing from these temple ruins?
They should be solid shapes.

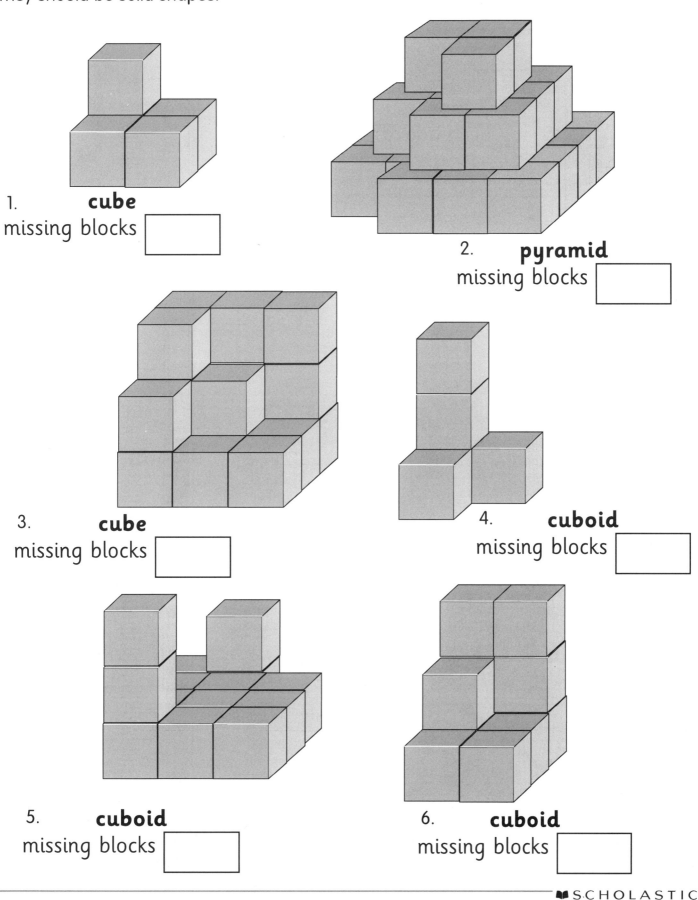

1.   **cube**
missing blocks

2.   **pyramid**
missing blocks

3.   **cube**
missing blocks

4.   **cuboid**
missing blocks

5.   **cuboid**
missing blocks

6.   **cuboid**
missing blocks

Making allowances

● Record the readings.

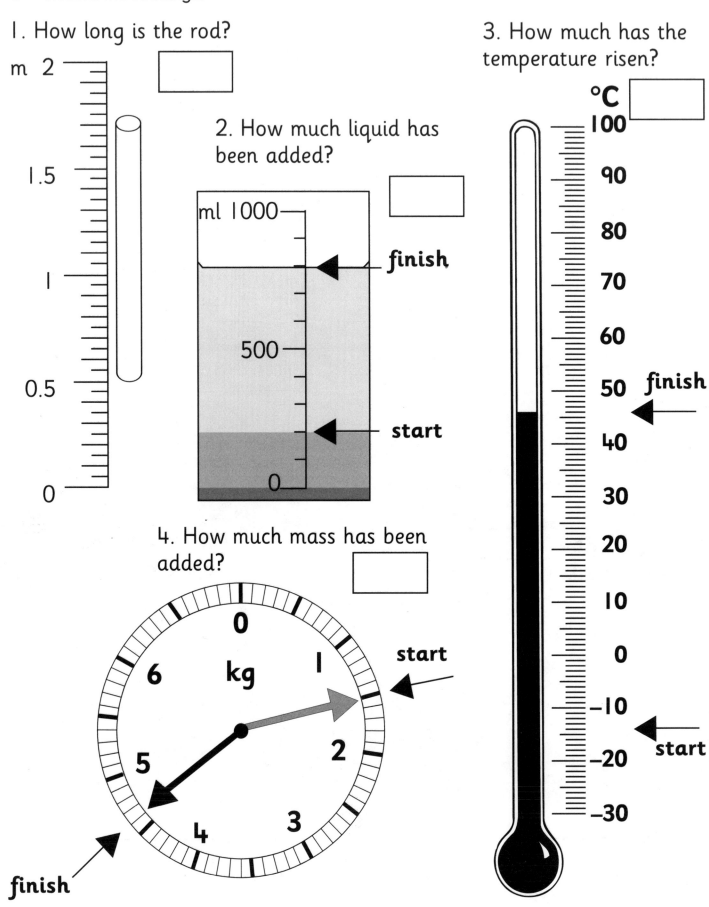

1. How long is the rod?

m 2

1.5

1

0.5

0

2. How much liquid has been added?

ml 1000

500

0

finish

start

3. How much has the temperature risen?

°C

100

90

80

70

60

50 — finish

40

30

20

10

0

−10

−20 — start

−30

finish

start

4. How much mass has been added?

0

6   kg   1

5   2

4   3

start

finish

Missing map

Someone has spilled coffee on the map!

● Write in the missing distance numbers on the stains.

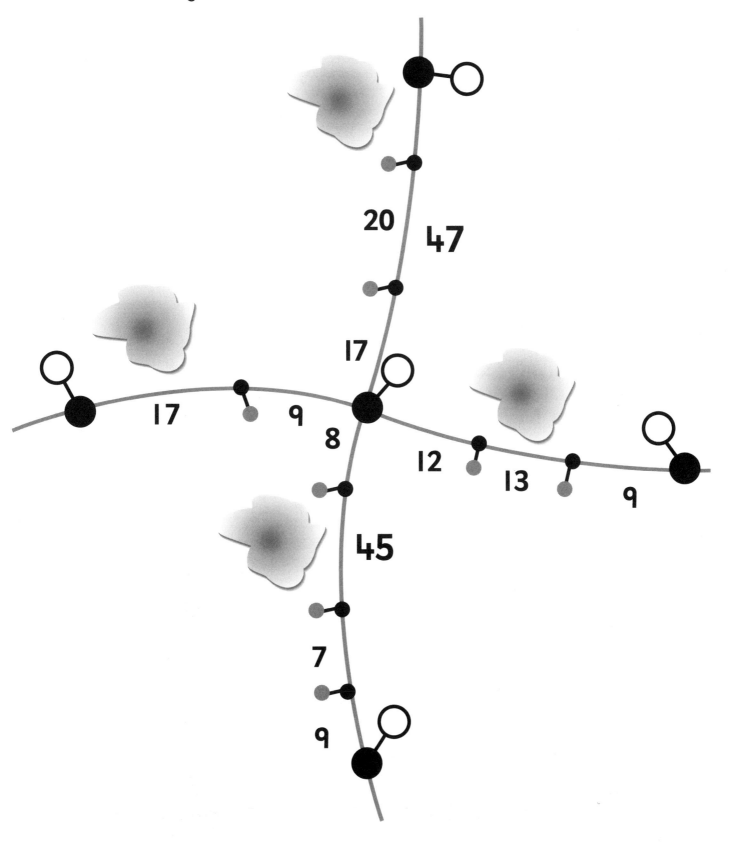

Name

1. Complete the table of temperature readings.

start temperature	finish temperature	temperature rise
°C	°C	°C

2. Find the total for this bill.

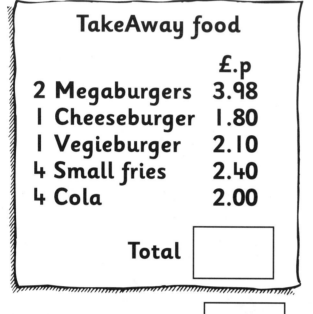

TakeAway food

	£.p
2 Megaburgers	3.98
1 Cheeseburger	1.80
1 Vegieburger	2.10
4 Small fries	2.40
4 Cola	2.00

Total ☐

How much does 1 Cola cost? ☐

Which costs more –
a Vegieburger ☐ or a Megaburger? ☐
☐ (Tick the right one.)

How much would 6 small fries cost? ☐

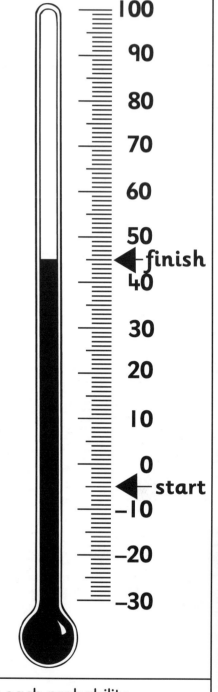

°C
— 100
— 90
— 80
— 70
— 60
— 50
◀ finish
— 40
— 30
— 20
— 10
— 0
◀ start
— –10
— –20
— –30

3. Estimate where these events go on the probability line. Mark each probability with an arrow.

Tossing heads with a fair coin.
A 75% chance of rain.
A 25% chance of rain.
Being at school at 3:00am tomorrow morning.
Falling asleep in the next 48 hours.

0 ├─────────────────────┼─────────────────────┤

100
Cross-curricular
Maths
Lessons

Lesson plans and photocopiable activity pages

Year 6

Term 1	Topics	Maths objectives	Cross-curricular objectives	Activities
Unit 1	Place value, ordering, rounding Using a calculator	Find the difference between a positive and a negative integer, or two negative integers, in a context such as temperature or the number line, and order a set of positive and negative integers.	**Science** To describe changes that occur when materials are heated or cooled. To be taught about reversible changes, including melting, boiling, condensing and freezing. Links to QCA Science Unit 6D: Reversible and irreversible changes.	**p95: Hot and cold** Sequence and find the difference between melting temperatures.
2–3	Understanding × and ÷ Mental calculation strategies (× and ÷) Pencil and paper procedures (× and ÷) Money and 'real-life' problems Making decisions and checking results, including using a calculator Fractions, decimals and percentages	Multiply by 10, 100, 1000 and explain the effect. Develop calculator skills and use a calculator effectively. Recognise and extend number sequences.	**Science** To use a food chain to show a feeding relationship. To know that nearly all food chains start with a green plant. Links to QCA Science Unit 6A: Interdependence and adaptation.	**p96: Food pyramids** Explore the mathematics of numbers in a food pyramid with a calculator.
		Use closely related facts in multiplication problems, for example by rounding, multiplying and then adjusting. Check with inverse operations or equivalent calculations. Use a calculator effectively.	**Geography** To carry out fieldwork investigations outside the classroom. Could be linked to QCA Geography Units 15: The mountain environment or 13: A contrasting UK locality..	**p97: What's the bill?** Explore and explain mental strategies for finding multiples of sums such as £1.99 and £2.05.
		Use related facts for mental multiplication, for example develop the 17 times table by adding facts from the 10 times table and the 7 times table.	**ICT** Work together to explore a variety of ICT tools. Links to QCA ICT Unit 6B: Spreadsheet modelling.	**p98: Beyond times 10** Produce multiplication tables beyond the 10 times table by adding times tables using a spreadsheet.
4–5	Ratio and proportion Handling data	Develop formal pencil and paper procedures for all four operations.	**History** A study of Victorian Britain. Links to QCA History Unit 11: What was it like for children living in Victorian Britain?	**p99: Victorian sums** Reproduce standard methods and story problems from a Victorian school mathematics book.
6	Using a calculator	Recognise the equivalence between the decimal and fractional forms of simple fractions. Express simple fractions as percentages.	**Science** To know that light is reflected from surfaces. To know that we see things only when light from them enters our eyes. Links to QCA Science Unit 6F: How we see things.	**p100: Colour fractions** Explore fractions in the context of sectors coloured on a colour wheel.
			Art and design To be taught about visual elements including colour.	
		Begin to convert a fraction to a decimal using division.	**ICT** Work together to explore a variety of ICT tools. Links to QCA ICT Unit 6B: Spreadsheet modelling.	**p101: Fractions and decimals** Use a spreadsheet to convert vulgar fractions into decimal fractions.
		Solve simple problems involving ratio and proportion.	**Design and technology** To explore how mechanisms can be used to make things move in different ways. Links to QCA Design and Technology Units 6C and 6D	**p102: Pulleys and gears** Investigate gear and pulley ratios.
		Solve a problem by representing data in tables and on line graphs.	**Science** To know that light cannot pass through some materials, and how this leads to the formation of shadows. Links to QCA Science Unit 6F: How we see things.	**p103: Shadow graphs** Measure and plot shadow size change with distance from light source.
		Begin to find the mean of a set of data. Calculate the area of rectangles. Use the vocabulary of estimation.	**Science** To carry out a complete scientific investigation. Links to QCA Science Unit 6H: Environmental enquiry.	**p105: Dandelions** Use a quadrant to estimate the number of dandelions in a field.
7	Assess and review			**See p113.**
8–10	Shape and space Reasoning about shapes Measures, including problems	Classify quadrilaterals, using criteria such as parallel sides, equal angles, equal sides...	**ICT** To develop and refine ideas by bringing together, organising and reorganising text, tables, images and sounds. Work together to explore a variety of ICT tools. Links to QCA ICT Unit 6A: Multimedia.	**p106: Multimedia shapes** Make a multimedia presentation about quadrilaterals.
11	Mental calculation strategies (+ and –) Pencil and paper procedures (+ and –) Money and 'real-life' problems Making decisions and checking results, including using a calculator Properties of numbers	To recognise where a shape will be after reflection: in a mirror line touching the shape at a point; in two mirror lines at right angles.	**Science** To know that light is reflected from surfaces. Links to QCA Science Unit 6F: How we see things.	**p107: It's all done with mirrors** Sketch reflections of shapes in single and double mirrors.
		Solve mathematical problems or puzzles. Suggest suitable measuring equipment to estimate or measure length, mass and capacity.	**Science** To make systematic observations and measurements. Could link to QCA Science Unit 6H: Environmental enquiry.	**p108: Mystery measures** Develop strategies for counting and measuring sheets of paper, blades of grass and grains of sand.
		Add several numbers mentally. Use informal and standard pencil and paper methods to support, record or explain additions and subtractions.	**Physical education** To take part in and design athletic challenges that call for stamina. To pace themselves in these challenges. Links to QCA Physical Education 31: Athletic activities.	**p109: Distance club** Make mental calculations based on distances run or walked.
		Recognise and extend number sequences, such as the sequence of square numbers, or the sequence of triangular numbers.	**ICT** Work together to explore a variety of ICT tools. Builds on QCA ICT Unit 5A: Graphical modelling.	**p110: Stacking numbers** Explore number sequences generated by regular stacking and arrays.
12	Reasoning about numbers		**Art and design** To explore pattern. Builds on QCA Art and Design Unit 5A: Objects and meaning.	
		Solve mathematical problems or puzzles, recognise and explain patterns and relationships. Explain a generalised relationship in words. Develop from explaining a generalised relationship in words to expressing it in a formula using letters as symbols.	**Design and technology** Develop design ideas and explain them clearly.	**p111: Building fences** Introduce simple formulae in the context of fence building.
		Find simple percentages of small whole-number quantities.	**PSHE & citizenship** To make choices and decisions, for example about how to spend money.	**p112: Discount fares** Complete a table of percentage discounts on basic fares.
13	Assess and review			**p113: Assessment 1**

YEAR 6

Term 2	Topics	Maths objectives	Cross-curricular objectives	Activities
1	Place value, ordering, rounding Using a calculator	Order fractions, Recognise equivalence between the decimal and fraction forms of $1/2$, $1/4$, $3/4$, $1/8$ and tenths. Express simple fractions as percentages. Begin to calculate the mean of a set of data.	**Physical education** To evaluate and improve performance. Could link to QCA Physical Education 26: Striking and fielding games.	**p114: Goal average** Order fractions and percentages derived from goal-scoring records.
2–3	Understanding × and ÷ Mental calculation strategies (× and ÷) Pencil and paper procedures (× and ÷) Money and 'real-life' problems	Multiply and divide decimals by 10 or 100, and integers by 1000 and explain the effect. Convert smaller to larger units of measurement and vice versa (eg m to km, cm or mm).	**Geography** To collect and record evidence. To use atlases and plans at a range of scales. To use secondary sources of information.	**p115: Times 10** Build up a table of lengths based on multiplying and dividing by 10.
		Recognise prime numbers to at least 20.	**History** To study the achievements of the ancient Greeks and the influence of their civilisation on the world today. Links to QCA History Unit 15 How do we use ancient Greek ideas today?	**p116: Prime numbers** Identify prime numbers to 100 using the sieve of Eratosthenes.
	Making decisions and checking results, including using a calculator Fractions, decimals and percentages	Describe and visualise properties of solid shapes. Make shapes with increasing accuracy. Visualise 3-D shapes from 2-D drawings.	**History** To study the achievements of the ancient Greeks and the influence of their civilisation on the world today. Links to QCA History Unit 15: How to we use ancient Greek ideas today?	**p117: Ideal shapes** Construct regular solids from nets. Classify solids by counting faces and edges.
4	Using a calculator Shape and space	Calculate the perimeter and area of simple compound shapes that can be split into rectangles. Round up or down depending on the context.	**Design and technology** Plan what they have to do. Measure and mark out a range of materials. Could link to QCA Design and technology Unit 6A: Shelters.	**p118: DIY** Calculate the areas and perimeters of various shaped rooms in the context of DIY.
5	Reasoning about shapes	Identify and use appropriate operations (including combinations of operations) to solve word problems involving numbers and quantities.	**PSHE & citizenship** To make choices and decisions, for example about how to spend money.	**p119: Best buys** Use a calculator to compare costs of different quantities.
		Solve a problem by extracting and interpreting data from charts and diagrams. Use, read and write standard metric units.	**Geography** Use maps and plans at a range of scales. Develop locational knowledge of the British Isles. Links to QCA Geography Unit 3: The mountain environment. Physical education Links to QCA Physical Education 32: Outdoor and adventurous activities.	**p120: Mountain maths** Interpret distances and heights on a map.
		To appreciate different times around the world.	**Science** To explore how the position of the Sun appears to change during the day. To know how day and night are related to the spin of the Earth on its own axis. **Geography** To develop locational knowledge of continents, countries and cities. To use appropriate geographical vocabulary.	**p121: Time zones** Explore time differences around the world.
		Find a simple percentage of small whole-number quantities. Identify and use appropriate operations to solve problems, including calculating percentages such as VAT.	**Literacy** To comment critically on the language, style and success of examples of non-fiction.	**p122: Plus VAT** Make VAT percentage calculations.
6	Assess and review			See p131.
7–8	Measures, including problems Handling data	Use, read and write standard metric units. Know imperial unit (mile, pint, gallon, lb, oz). Know rough equivalents of lb and kg, oz and g, miles and kilometres, litres and pints or gallons. Solve a problem by representing data on a line graph.	**History** To study changes that have taken place since 1930. Links to QCA History Unit 13: How has life in Britain changed since 1948?	**p123: Making conversions** Plot conversion charts/tables between various units.
9–10	Mental calculation strategies (+ and −) Pencil and paper procedures (+ and −) Money and 'real-life' problems Making decisions and checking results, including using a calculator Properties of numbers	To solve a problem by representing, extracting and interpreting data in tables and graphs, including those generated by computer.	**History** To learn how to find out about events, people and changes from an appropriate range of sources of information, including ICT-based sources. To investigate how an aspect of the local area has changed over a long period of time. Could be linked to QCA History Units 12: How did life change in our locality in Victorian times? and 13: How has life in Britain changed since 1948?	**p124: How have things changed?** To use the Internet to research local population and other changes since Victorian times.
		Make shapes with increasing accuracy. Calculate the surface area of a cuboid.	**Design and technology** Undertake focused practical tasks that develop a range of techniques, skills, processes and knowledge. Could also build on QCA Art and Design Unit 5B: Containers.	**p125: Box challenge** To investigate nets for open cuboid boxes and attempt to maximise the box capacity.
11	Reasoning about numbers	Express simple fractions as percentages. Use a fraction as an 'operator' to find fractions of numbers or quantities. Begin to convert a fraction to a decimal using division. Solve a problem by interpreting data in tables.	**Geography** To investigate an environmental issue, for example increasing traffic congestion. Builds on QCA Geography Units 12: Should the high street be closed to traffic? and 20: Local traffic – an environmental issue.	**p126: Traffic trouble** Make estimates based on traffic and population data.
		Identify and use appropriate operations to solve 'real-life' problems involving money, using one or more steps. Solve a problem by extracting and interpreting data in tables.	**Geography** To study a range of places and environments in different parts of the world. Links to QCA Geography Unit 18: Connecting ourselves to the world.	**p127: Holiday choice** Investigate holiday choices from travel brochure tables.
		Use and understand appropriate mathematical vocabulary.	**Literacy** To use prefixes and suffixes as a support for spelling. To understand the function of an (etymological) dictionary to study words of interest and significance. History Could link to QCA History Unit 15: How do we use ancient Greek ideas today?	**p128: Number words** Explore mathematical and related vocabulary derived from Greek number words.
		Use and understand appropriate mathematical vocabulary. Solve mathematical problems and puzzles.	**Literacy** To practise and extend vocabulary, e.g. through inventing word games such as crosswords.	**p129: Mathematical crosswords** Solve and devise crosswords based on calculations and mathematical vocabulary.
		Use the language associated with probability to discuss events, including those with equally likely outcomes.	**ICT** To learn how to organise tables. To work with others to explore a variety of ICT tools. Links to QCA ICT Unit 6B: Spreadsheet modelling.	**p130: Heads or tails?** Investigate the probability of different outcomes when tossing coins.
Unit 12	Assess and review			**p131: Assessment 2**

Term 3	Topics	Maths objectives	Cross-curricular objectives	Activities
1	Place value, ordering, rounding	Order fractions, decimal fractions and percentages.	**ICT** To learn how to organise and reorganise images. To work with others to explore a variety of ICT tools. Builds on QCA ICT Unit 5A: Graphical modelling.	**p132: Fraction sequence** Represent fractions using computer graphics. Make a fraction-sequencing game.
	Using a calculator	Recognise the equivalence between fractions, decimal fractions and percentages.		
2–3	Understanding × and ÷	Recognise relationships between fractions. Reduce a fraction to its simplest form by cancelling common factors. Know imperial units.	**History** To study changes since Victorian times and the 1930s. Could link to QCA History Units 11 and 13	**p133: Equal fractions** Identify equivalent fractions in the context of fractions of an inch on an imperial ruler.
	Mental calculation strategies (× and ÷)		**History** To study the achievements of the ancient Greeks and the influence of their civilisation on the world today. Links to QCA History Unit 15: How do we use ancient Greek ideas today?	**p134: Finding factors** Develop a standard method for resolving a composite number into prime factors.
	Pencil and paper procedures (× and ÷)	Factorise numbers to 100 into prime factors.		
	Money and 'real-life' problems		**History** To study changes since Victorian times. Links to QCA History Units 11: What was it like for children living in Victorian Britain? and 12: How did life change in our locality in Victorian times?	**p135: Changing families** Use the mode, median and mean to explore changes in household size since the Victorian era.
	Making decisions and checking results, including using a calculator	To find the mode. Begin to find the median and mean of a set of data.		
	Fractions, decimals and percentages	Read and plot coordinates in all four quadrants.	**Geography** To use and draw maps and plans at a range of scales.	**p136: Where are you?** Read and plot coordinates in all four quadrants on a map of an archaeological site.
4–5	Ratio and proportion			
	Handling data	Recognise where a shape will be after two translations.	**Art and design** Work on their own and with others in projects in two dimensions at different scales. Use a range of materials and processes. Links to QCA Art and Design Unit 6A: People in action.	**p137: Animated shapes** Explore rotation and translation by creating simple animations.
6	Using a calculator	Recognise where a shape will be after rotation through 90° about one of its vertices.		
		To classify quadrilaterals, using criteria such as parallel sides, equal angles, equal sides. To use mathematical vocabulary and language.	**Literacy** To extend vocabulary through working with explanations linked to work from other subjects; reference texts, including ICT sources.	**p138: Internet search** Use the Internet to search for information on a mathematical topic.
			ICT To work with others to explore a variety of information sources, for example searching the Internet for information. Links to QCA ICT Unit 5B: Analysing data.	
		Use the language associated with probability to discuss events, including those with equally likely outcomes.	**ICT** To learn how to organise and reorganise text and tables. To work with others to explore a variety of ICT tools. Links to QCA ICT Unit 6B: Spreadsheet modelling.	**p139: Making spinners** Investigate the properties of spinners for selecting 'random' numbers.
			Design and technology To undertake focused practical tasks.	
7	Assess and review			**See p145.**
8–10	Shape and space	Recognise and estimate angles. Use a protractor to measure acute and obtuse angles to the nearest degree. Check that the sum of the angles of a triangle is 180°, for example by measuring and paper tearing.	**History** To study beliefs and achievements in ancient Greece. Links to QCA History Unit 15: How do we use ancient Greek ideas today?	**p140: Shapes and angles** Use a protractor to investigate the internal angles of triangles and other polygons.
	Reasoning about shapes			
	Measures, including problems	Visualise 3-D shapes from 2-D drawings.	**Art and design** Be taught about visual elements including form and space. Links to QCA Art and Design Unit 6C: A sense of place.	**p141: Viewpoints** Sketch 3-D shapes from different viewpoints.
11	Mental calculation strategies (+ and –)			
	Pencil and paper procedures (+ and –)	Record readings from scales to a suitable degree of accuracy.	**Science** To learn how to measure forces and identify the direction in which they act. Links to QCA Science Unit 6E Forces in action	**p142: Floating force** Weigh objects in and out of water. Find weight differences.
	Money and 'real-life' problems	Use a fraction as an 'operator' to find fractions. Express simple fractions as percentages. Recognise and estimate angles. Solve a problem by representing and extracting data from pie charts.	**Geography** To analyse evidence and draw conclusions. Could build on QCA Geography Unit 12: Should the high street be closed to traffic?	**p143: Fraction pies** Interpret and create simple pie charts.
	Making decisions and checking results, including using a calculator			
	Properties of numbers	Use the language associated with probability to discuss events, including those with equally likely outcomes.	**English** To take part in group discussion, considering alternatives and reaching agreement.	**p144: Lucky draw** Play a team game based on the probabilities of drawing numbered balls from a bag.
12	Reasoning about numbers			
13	Assess and review			**p145: Assessment 3**

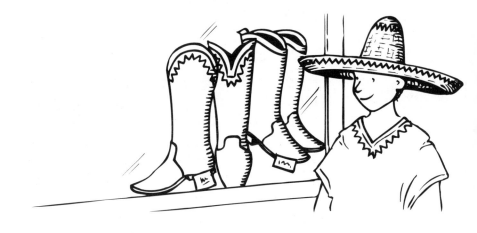

Linked to
Science

1 Hot and cold

Objectives

Numeracy
Find the difference between a positive and a negative integer, or two negative integers, in a context such as temperature or the number line, and order a set of positive and negative integers.

Science
To describe changes that occur when materials are heated or cooled.
To be taught about reversible changes, including melting, boiling, condensing and freezing.
Could be linked to QCA Science Unit 6D: Reversible and irreversible changes.

Resources

A copy of photocopiable page 146 for each child, a large demonstration thermometer with scale, a flip chart or board.

Vocabulary

positive number
negative number
temperature scale
difference
degrees Celsius

Background

As materials are heated or cooled, their state may change. Children are familiar with water freezing at 0°C and boiling at 100°C. Other materials change their state in a similar way, but the temperatures may be more extreme. The lava pouring from a volcano melts at 1200°C. The liquid oxygen in a space shuttle's fuel tanks *boils* at −183°C (183°C *below* freezing). A temperature scale is a number line along which children can sequence positive and negative numbers. In this lesson, they work in the context of the melting temperatures of different substances.

Preparation

Copy and distribute the worksheets. Set up the thermometer.

Main teaching activity

Introduce the lesson by reminding the children about temperature and its measurement. What is a typical temperature in a comfortable room, on a cold winter day, on a hot day near the Equator? Show the children the thermometer and indicate the temperatures you discuss on the scale. Describe how the scale is fixed by the changes to water as it is heated or cooled. Explain the significance of negative temperatures as temperatures below 0°C, the melting temperature of ice. Ask the

children to think about other substances changing their state. Can metal and rock melt? What temperatures would be required – very high or very low? Can air condense and freeze? How cold would it have to get?

Set the children to work in pairs or small groups on questions 1 and 2 on the worksheet.

Review the activity with the class, discussing how they judged the position of the various temperatures relative to the scale markings.

Proceed to discuss question 3, in which the children must find temperature differences from the scale. Discuss the strategy for finding the difference between a positive and a negative quantity and the difference between two negative quantities.

Differentiation

All children should be able to locate the temperatures on the scale with reasonable accuracy. Less able children may need some support to calculate temperature differences. A fail-safe method is to draw a number line and count on from the smaller number to the larger one. This works whether or not you cross 0 in the process.

Challenge more able children to research further melting and boiling points, for example which metal has the highest melting point?

the difference
between −3 and −5
−3 − (−5) = 2

the difference
between 4 and −2
4 − (−2) = 6

| −5 | −4 | −3 | −2 | −1 | 0 | 1 | 2 | 3 | 4 | 5 |

Plenary

Review the worksheet answers as a class. Ask the children to record their own record temperatures. Where is the coldest/hottest place they have been? What was the temperature when they were there? The answers are:

1. oxygen, mercury, water, lead, gold, iron
3. 476°C, 736°C, 367°C, 180°C

2 Food pyramids

Background

A food chain is a sequence of plants (producers), herbivores (consumers), carnivores and omnivores (secondary consumers) – each feeding on the level of living thing below.

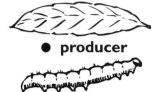

● **producer**

● **consumer**

● **secondary consumer**

● **tertiary consumer**

Green plants produce food from sunlight, water and carbon dioxide. Caterpillars are primary consumers eating plants; great tits are secondary consumers eating caterpillars; hawks are tertiary consumers eating great tits, and so on.

When we take account of the numbers of individuals consumed at each stage, the chain becomes a pyramid. At the top of the pyramid sits a hawk. To survive for a year 1 caterpillar might eat 10 leaves, 1 great tit might eat 1000 caterpillars, and 1 hawk might eat 100 great tits. The numbers multiply up as below. In effect, the hawk consumes about one million leaves – about 100 trees. This explains why

hawks are much rarer than trees and caterpillars! In this lesson, children explore number sequences generated by various food pyramids.

Preparation

Copy and distribute the worksheets and the calculators.

Main teaching activity

Introduce the lesson by reminding the children about predators and prey, and discussing the food chains illustrated on the worksheet. Who eats whom? Are there more great tits or hawks? What would happen if there were more great tits than worms, or more lions than antelopes? Why are big fierce animals quite rare?

Develop the lesson by introducing the concept of a food pyramid. Draw the number table below on the board and fill in the cells, showing the children how to calculate the numbers at each level.

Set the children to complete the number tables on the worksheet.

Differentiation

Less able children should concentrate on completing the basic activity, using calculators to check the numbers. Discuss the effect of multiplying by 10, 100, 1000 on the initial numbers at the various stages. Stress moving the numbers relative to the decimal point – *not* adding noughts.

Challenge more able children to pursue the question at the bottom of the worksheet. Can they explain why large predators usually defend a large territory?

Plenary

Review the worksheet answers with the whole class. Can the children now explain why big fierce animals are relatively rare?

The answers are:
1. 100 frogs, 10 000 worms, 100 000 leaves
2. 20 seals, 40 000 large fish, 8 000 000 small fish.

food pyramid	how many does one consume?	multiply up	total number in pyramid
hawk		1	1 hawk
great tit	1 hawk eats 100 great tits	1×100	100 great tits
caterpillar	1 great tit eats 1000 caterpillars	1 × 100×1000	100 000 caterpillars
leaf	1 caterpillar eats 10 leaves	1 × 100×1000 ×10	1 000 000 leaves

3 What's the bill?

Objectives

Numeracy
Use closely related facts in multiplication problems, for example by rounding, multiplying and then adjusting.
Check with inverse operations or equivalent calculations.
Use a calculator effectively.

Geography
To carry out fieldwork investigations outside the classroom.
Could be linked to QCA Geography Units 15: The mountain environment or 13: A contrasting UK locality.

Resources

Calculators, pencils and paper.

Vocabulary

round
multiply
adjust

Background

Rarely are purchases made in integer numbers of pounds. Shopkeepers' psychology is to set prices such as £5.99, £1.95 or 99p, rather than £6, £2 or £1. They must believe that the slightly lower prices seem significantly cheaper, and will therefore encourage more purchases. Such prices complicate the calculation of totals, but by rounding to the nearest pound, adding or multiplying as appropriate, and then adjusting, mental calculations such as six tickets at £1.95 each can be performed rapidly and efficiently. In this lesson, children practise the strategy of rounding and adjusting in the context of money calculations for a planned Geography field trip. They use their developing calculator skills to check their results.

Preparation
Distribute the calculators, pencils and paper.

Main teaching activity
Introduce the lesson by saying that the children are going to rehearse some money calculations they may make on a planned Geography field trip. A party of eight arrives at the station. The fare is £2.99. Can the children calculate mentally the total cost? Explain the strategy:

Round £2.99 to £3.00
£3.00 × 8 = £24.00
1p × 8 = 8p
£24.00 − 8p = £23.92

Explain the calculation again, emphasising how you have rounded and then adjusted.

Proceed to develop the scenario, introducing further examples of the 'rounding and adjusting' strategy. For example, on the train six children purchase drinks. The drinks are 95p each – how much do they cost altogether? When they arrive at their destination, four children buy hot dogs. The hot dogs are £1.49 each. How much do they cost altogether?

Set the children to work in pairs to solve the following word problems:
1. Seven tickets at £9.99 each.
2. Five magazines at £1.95 each.
3. Eight drinks at 99p each.
4. Ten burgers at £1.45 each.
5. Six meals at £3.95 each.
6. Seven books at £2.98 each.
7. Four souvenirs at 97p each.
8. Eight T-shirts at £5.80 each.
9. Five DVDs at £14.90 each.
10. Three pairs of trainers at £39.93 each.

Explain that they should attempt each problem mentally, talking through their answer with their partner. When they have agreed an answer, they should check it by making the reverse calculation with a calculator. For example, if the total price for 8 tickets is £23.92, the price for one ticket is £23.92 ÷ 8 = £2.99.

Differentiation
Less able children should concentrate on the first five problems, which involve making adjustments by multiples of 1p or 5p.

More able children can proceed to the later problems, which require adjustments involving more difficult multiplications.

Plenary
Review the children's answers as a class. Select appropriate pairs to talk through their mental calculations for the various problems.
The answers are: **1.** £69.93, **2.** £9.75, **3.** £7.92, **4.** £14.50, **5.** £23.70, **6.** £20.86, **7.** £3.88, **8.** £46.40, **9.** £74.50, **10.** £119.79.

4 Beyond times 10

Objectives

Numeracy
Use related facts for mental multiplication, for example develop the 17 times table by adding facts from the 10 times table and the 7 times table.
ICT
Work together to explore a variety of ICT tools.
Links to QCA ICT Unit 6B: Spreadsheet modelling.

Resources

Computers running spreadsheet software, for example *Microsoft Excel* or *Textease*; printers and paper, flip chart or board.

Vocabulary

times table
grid
cell
column
row
formula

Background

A mental strategy for calculating 17 × 5 would be to say 10 × 5 = 50, 7 × 5 = 35, 50 + 35 = 85. The strategy combines facts from two multiplication tables that we know or can derive rapidly, to perform a more complex multiplication. A spreadsheet is a good tool with which to explore the effect of adding multiplication tables in preparation for using this strategy in mental calculations. It can be programmed to complete repetitive calculations quickly, and can easily be amended to explore the effect of changing input values.

Preparation

Set up the computer running your chosen software. Check that you can use it confidently to produce times tables. The sample spreadsheet shown was produced in *Excel* as follows. Enter the 'header' values into row 1. Enter '1' in cell A2. Select cell A3, enter the formula '=A2+1' and press return. The number 2 will be displayed in A3. Click and drag to highlight cells A3–A11, then select 'Fill down' from the *Edit* menu to copy the formula from A3 down the column. The numbers 3–10 will appear. Enter the following formulae in cells B2, C2, D1, then use the 'fill down' technique to complete the table:
B2=$A2×B$1
C2=$A2×C$1
D1=B1+C1

Column B shows the 7 times table, column C the 10 times table and column D the sum of the two tables, that is, the 17 times table.

Main teaching activity

Introduce the lesson with some oral times-table questions. Develop the questioning to include multiplication of teen numbers by single-digit numbers. Suggest that the problems can be solved by adding times-table facts known already – explain 17 × 5 and similar examples.

Tell the children they are going to use spreadsheets to explore the addition of times tables 1 to 10 to generate new times tables. Set them to work in small groups at the computer. Show them how to set up the spreadsheets and enter the appropriate formulae into the cells. Demonstrate how, when a number in a cell to which the formulae refer is changed, the spreadsheet updates the values in the other cells.

Let the children explore the effect of changing the numbers in the header row to generate different times tables. They should print their results out for discussion in the plenary session.

Differentiation

Less able children may find the process of programming a spreadsheet too demanding. Let them work with a spreadsheet you have programmed in advance of the lesson.

Challenge more able children to program a grid similar to the one below.

Plenary

As a class, look at the grids the children have produced. Discuss the techniques they used. What formulae did they use? Make a display of the times tables they have printed.

5 Victorian sums

Objectives

Numeracy
Develop formal pencil and paper procedures for all four operations.
History
A study of Victorian Britain
Links to QCA History Unit 11: What was it like for children living in Victorian Britain?

Resources

A copy of photocopiable page 148 for each child; pencils and paper, calculators. If possible, a collection of old arithmetic books and pictures of Victorian classrooms (see for example www.nettlesworth. durham.sch.uk/time/victorian/vschool.html)

Vocabulary

calculate
method
addition
subtraction
multiplication
division

Background

Teaching methods are constantly changing and evolving. How did learning mathematics in Victorian times compare with maths lessons today? In 19th-century schools, lessons were based on rote learning and practice of formal methods for doing arithmetic. In this lesson, children look at arithmetic questions from old textbooks, compare them with the problems they solve today, and practise their own pencil and paper calculation skills.

Preparation

Copy and distribute the worksheets, pencils and paper. Assemble the other resources.

Main teaching activity

Introduce the lesson by showing the children the Victorian classroom pictures and old textbooks. Discuss how schools have changed since the first 'Board Schools' were founded towards the end of the Victorian age. How many children were in a class then? How many now? What sort of activities did Victorian children do at school? What teaching resources do we have now that the Victorians did not have? How were their textbooks different from ours?

Look through old mathematics textbooks with the children and compare them with the books they use today. Are they more difficult or easier? Are they more interesting or duller? Set the children to work on the problems on the worksheet. Can they solve them with a calculator? Could they solve them without a calculator? Demonstrate and discuss the formal paper and pencil procedures that Victorian children would

have needed to solve the problems.
Also describe the problems associated

```
    382              32 remainder 5
  x  26          17) 549
  2292               51
  7640               39
  9932               34
                      5
```

with money sums. Children had to remember that there were 12 pennies in a shilling and 20 shillings in a pound. Can the children explain this sum?

```
 £  s  d
 5 12  9
 9 19  6
15 12  3
```

Differentiation

Less able children will find many of the problems too difficult to solve with pencil and paper. Encourage them to use their calculators to find the answers.

Challenge more able children to reproduce the formal methods Victorians would have used.

Plenary

Review the worksheet answers as a class. Discuss the children's feelings about the questions. Would they have liked to spend their days at school solving similar problems? The answers are:

Multiplication
1. 5382
2. 8772
3. 35 952
4. 21 199
5. 42 143
6. 89 726
7. 359 923
8. 682 038
9. 424 656

Division
1. 32
2. 36 remainder 3
3. 37 remainder 6
4. 71
5. 21 remainder 14

6. 226 remainder 3
7. 352
8. 317 remainder 18
9. 760 remainder 1
10. 456 remainder 9

Find the cost
1. £72
2. £384
3. £7332
4. £250
5. £2400
6. £675
7. £2250
8. £2520
9. £272
10. £4958.33

Linked to
Science
Art & Design

6 Colour fractions

Objectives

Numeracy
Recognise the equivalence between the decimal and fractional forms of simple fractions. Express simple fractions as percentages.
Science
To know that light is reflected from surfaces.
To know that we see things only when light scattered from them enters our eyes.
Links to QCA Science Unit 6F: How we see things.
Art and design
To be taught about visual elements including colour.

Resources

A copy of photocopiable page 149 for each child; scissors, card, nuts and bolts, hand drills; red, green and blue felt-tipped pens or paints; calculators.

Vocabulary

simple fraction
decimal fraction
percentage
disc
angle

Background

All the colours on TV and computer screens are produced by mixing just three primary light colours. If red, green and blue light are mixed in equal proportions, the result is white light. Many computer painting packages include colour mixing palettes that children can use to explore the effect of mixing red, green and blue light in different proportions.

Colour mixing of light can also be investigated with a colour wheel on which different fractions have been shaded red, green or blue. When the wheel is spun, the colours combine to produce a single new colour. (This is a different process from mixing coloured paints in a pot. Spinning mixes the reflected light, not the pigments themselves.) In this lesson, children explore colour mixing with computers and colour wheels.

Preparation

Copy the worksheets on to card and distribute them in preparation for group work. Set out the practical materials. Make up a sample colour wheel as illustrated below. The card disc is 50% red and 50% blue; a small bolt is pushed through a hole at the centre of the disc and fixed in place by a nut. The end of the bolt is held in the chuck of a hand drill and the disc is spun by turning the drill handle. You will need to remind children to take care when handling tools for this activity.

Main teaching activity

Introduce the lesson by talking about colour mixing. Explain that on a television or computer screen all the colours are produced by mixing three primary light colours: red, green and blue. You could demonstrate colour mixing using the custom colour palette in *Microsoft Word* or *Paint*. Explain that the children's task is to make colour wheels to investigate how mixing different amounts of primary colours affects the colour seen. Demonstrate your sample colour wheel.

Set the children to work in pairs or small groups. They should cut out card discs using the template on the worksheet. The table gives colour percentages to investigate. Once the children have completed a wheel, they should spin it using a hand drill and record the colour observed.

Differentiation

Less able children will need help to colour their discs with the correct percentages.

More able children could investigate colour mixing on the computer. Can they reproduce the colours they see on their spinning wheels?

Plenary

Ask selected children to demonstrate their colour wheels. Ask them to describe the colours they have used, expressing them as fractions, decimals and percentages, for example 'This disc is $^3/_5$ green and $^2/_5$ red; that's 0.6 green, 0.4 red; or 60% green, 40% red.' What colours do the other children see when the discs are spun? Make a display of discs labelled with the colour fractions in the alternative forms.

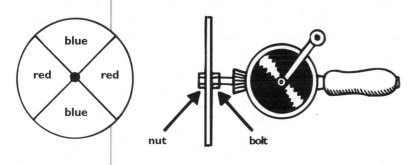

blue

red   red

blue

nut   bolt

Linked to
I C T

7 Fractions and decimals

Background

A simple fraction such as $^3/_8$ can be converted into a decimal by dividing the denominator into the numerator: $3 ÷ 8 = 0.375$. Some simple fractions correspond to exact decimals: $^1/_2 = 0.5$, $^1/_4 = 0.25$, $^1/_8 = 0.125$ and so on. However, other simple fractions do not have an exact decimal equivalent: $^1/_3 = 0.333...$, the digit 3 recurs an infinite number of times; $^1/_7 = 0.142\ 857\ 142\ 857...$, the digits 142 857 recur for ever. The convention for writing a recurring decimal is to place a dot over the first and last figure of the group of recurring digits: $^1/_3 = 0.\dot{3}$, $^1/_7 = 0.\dot{1}42\ 85\dot{7}$. In this lesson, children use a spreadsheet to explore fraction to decimal conversions.

Preparation

Set up the computer running your chosen software package. Check that you can use it confidently to convert a fraction to a decimal by entering an appropriate formula. The sample spreadsheet shown below was produced in *Excel* as follows. Enter the formula 'C2=A2/B2' in cell C2. When the numerator and denominator values are entered in cells A2 and B2, the spreadsheet calculates the decimal and displays it in cell

numerator	denominator	numerator ÷ denominator
1	2	0.5
1	3	0.33333333333333
1	4	0.25
1	5	0.2
1	6	0.16666666666667
1	7	0.14285714285714
1	8	0.125
1	9	0.11111111111111
1	10	0.1
1	11	0.09090909090909
1	12	0.08333333333333
2	3	0.66666666666667
2	4	0.5
2	5	0.4
2	6	0.33333333333333
2	7	0.28571428571429
2	8	0.25
2	9	0.22222222222222
2	10	0.2
2	11	0.18181818181818

C2. The formula can be copied down column C by highlighting the cells and selecting the 'Fill Down' option from the *Edit* menu.

Main teaching activity

Introduce the lesson by reminding children of the equivalence between familiar simple and decimal fractions: $^1/_2 = 0.5$, $^1/_4 = 0.25$, $^3/_{10} = 0.3$ and so on.

Explain how to calculate the decimal equivalent of a fraction using the calculator. Write a list of fractions on the board for the children to convert. These should include $^1/_3$, $^2/_3$, $^1/_7$, $^1/_{11}$ and other fractions that produce recurring decimals. Discuss the results the children obtain, and introduce the notation for writing recurring decimals.

Tell the children they are going to use computer spreadsheets to explore fraction conversions. Set them to work in small groups at the computer. Show them how to set up the spreadsheets and enter the appropriate formulae into the cells. Demonstrate how, when a number in a cell to which the formulae refer is changed, the spreadsheet updates the other cells.

Let the children explore a range of fractions and their decimal equivalents. Children should print sample tables for discussion in the plenary session.

Differentiation

Less able children may find the process of programming a spreadsheet too demanding. Let them work with a spreadsheet you have programmed in advance of the lesson.

Challenge more able children to use their spreadsheets to investigate these questions: *Which denominators produce recurring decimals? Do they always produce recurring decimals, whatever the numerator?*

Plenary

As a class, look at the spreadsheets the children have produced. Discuss the techniques they used. Have any of the children used their spreadsheets to make the suggested investigations? What conclusions have they drawn?

8 Pulleys and gears

main sprocket (gear) number of teeth	rear sprockets (gears) number of teeth	ratio	number of turns of rear wheel for one pedal turn
48	32	48:32 = 1.5:1	1.5
48	28	48:28 = 1.7:1	1.7
48	24	48:24 = 2:1	2
48	20	48:20 = 2.4:1	2.4
48	16	48:16 = 3:1	3

Objectives

Numeracy
Solve simple problems involving ratio and proportion.
Design and technology
To explore how mechanisms can be used to make things move in different ways.
Links to QCA Design and Technology Units 6C: Fairground and 6D: Controllable vehicles.

Resources

A mountain bike with visible gears; construction kits with gears and pulleys; rulers, pencils and paper, a flip chart or board.

Vocabulary

ratio
for every
fraction

Background

Gears and pulleys are used in machines to pass on turning motion from one place to another, and to change the speed and/or direction of rotation. For example, on a bicycle gears are selected to change the ratio between the rate at which you pedal and the rate at which the back wheel turns. The 'gear ratio' is the ratio between the number of turns of two linked gears or pulleys. If the gears have the same number of teeth, or the pulley wheels are the same size, the ratio is 1 to 1 and they will turn at the same rate. If the second gear has twice as many teeth as the first (or the second pulley wheel is twice the diameter of the first) then the ratio is 2 to 1; the smaller gear or pulley turns twice as fast as the larger one. In this lesson, children investigate ratios in the real-life context of

gear ratios for bicycles and construction kit models.

Preparation

Turn the mountain bike upside-down. Set out construction kits, rulers, pencils and gears in preparation for group work.

Main teaching activity

Introduce the lesson with a discussion of the mountain bike gears. Have the children got bikes? How many gears do they have? What is the purpose of gears? How does selecting different gears change the ease of peddling and the speed of the bike?

Investigate the mountain bike gears. Construct a table similar to the one above on the board. (**Safety:** you should turn the pedals as the children count the rotations. Don't let children place their fingers near the moving parts.)

Ask the children, using construction kits, to build and investigate simple models, including pulleys or gears. They should complete tables of gear ratios for their models. Explain that, for linked gears they must count the teeth to find the ratio; for pulleys, they should measure the diameters.

Differentiation

Less able children should concentrate on making a simple link between two different-sized gear wheels. They should relate the ratio of number of teeth to the ratio of numbers of turns.

Challenge more able children to produce more complex gear systems with three or more gear wheels linked in different ways. What is the overall gear ratio for their machine? How is it related to the number of teeth on the wheels?

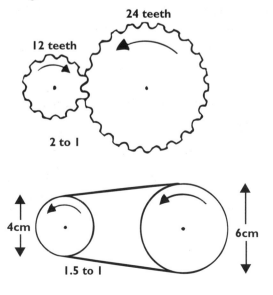

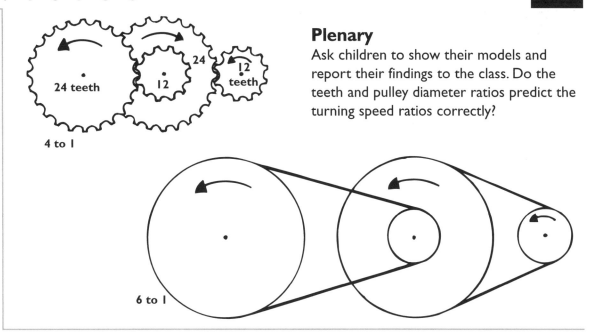

4 to 1

6 to 1

Plenary

Ask children to show their models and report their findings to the class. Do the teeth and pulley diameter ratios predict the turning speed ratios correctly?

9 Shadow graphs

Objectives

Numeracy
Solve a problem by representing data in tables and on line graphs.
Science
To know that light cannot pass through some materials, and how this leads to the formation of shadows.
Links to QCA Science Unit 6F: How we see things.

Resources

Torches, tape measures, rulers and card discs; paper and pencils, graph paper; a darkened room, a table lamp.

Vocabulary

data
line graph
table
coordinates
label
axis
title

Background

Plotting a line graph on squared paper is a skill that requires much practice. There are a number of decisions to make and processes to apply to produce a good graph from even the simplest data: choosing scales, labelling the axes, locating the point coordinates and plotting points. In this lesson, children use their measuring skills in a science investigation of shadows. They record their data in a table and use it to plot a simple line graph.

Main teaching activity

Introduce the lesson with a discussion of shadows. Demonstrate shadow formation on the wall by holding up objects in front of the table lamp. Discuss and demonstrate how the size of the shadow depends on the object's position between the wall and the light source. Show how the shadow gets smaller as you move the object away from the lamp.

Explain that the children's task is to investigate the relationship between shadow size and object position. Show them the apparatus and discuss plans for a suitable experiment. Sketch the arrangement illustrated below as one possible method. (If children suggest alternatives, encourage them to pursue their plans.)

Preparation

Set out the resources in preparation for the group investigations. Darken the room.

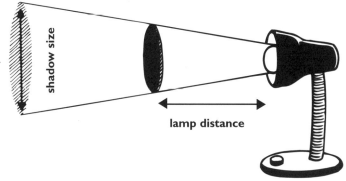

shadow size

lamp distance

Children should plan how they are going to measure and record their data. Lead them to draw up a table to record the measurements, as follows.

distance of object from lamp in cm	shadow size in cm
20	150
40	75
60	50
80	38
100	30
120	25
140	21
160	19
180	17
200	15

When children have recorded their results, suggest they plot their data as a line graph. Discuss the process of plotting the graph from the data in the table, showing the children how to label axes and plot points. Since intermediate points could have been

plotted, it is appropriate to join the points with a smooth line.

Differentiation

Less able children will need considerable support to plot their graphs. If necessary, draw and label the axes for them, then ask the children to plot the points.

More able children could transfer their data to the computer once they have completed the manual graph-plotting exercise, experimenting with the scales chosen for the axes to produce the clearest graph.

Plenary

Ask selected children to show their graphs and describe their findings. How did the experiment show the shadow size changing? How does the graph help in describing and interpreting the findings? The graph below shows that the shadow size changes quickly when the object is close to the lamp, but more slowly when it is closer to the wall.

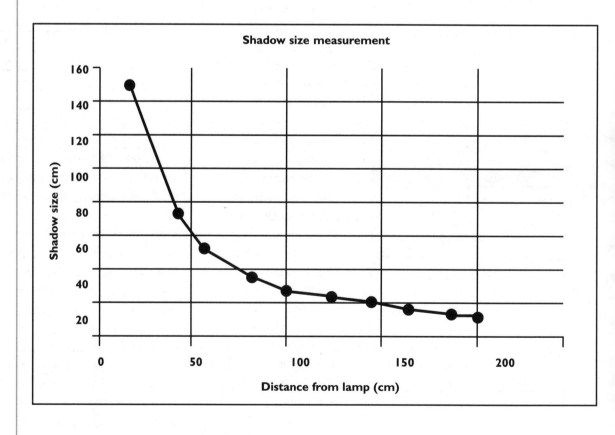

Linked to
S c i e n c e

10 Dandelions

Objectives

Numeracy
Begin to find the mean of a set of data.
Calculate the area of rectangles.
Use the vocabulary of estimation.
Science
To carry out a complete scientific
investigation.
Links to QCA Science Unit 6H:
Environmental enquiry.

Resources

Quadrats (made from strips of cardboard
or plastic taped together at the corners to
surround a 1m square opening); pencils and
paper, tape measures; the school field or
other grass area, tennis balls.

Vocabulary

mean
random
sample
estimate
area

Background

How many dandelions are there are on the school field? Are there more in a shady area or in a sunny area? Counting every dandelion plant in a field, every bird in a flock or every leaf on a tree are clearly impractical tasks. Such investigations demonstrate the need to develop and apply procedures for counting samples to make estimates for a whole population. In this lesson, children investigate methods for estimating plant numbers using quadrats. They record dandelions in random unit areas of the school field, calculate a mean, and apply their knowledge of area calculations to estimate the number on the whole field.

Preparation

Make quadrats. Issue paper, clipboards, pencils and tape measures. This investigation is best undertaken in spring or summer when dandelion plants can be recognised easily.

Main teaching activity

Introduce the lesson by describing the procedure. Explain that the children are going to estimate the number of dandelion plants on the school field. To do this they will count the number of dandelions in random 1m squares, find the mean number per square, and multiply this by the total area of the field to find the total number of plants. Explain the importance of selecting the squares at random with quadrats to make the estimate 'fair'.

Take the children onto the field and divide them into groups. Set half the children to measure the field with tape measures. They should sketch the field and label the sketch with their measurements. Set the other groups to make measurements with the quadrats. Demonstrate how to place the quadrats in random locations (for example, by tossing a tennis ball over your shoulder and placing the quadrat where it lands) and how to identify dandelion plants. They should record their observations in a table as shown below.

Return to the classroom. Combine the data from the groups to find an overall mean value for the number of dandelions per square metre. Make a sketch of the field and use the children's measurements to calculate its total area. Hence calculate the total number of dandelion plants.

quadrat number	number of dandelions counted in quadrat
1	3
2	0
3	4
4	2
5	1
Total	10
Mean number	10 ÷ 5 = 2

Our estimate of the number of dandelions on the school field = 2 × 2250 = 4500

Differentiation

Less able children can concentrate on the basic identification and counting activity.

Challenge more able children to extend the activity to investigate variations in dandelion plant numbers in different parts of the field. Do dandelion plant numbers differ between areas in the shade of trees and buildings, and areas in full sunlight? Are there more dandelions in frequently mown areas or in areas that are mown less often?

Plenary

Create a display of the children's findings. Devise a visual means of presenting the data, perhaps using pictograms or a bar chart.

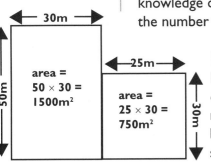

area =
50 × 30 =
1500m²

area =
25 × 30 =
750m²

30m

25m

50m

30m

Total area = 1500m² + 750m² = 2250m²

1m
quadrat

1m

11 Multimedia shapes

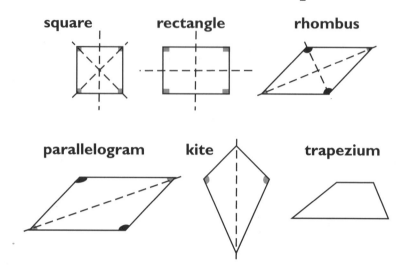

square   rectangle   rhombus

parallelogram   kite   trapezium

Objectives

Numeracy
Classify quadrilaterals, using criteria such as parallel sides, equal angles, equal sides…
ICT
To develop and refine ideas by bringing together, organising and reorganising text, tables, images and sounds.
Work together to explore a variety of ICT tools.
Links to QCA ICT Unit 6A: Multimedia presentation.

Resources

Computers running software suitable for creating simple multimedia presentations, for example *Textease* or *Microsoft PowerPoint*; a chart of quadrilateral features, paper and pencils.

Vocabulary

quadrilateral
angle
regular
side
parallel
equal
square
rectangle
rhombus
kite
parallelogram
trapezium

Background

The facts that children should know about quadrilaterals are summarised in the table opposite. In a multimedia presentation based on this table, the different classes of quadrilateral can be shown visually, and their key features described using graphics, text and audio. For example, a page illustrating each quadrilateral could link to individual pages on their key features.

linked pages and record sounds. For example, with *Textease* quadrilaterals can be drawn with the polygon drawing tool; standard shapes can be dragged onto the page from a selection window opened when the right mouse button is clicked over the polygon tool; shapes can be formatted by opening the *Effects* window; links can be created between objects by clicking on the 'Link' button (shown with a chain-link icon); sounds can be recorded by selecting the 'Record sound' option from the *Tools* menu.

Main teaching activity

Introduce the lesson by explaining that the children are going to produce a multimedia presentation about quadrilaterals. Discuss multimedia presentations, including the combined use of images, text and audio. Explain that the presentation should give the key features of quadrilaterals in a way that is simple to navigate to find the information. Discuss how 'hot links' (highlighted pieces of text, images or icons) are used to connect one piece of information to another.

Set the children to work in groups to plan their presentations. Suggest they start with a simple idea, which can be elaborated later. For example, they could have a menu screen showing different types of quadrilateral; clicking on a shape should give further information about it.

Once the groups have formulated some ideas, set them to work at the computer to translate their plans into a presentation.

Preparation

This lesson should build on a previous lesson on the properties of quadrilaterals. Make sure you are familiar with the multimedia capabilities of your chosen software and can use it confidently to draw shapes, create

quadrilateral name	sides	angles	number of symmetry lines
square	all equal, opposite sides parallel	all 90°	4
rectangle	opposite sides equal and parallel	all 90°	2
rhombus	all equal, opposite sides parallel	opposite angles equal	2
parallelogram	opposite sides equal and parallel	opposite angles equal	0
kite	two pairs of equal adjacent sides	two equal angles	1
trapezium	two parallel sides		0

Children will need guidance to start using the multimedia features of the software. In particular, they will need help to create links between objects.

Differentiation
Less able children could aim to record a sound file to play when a shape is selected.

With more able children, the sky is the limit. They could extend their work to create multimedia presentations of a whole range of mathematical topics.

Plenary
Ask groups to demonstrate their presentation to the whole class. Is it easy to understand? Is it easy to navigate forwards and backwards through the screens?

Linked to
S c i e n c e

12 It's all done with mirrors

Objectives

Numeracy
To recognise where a shape will be after reflection: in a mirror line touching the shape at a point; in two mirror lines at right angles.
Science
To know that light is reflected from surfaces.
To make systematic observations.
Links to QCA Science Unit 6F: How we see things.

Resources

A copy of photocopiable page 150 for each child; safety mirrors; a flip chart or board; a torch, a kaleidoscope, protractors.

Vocabulary

symmetry
symmetrical
shape
mirror
mirror line
reflection
angle

Background
Sketching the reflection of a shape is a skill that requires understanding of the connection between an object and its mirror image. Corresponding points in the image and object are on either side of the mirror, at equal distances from the mirror line. The line connecting an object point and its image is perpendicular to the mirror. The overall effect of the mirror is to 'flip' the shape over, about the mirror line.

When two mirrors are at an angle, multiple images are produced. If the mirrors are at right angles, three reflections of the original shape can be seen. If the mirrors are at 60°, five reflections can be seen – the object and its reflections are arranged with the symmetry of a hexagon. This is how the patterns in a kaleidoscope are produced.

Work on sketching reflections in mathematics links to work on light in science. The light that illuminates objects (and is scattered into our eyes so that we see them), is also reflected in a regular way by a mirror. Our eyes see the reflected light as if it is coming from behind the mirror, hence we see images, or 'reflections', of objects.

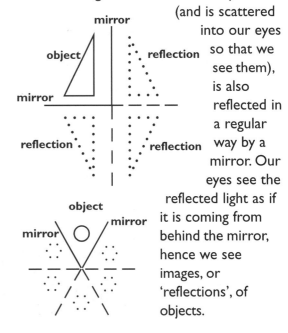

Preparation

Distribute the worksheets and mirrors.

Main teaching activity

Remind the children about mirrors and reflections. What is the relationship between a shape and its reflection? Explain that the shape and its reflection are on 'opposite sides' of the mirror. Demonstrate this with a mirror and some simple shapes. Consider the effect of two mirrors placed at an angle.

Set the children to work in small groups on the first part of the worksheet. They investigate the number of reflections they see as they adjust the angle between the mirrors. Demonstrate the kaleidoscope. Relate it to the pattern the children produce in two angled mirrors.

Let the children proceed to the second worksheet activity. Suggest that they check their work by using a mirror to look at the reflections of the original shape.

Differentiation

Less able children may require considerable assistance to draw the reflections.

More able children could use a computer to create shapes and generate their reflections by using the 'flip' options in a computer drawing package. Can they copy and paste the shapes correctly to illustrate reflections in two perpendicular mirrors?

Plenary

Review the children's worksheet answers. Use a mirror to check their drawings.

Linked to
Science

13 Mystery measures

Objectives

Numeracy
Solve mathematical problems or puzzles. Suggest suitable measuring equipment to estimate or measure length, mass and capacity.
Science
To make systematic observations and measurements.
Could link to QCA Science Unit 6H: Environmental enquiry.

Resources

Flip chart or board; cotton on cotton reels, empty cotton reels, a digital balance, rulers, pencils and paper, calculators, samples for measuring/estimating activities. These could include: pasta shapes, lentils, dried beans, sand, rice, beads, blocks of paper, boxes of paper clips.

Vocabulary

estimate
measure
thickness
millimetre
weight
gram
approximately

Background

How can you estimate the number of dried peas in a jar or the number of grains in a spoonful of sand without counting every one? How can you measure the thickness of a sheet of paper or the weight of a grain of rice without using special measuring equipment? These questions require some practical problem-solving skills involving multiplying up or dividing down quantities that are more readily counted or measured.

For example, the thickness of a single sheet of paper can be measured by measuring the thickness of a stack of 500 sheets with a ruler. Divide the thickness of the stack by 500 to find the thickness of a single sheet.

The weight of a single grain of rice can be estimated by weighing 100g of rice and estimating the number of grains. This can be done by progressive halving. By eye, divide the 100g of rice into two 50g piles, divide one pile in half again, and repeat until you are left with a reasonable number of rice grains to count. Count the grains and repeatedly double the answer the same number of times as you halved the original pile. You then know the number of grains in 100g, and can calculate the weight of a single grain.

Preparation

Prepare a series of measurement questions to accompany the items you have collected. Write questions on cards to place with the items and set them out in preparation for group work. For example:
Can you estimate:
● *the number of grains of rice in this jar?*
● *the thickness of a sheet of this paper?*
● *the weight of a sheet of this paper?*
● *the weight of a grain of this sand?*
● *the number of grains of sand in this jar?*

- *the thickness of this cotton thread?*
- *the weight of 1m of this cotton thread?*

Main teaching activity

Start by solving one or two problems of the type shown in Background. For example: *Measure the thickness of a sheet of paper; Estimate the number of rice grains in a jar and the mass of each grain.*

Explain that the children's task is to devise methods to count and measure the items you have set out around the class.

Set the children to work in small groups on the various measuring activities.

Differentiation

Less able children should tackle some

straightforward problems such as paper thickness measurements or estimating the number of lentils in a jar.

Challenge more able children with problems such as weighing a grain of sand or finding the thickness of a cotton thread (for example, by winding 100 adjacent turns on a pencil, measuring the total length of the winding, and dividing by 100).

Plenary

Ask representatives from the groups to report their measurements and describe the techniques they developed to make them. Write up the results on the board. Discuss with the class whether or not they seem reasonable.

Linked to
P E

14 Distance club

Objectives

Numeracy
Add several numbers mentally.
Use informal and standard pencil and paper methods to support, record or explain additions and subtractions.
Physical education
To take part in and design athletic challenges that call for stamina. To pace themselves in these challenges.
Links to QCA Physical Education 31: Athletic activities.

Resources

A copy of photocopiable page 151 for each child; notebooks and pencils, tape measures, calculators.

Vocabulary

addition
subtraction
distance
km
measure
circumference

Background

In PE, children build up their stamina by walking or running regularly. The class could start 50km and 100km clubs. Children keep a diary of distances walked or run over a period of weeks, with the goal of joining the '50k' and '100k' clubs when they have passed these targets. They will need to use their addition skills to total the distance covered during a period, and subtraction to find the distance still to go. Measurement is required to establish the length of the track or route along which the children walk or run, for example the perimeter of the school field.

Preparation

Copy and distribute the worksheets with the notebooks and pencils. You could prepare 25k, 50k and 100k certificates to be awarded to members of the distance clubs when they reach these targets. Desktop publishing packages usually include certificate designs that you can adapt.

Main teaching activity

Introduce the lesson with a discussion of regular exercise. Why is it good to walk or run regularly? Explain the idea of a distance club and the process of keeping a record of distances covered in a notebook. Show the children the certificates that will be awarded to club members who reach the various targets.

Look at the worksheet together. It shows imaginary entries in the diaries of two distance club members. Set the children to work in pairs or small groups to answer the accompanying questions. They should calculate the totals indicated and find the dates on which the various certificates were awarded.

Differentiation

Less able children could work out the answers with the aid of calculators.

Challenge more able children to make the calculations mentally and then check them with the aid of paper and pencil jottings.

Plenary

Review the answers to the worksheet questions as a class. Conclude the lesson with a discussion of the conditions for the class distance club. Where should the children do their walking or running? Organise some volunteers to measure the length of the course. Can the children estimate how many weeks it will take them to join the 100k club? Suggest that children keep their records either in the notebooks provided, or as spreadsheets on the computer. The answers are:

1. Shane: 34km, Sophie: 41.5km
2. 13 May
3. 10 May
4. Shane: 2.1km, Sophie: 2.6km

Linked to
ICT
Art & Design

15 Stacking numbers

Objectives

Numeracy
Recognise and extend number sequences, such as the sequence of square numbers, or the sequence of triangular numbers.
ICT
Work together to explore a variety of ICT tools.
Builds on QCA ICT Unit 5A: Graphical modelling.
Art and design
To explore pattern.
Builds on QCA Art and Design Unit 5A: Objects and meanings.

Resources

Flip chart or board; circular counters; computers running software with object drawing capabilities, for example *Textease* or *Microsoft Word*.

Vocabulary

pattern
sequence
array
square number
triangular number

Background

Whole numbers can be represented by arrays or patterns of counting objects. Some numbers correspond to regular arrays with particular geometrical features, for example the square numbers 1, 4, 9, 16… can be represented as square arrays of dots:

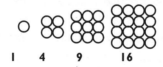

The triangular numbers 1, 3, 6, 10… correspond to triangular dot patterns.

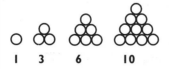

The number sequences generated by patterns like these are readily explored with counters or computer graphics. In this lesson, children use this practical approach to investigate number sequences including square, triangular and rectangular numbers. The patterns produced could be used as the basis for some creative mathematical designs linking to work in art and design.

Preparation

Set out trays of counters. Set up the computer running your chosen software and make sure that you can use it confidently to draw arrays of circular objects.

Main teaching activity

Introduce the lesson by showing how counters can be used to generate sequences of rectangular numbers representing times tables. For example, this pattern of rectangles shows how the 3 times table is developed:

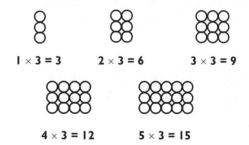

Develop the lesson by exploring the sequence of square numbers and their corresponding patterns. Set out or draw the squares corresponding to 1, 4 and 9. Set the children to work in pairs or small groups to continue the sequence, with counters or computer graphics. What are the next four numbers in the sequence?

Proceed to explore triangular numbers. Again, start the sequence with the children and ask them to continue it practically. Can any children discover a relationship between triangular numbers and square numbers? (The sum of two adjacent triangular numbers is always equal to a square number, as illustrated below.)

1 + 3 = 4   3 + 6 = 9   6 + 10 = 16

Differentiation
Less able children should concentrate on identifying the numbers in the sequences and setting out or drawing arrays to show them.

More able children should be able to identify the sequence rule and describe it in words: 'The number of counters in the fifth square number is 5 × 5. The number in the eighth will be 8 × 8…' You could challenge the most able children to identify formulae for the number of counters in pattern number n of the sequence they are working with. For example, number n in the 5 times table is $5n$; number n in the sequence of square numbers is n^2. (Number n in the sequence of triangular numbers is $n(n+1)/2$, but don't expect them to discover this!)

Plenary
Ask representatives of the various groups to show some of the patterns they have created and to describe their findings. Make a display of number sequences.

Linked to
D & T

16 Building fences

Objectives

Numeracy
Solve mathematical problems or puzzles, recognise and explain patterns and relationships.
Explain a generalised relationship in words.
Develop from explaining a generalised relationship in words to expressing it in a formula using letters as symbols.
Design and technology
Develop design ideas and explain them clearly.

Resources

A copy of photocopiable page 152 for each child; flip chart or board.

Vocabulary

formula
pattern
equation

Background
Planning a practical task requires calculation of the quantities of materials required. For example, the number of fence posts, cross bars and nails needed to build a fence. With a regular repeating structure such as a fence, the number of repeating units determines the quantities. For a fence, the number of posts is one more than the number of gaps between the posts. In this lesson, children generalise the relationships between quantities in their own words. The most able begin to express the relationships as formulae using letters as symbols. The activity should build on previous numeracy lessons in which simple formulae have been introduced (for example, the cost of n apples at 15p each = $15n$).

Preparation
Copy and distribute the worksheets.

Main teaching activity
Introduce the lesson by making a drawing of the basic fence design below on the board. Explain that a farmer must calculate the quantities of fence posts, cross bars and nails needed to make different lengths of fence. The first metre of fence requires 2 posts, 2 bars and 4 nails. Each extra metre needs 1 more post, 2 more bars and 4 more nails.

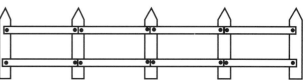

Draw diagrams to illustrate how the number sequences work out. These are summarised in the table overleaf.

length of fence in metres	number of posts	number of bars	number of nails
1	2	2	4
2	3	4	8
3	4	6	12
4	5	8	16
n	n + 1	2n	4n

Set the children to complete the table on the worksheet.

Differentiation

Less able children should concentrate on the basic calculations and describing the relationships in words.

Stretch more able children by explaining how the relationships can be expressed as

formulae. The formulae for the quantities for n metres of fence using this design are:
number of posts = $n + 1$
number of bars = $2 \times n = 2n$
number of nails = $4 \times n = 4n$

Explain that in formulae $2 \times n$ is usually written as $2n$.

Set some calculations based on the formulae. How many nails would you need for 100 metres of fence? How many posts?

Plenary

Review the answers to the worksheet problems. Ask selected children to read out their relationships in words. Discuss them as a class.

Linked to
P S H E

17 Discount fares

Objectives

Numeracy
Find simple percentages of small whole-number quantities.
PSHE & citizenship
To make choices and decisions, for example about how to spend money.

Resources

A copy of photocopiable page 153 for each child; calculators.

Vocabulary

percentage
discount
fraction
reduction
cost
saving

Background

Bus and train fares are marketed with a wide range of special offers and discounts. There are discounts for early booking, last-minute booking, group bookings, season tickets, pensioners, students and children. Children might have termly bus passes, or families may have rail cards. In this lesson, children calculate discounts as percentage reductions, to find both the discounted price and the saving on the standard price. As they compare prices and savings and make purchasing decisions, children begin to develop the numeracy skills required to manage money.

Preparation

Copy and distribute the worksheets with the calculators.

Main teaching activity

Introduce the lesson by talking about fares and discounts on transport services. Does everyone pay the standard fare, or are some fares discounted? What does a 10% discount mean and how is it calculated? How much do you pay compared with the standard fare? How much do you save? Should you buy a season ticket, or will you not use it enough to justify the discount?

Remind the children about percentages as fractional quantities, expressing the number of parts in every 100. Ask them to recall the percentage equivalents of $\frac{1}{2}$, $\frac{1}{4}$, $\frac{1}{5}$ and $\frac{1}{10}$. Write the following list on the board:
$\frac{1}{2}$ = 50%
$\frac{1}{4}$ = 25%
$\frac{1}{5}$ = 20%
$\frac{1}{10}$ = 10%

Explain how to calculate simple percentages of small whole-number quantities mentally by using these relationships. For example, 50% of £8 is £4; 10% of £8 is 80p; 5% is half 10% so 5% of £8 is 40p; 15% = 10% + 5%, so 15% of £8 = 80p + 40p = £1.20; and so on. Ask the class some oral problems based on the strategy.

Develop the questioning by introducing the vocabulary of discount calculations. For example: *The full fare is £100. There is a 20% discount for early booking. How much do you pay? How much do you save?*

When you feel the children have understood the concept of discounts correctly, set them to work in pairs or small groups on the worksheet.

London return

fare type	discount	saving	fare
Standard	–	–	£100
Young person	50%	£50	£50
OAP	25%	£25	£75
Weekend	10%	£10	£90
Early booking	20%	£20	£80
Last minute	75%	£75	£25
Family rail card	40%	£40	£60

Paris return

fare type	discount	saving	fare
Standard	–	–	£200
Young person	50%	£100	£100
OAP	25%	£50	£150
Weekend	10%	£20	£180
Early booking	20%	£40	£160
Last minute	75%	£150	£50
Family rail card	40%	£80	£120

Birmingham return

fare type	discount	saving	fare
Standard	–	–	£80
Young person	50%	£40	£40
OAP	25%	£20	£60
Weekend	10%	£8	£72
Early booking	20%	£16	£64
Last minute	75%	£60	£20
Family rail card	40%	£32	£48

Differentiation

Less able children should complete the first table of discount calculations on the worksheet.

More able children should proceed to the more challenging calculations in the second and third tables.

Plenary

Review the answers to the worksheet problems as a class. Conclude with some more rapid mental discount calculations. The answers are shown on the left.

18 Assessment 1

Objectives

The assessment activities in this book are designed to introduce Key Stage 2 children to SAT-style questions. They are set in cross-curricular contexts based on the preceding term's lessons. The questions in Assessment 1 test the children's progress in: ordering and finding the difference between positive and negative integers; finding percentages of whole number quantities; using the vocabulary of estimation and finding the mode, median and mean of a set of data.

Resources

A copy of photocopiable page 154 for each child; a large sheet of squared paper; pairs of identical plastic/card triangles.

Preparation
Make copies of the assessment sheet. If you feel that the sheet is too 'busy', the three activities could be separated and enlarged on individual sheets. Rule a single line and two perpendicular lines on the squared paper to represent mirrors.

Lesson introduction
Review the relevant cross-curricular topics covered during the term. Remind the children of some of the work they have undertaken, and ask them to recall and recount it. Stress the mathematical content – for example: *How did we estimate the number of dandelions on the school field?*

Main assessment activity
Distribute the worksheets and ask the children to work on them individually. Guide the whole class through the questions one at a time, reading the text with them, and prompting them to work out and fill in their answers. Try to make the whole activity enjoyable!

Practical activity
Position a triangle next to the mirror line ruled on the squared paper. Ask the children to position an identical triangle to represent the reflection of the first triangle in the mirror. Repeat with shapes in different orientations and with two perpendicular mirror lines.

Plenary
Review the answers to the questions as a class. Collect the completed question sheets to use as an aid to judging individual children's progress, and to include in your records.

The answers are:
1. 18°C, 17°C
2. £15, £6.40, £8, £7.50
3. mode = 2, median = 2, mean = 2.4, estimate = 2.4 × 5000 = 12 000

Linked to
P E

19 Goal average

Objectives

Numeracy
Order fractions.
Recognise equivalence between the decimal and fraction forms of $\frac{1}{2}$, $\frac{1}{4}$, $\frac{3}{4}$, $\frac{1}{8}$ and tenths.
Express simple fractions as percentages.
Begin to calculate the mean of a set of data.
Physical education
To evaluate and improve performance.
Could link to QCA Physical Education 26: Striking and fielding games.

Resources

A copy of photocopiable page 155 for each child; calculators, sports statistics from newspapers.

Vocabulary

mean
average
statistics
table
percentage
proportion

Background

Scoring systems and statistics for football and other games are a motivating context for mathematics for some children. Complex tables of football statistics, for example, are published regularly in the national papers. These include information such as goal averages, points averages per game home and away, top goalscorers, fouls per game, red and yellow cards received. In this lesson, children interpret a table of goals scored by imaginary teams and players. They calculate team goal averages and the scoring percentages of the players.

Preparation

Copy and distribute the worksheets. Collect together a selection of statistical tables and charts from newspaper sports pages.

Main teaching activity

Introduce the lesson by showing the children sporting statistics you have selected from newspapers. Discuss the information that these tables present. What is meant by a goal average? How do you calculate such an average? (Divide the total number of goals scored by the number of games played to find the average number per game.) Explain that mathematicians call an average calculated in this way the 'mean'. Make some calculations of averages with the whole class on the board. For example, City score 3, 3, 2, 1, 2, 0, 3, 2 goals in eight successive games. What is their a goal average? Total goals = 3 + 3 + 2 + 1 + 2 + 0 + 3 + 2 = 16. Goal

average = 16 ÷ 8 = 2.

Develop the lesson by considering scoring percentages. Rovers' top scorer has played 20 games and scored 15 goals. On average, in what proportion of games does he score? ($\frac{15}{20}$ = ¾ – 'three out of four'). In what percentage of the games he plays does he score? (¾ = 75%)

Set the children to work in pairs or small groups on the two worksheet tasks. The first task is to calculate goal averages for the teams. The second is to calculate the scoring percentages of the top players. Which player has the best scoring record per game played?

Differentiation

Less able children should concentrate on the less challenging goal average activity.

More able children should tackle both activities and compile tables of their favourite teams and players based on goal averages and scoring percentages.

Plenary

Review the worksheet answers as a class. Suggest that the children produce similar tables of statistics for school football and netball teams and create a display in the school entrance hall. The answers are:
1. Rovers 2, United 2, Town 1, City 3, Albion 2, Wanderers 2.5; the best is City.
2. Jones 75%, Evans 40%, Taylor 33.3%, Driver 30%, Cooper 25%; the best is Jones.

Linked to Geography

20 Times 10

Background

The width of a child's little finger is about 1cm. With this as a reference length, the lengths children talk about in the classroom cover many multiples of 10, from $1/100$th of a finger width (about the thickness of a sheet of paper) to 1 000 000 finger widths (about the height of Mount Everest) and beyond. In this lesson, children research 'typical' lengths for multiples and sub-multiples of 1cm. In so doing, they will increase their knowledge of the relative size of measurements and measurement units.

Preparation

Assemble the rulers, tape measures and reference materials and set them out in preparation for group work.

Main teaching activity

Introduce the lesson by writing the following table on the board.

length	example
1 000 000cm	
100 000cm	
10 000cm	
1000cm	
100cm	
10cm	
1cm	
0.1cm	
0.01cm	

Discuss how each quantity is related to the one above and below by multiplication or

division by 10. Discuss the units, mm, m and km, and identify them with the quantities in the table.

Explain that the children's task is to find examples of 'typical' objects or dimensions which each of the measures represents, for example a finger's width for 1cm. They should copy the table and fill in the empty column. Set the children to work in pairs or small groups on the task. They can use the rulers and tape measures to measure objects around the school to help fill in some of the blanks.

Differentiation

Less able children should concentrate on filling items in the range 0.1cm to 1000cm, all of which they should be able to find around them.

Challenge more able children to extend the table in either direction by researching examples of objects that are typically 0.001cm and smaller or 10 million cm and bigger.

Plenary

Ask representatives from the groups to report back the objects they have identified corresponding to the different size scales. Compile an overall summary chart to form a classroom display.

Linked to History

21 Prime numbers

Objectives

Numeracy
Recognise prime numbers to at least 20.
History
To study the achievements of the ancient Greeks and the influence of their civilisation on the world today.
Links to QCA History Unit 15: How do we use ancient Greek ideas today?

Resources

A photocopy of a 100-square grid (photocopiable resource page XX) for each child; a large display 100-square grid.

Vocabulary

prime number
factor
multiple

Background

A prime number is a number whose only factors are itself and 1. The first prime number is 2 (1 is not considered to be prime, since it has no factors other than 1), the only even prime number. The next prime number is 3. The number 4 is not prime, since its factors are 1, 2 and 4. The ideas about prime numbers we use today were developed by the ancient Greeks. The mathematician and philosopher Eratosthenes devised a systematic method for finding prime numbers, which children can apply, called the 'sieve of Eratosthenes'. Work on primes can thus be linked to work in history on the ancient Greeks and their ideas. See also Lessons 22, 39 and 45.

Preparation

Prepare and distribute the 100-square grids, with coloured pencils.

Main teaching activity

Introduce the concept of a prime number by discussion with the whole class. Explain that a prime number can be divided only by itself or 1 without giving a remainder. A prime number's only factors are itself and 1. Mentally investigate and discuss which of the numbers 2 to 10 are prime (2, 3, 5, 7).

Explain that prime numbers were investigated by the ancient Greek philosophers. Today they are very important for creating 'unbreakable' secret codes used for computer security. A Greek mathematician called Eratosthenes devised a method for finding prime numbers that the children are going to use. He called it a sieve.

Show the children the enlarged 100-square grid and explain how to use Eratosthenes' sieve as follows.

Put a ring around 2 – the first prime number. Cross out all multiples of 2, since none of these can be prime numbers. Put a ring around 3 – the second prime number. Cross out all multiples of 3 not already crossed out, since none of these can be prime numbers. Put a ring around 5 – the third prime number. Cross out all multiples of 5 not already crossed out, since none of these can be prime numbers.

Continue this procedure until you can go no further (in fact, there are no more numbers to cross out beyond multiples of 11). You have then 'sieved out' all numbers that are multiples of numbers other than 1 and themselves. The numbers that are not crossed out are all primes and should be ringed.

1	②	③	4	⑤	6	⑦	8	9	10
⑪	12	⑬	14	15	16	⑰	18	⑲	20
21	22	㉓	24	25	26	27	28	㉙	30
㉛	32	33	34	35	36	㊲	38	39	40
㊶	42	㊸	44	45	46	㊼	48	49	50
51	52	㉝	54	55	56	57	58	㊾	60
㊶	62	63	64	65	66	㉮	68	69	70
㉛	72	㉝	74	75	76	77	78	㉙	80
81	82	㉝	84	85	86	87	88	㉙	90
91	92	93	94	95	96	㉧	98	99	100

Differentiation

Less able children could use a smaller number grid to investigate prime numbers to, say, 20 or 50.

More able children can extend the process to numbers up to 200 and beyond.

Plenary

Make a display of prime numbers on a 100-square grid. Conclude the lesson with some 'is it prime?' questions: *Is 17 a prime number? What is the next prime number after 19? Is 27 a prime number?*

Linked to
H i s t o r y

22 Ideal shapes

Objectives

Numeracy
Describe and visualise properties of solid shapes.
Make shapes with increasing accuracy.
Visualise 3-D shapes from 2-D drawings.

History
To study the achievements of the ancient Greeks and the influence of their civilisation on the world today.
Links to QCA History Unit 15: How do we use ancient Greek ideas today?

Resources

Copies of photocopiable pages 156 and 157; card, glue, scissors and paints.

Vocabulary

polygon
polyhedron
regular
solid shape
edge
face
angle
vertex

Background

A polyhedron is a solid shape with plane faces, such as a cube or a pyramid. In a regular polyhedron, all the faces are identical regular polygons. All the edges of a regular polyhedron are equal in length, and all angles between the edges are equal. The ancient Greek mathematicians discovered that there are only five regular polyhedra. These are called the *Platonic solids*, after the philosopher Plato who considered them to be perfect or 'ideal' shapes. In this lesson, the children use nets to make models of the Platonic solids.

or are they all the same? Explain that the cube is an example of a regular solid made from identical faces, each of which is an identical regular polygon. *Are there any other regular solids?* Ask for suggestions. Discuss the features of the shapes suggested by the children and decide whether or not they qualify as regular.

Develop the lesson by explaining that the ancient Greeks studied this question more than 2000 years ago. They eventually discovered that there are just five 'ideal shapes', known as the *Platonic solids*: tetrahedron, cube, octahedron, dodecahedron and icosahedron. Explain that the children's task is to make models of the shapes from the nets on the worksheets.

Set the children to work in pairs or small groups on the practical activity. They should cut out a net, glue it to thin cardboard, fold along the lines and glue the tabs to make their shapes.

Differentiation

Less able children should concentrate on making the tetrahedron, cube and octahedron. They may find this easier with a construction kit such as Polydron; or they could make shape 'frameworks' with a construction kit such as K'nex.

More able children can make the dodecahedron and icosahedron, then count the sides, edges and corners of each shape.

Plenary

When the children have completed their model-making activity, review the properties of the five shapes. Make a table giving the shape names and the numbers of faces and edges for each shape.

tetrahedron   dodecahedron   cube

icosahedron   octahedron

Preparation

Copy the worksheets and distribute the craft materials for group work. You may wish to enlarge the sheets to make larger models and/or copy them onto thin card to make the models more durable.

Main teaching activity

Introduce the lesson by showing the children a cube. Ask them to count the faces and edges, and to describe the key features of a cube. Are any of the faces or edges special,

shape	number of faces	number of edges	number of vertices (corners)
tetrahedron	4	6	4
cube	6	12	8
octahedron	8	12	6
dodecahedron	12	30	20
icosahedron	20	30	12

Linked to
D & T

23 DIY

Objectives

Numeracy
Calculate the perimeter and area of simple compound shapes that can be split into rectangles.
Round up or down depending on the context.

Design and technology
Plan what they have to do.
Measure and mark out a range of materials.
Could link to QCA Design and Technology Unit 6A: Shelters.

Resources

A copy of photocopiable page 158 for each child; sample floor tiles and skirting board (a local DIY store may be able to supply some samples or old stock); flip chart or board.

Vocabulary

area
perimeter
measure
calculate
divide
estimate
round

Background

DIY projects pose many mathematical problems. For example, to tile a floor the floor area must be calculated then divided by the area covered per pack of tiles to find how many packs must be purchased. The number obtained should be rounded up to find the minimum number of packs required. Similarly, to calculate the length of skirting board needed for a room, the perimeter of the room must be found, then divided by the length in which board is supplied, to find the number of lengths needed. In this lesson, children apply their calculation skills and knowledge of area and perimeter calculations to solving DIY problems. An investigation of the properties of flooring materials (such as friction – is it slippery?) makes a good science link. Flooring materials and patterns can also be investigated in relation to art and design and the construction of shelters and homes.

Preparation

Copy and distribute the worksheets. Set out your DIY samples for discussion.

Main teaching activity

Introduce the lesson by sketching an L-shaped room on the board. Pose the problem of tiling the floor. Show (or describe) a packet of floor tiles to the children. Identify the figure giving the area that the tiles in the packet cover. How many packets should be purchased? Lead the

children to solve the problem of calculating the floor area by dividing the room into rectangles. Discuss how the total area must be divided by the area per packet to find the number of packets required. Should the division calculation be rounded up or down?

Develop the lesson by stating that you now wish to finish the job by fixing skirting board all the way around the room. How much skirting board is required? Discuss the process of calculating the perimeter of the room from the dimensions on the diagram. Consider how to calculate the total number of boards required if the board is purchased in 3m lengths.

Set the children to work in pairs or small groups on the worksheet activities.

Differentiation

Less able children should concentrate on the basic area and perimeter calculations.

More able children can extend their investigations to include quantity and cost estimates, as suggested on the worksheets.

Plenary

Review the answers to the worksheets with the whole class. Suggest that children make measurements of the area and perimeter of their bedroom. How many floor tiles would they need to cover the floor? What floor material would they choose?

The answers are:
1. kitchen: 6.5m², lounge: 9.5m²
2. lounge: 8, kitchen: 6
3. kitchen: 12m, lounge: 14m
4. 7

Linked to
P S H E

24 Best buys

Objectives

Numeracy
Identify and use appropriate operations (including combinations of operations) to solve word problems involving numbers and quantities.
PSHE & citizenship
To make choices and decisions, for example about how to spend money.

Resources

A copy of photocopiable page 159 for each child. If possible, some sample products for comparison, for example different brands of baked beans in different-sized tins; calculators.

Vocabulary

price
cost
amount
value
compare
kilogram
gram
litre
millilitre

Background

A tour of local shops and supermarkets shows that effective shopping requires good numeracy skills. Products, for example tomato sauce or cheese, are sold in packages of varying types and sizes. Comparing the relative costs of different-sized packages or multi-packs of a product to select the 'best buy' can be a challenging task. Larger quantities are usually relatively cheaper, but an estimate must be made of whether or not you will use the quantity before the 'best before' date. Large supermarkets now display prices per kilo or per litre next to products, to help customers compare different pack sizes and brands. In this lesson, children make 'price per quantity' calculations to compare prices and make judgements of value for money.

Preparation

Copy and distribute the worksheets. Set out the baked beans or similar products with their prices displayed.

Main teaching activity

Show the children the bean cans or other samples. Explain that the problem is to find the best value beans. Discuss how the relative costs of the product in different-sized containers can be compared. Demonstrate how to calculate the price per kilo or price per litre for your examples. An example is illustrated above right.
Go on to discuss the pros and cons of buying large-sized containers or multi-packs of products. Have the children seen the 'cost per kilo' and 'cost per litre' labels in the supermarket that help them make comparisons?
Set the children to work in pairs or small groups to solve the worksheet problems.

Differentiation

Less able children should concentrate on completing the first table.
More able children can proceed to the calculations in the second table, which involve more steps. Make sure they understand that they must convert quantities to the same units (for example, kilos or litres) to make valid comparisons.

Plenary

Review the answers to the worksheet (shown in the tables on the right) as a class. Suggest that the children look out for price comparison labels the next time they go to a large shop.

Baked Beans 250g 38p

250g = 0.25kg
cost per kg = 38p ÷ 0.25
= 152p = £1.52

Baked Beans 500g 72p

500g = 0.5kg
cost per kg = 72p ÷ 0.5
= 144p = £1.44

Potatoes

product description	price per kg	rank
new potatoes	£1.20	5
baking potatoes	90p	4
washed potatoes	80p	3
small sack	75p	2
large sack	60p	1

Crisps

product description	price per g	rank
small packet	1.5p	4
large packet	1.2p	2
family pack	1p	1
multi-pack	1.4p	3
pan fried	2p	5

Lemonade

product description	price per litre	rank
value lemonade	49p	1
deluxe lemonade	£1.05	5
kid's bottle pack	80p	2=
single can	90p	4
6-pack	80p	2=

Linked to
Geography
P E

25 Mountain maths

Background

Mount Snowdon is the highest mountain in England and Wales. Its summit is 3560ft (1085m) above sea level. The ascent of Mount Snowdon is a challenging walk that some children may have made on summer holidays. There are several well-known, named routes. An alternative and equally enjoyable way up the mountain is on the mountain railway that runs from Llanberis to the summit station.

Planning the ascent of the mountain by the alternative walking routes or on the train is a good exercise to develop map-reading skills and practise the associated mathematics.

Preparation

Copy and distribute the worksheets with the other resources. Pin up the maps for class discussion.

Main teaching activity

Introduce the lesson with a discussion of the highest mountains in England, Wales and Scotland. The highest mountain in England is Scafell Pike in the Lake District, height 977m. Mount Snowdon is 108m higher and is the highest peak in Wales. Ben Nevis, at 1343m, is the highest mountain in Great Britain, and is found in mid-west

Scotland. Locate the mountains on the map.

Explain that the children's task is to plan an ascent of Snowdon. They should complete the table on the worksheet, comparing the alternative routes. They should use the spot heights and information on the map scale to fill in the blanks.

Differentiation

Less able children should concentrate on the worksheet exercise.

Challenge more able children to research routes on Snowdon in more detail using the Ordnance Survey maps. Discuss how contours are lines that join points at the same height. They are labelled every 50m above sea level. Where the ground is flat or gently sloping, the contours are widely spaced; where it is steep, they are close together. Can the children make a judgement of the difficulties of the alternative routes from the spacing of the contours they cross? Can they compare the lengths of the routes?

Plenary

Conclude the lesson with a discussion of the children's conclusions about their chosen route. Check their calculations. Which is the most straightforward walking route? Why might other routes be dangerous without proper experience or equipment? Why might any route on Snowdon be dangerous in winter? The answers are:

path	name	start height	height gained	description
1.	Rhd-Ddu path	190m	895m	very steep
2.	Ranger path	145m	940m	steep
3.	Llanberis path	120m	965m	steady going
4.	Crib Goch	356m	729m	dangerous
5.	Pyg track	356m	729m	very steep
6.	Watkin path	55m	1030m	very steep

26 Time zones

Objectives

Numeracy
To appreciate different times around the world.
Science
To explore how the position of the Sun appears to change during the day.
To know how day and night are related to the spin of the Earth on its own axis.
Geography
To develop locational knowledge of continents, countries and cities.
To use appropriate geographical vocabulary.

Resources

A copy of photocopiable page 161 for each child; notebooks and pencils; a globe, a torch.

Vocabulary

am
pm
noon
midnight
today
yesterday
tomorrow
before
after
hour
minute
24-hour clock
Greenwich Mean Time
British Summer Time
International Date Line

Background

The Earth rotates on its axis once a day. As the Earth's surface moves from west to east, the Sun appears to rise in the east and set in the west. Noon is the time at which the Sun reaches its highest point in the sky. By international convention, time zones around the world refer to Greenwich Mean Time (GMT). Noon GMT is the time at which the Sun is overhead on the Greenwich meridian – longitude 0°. Because of the rotation of the Earth, noon occurs earlier at longitudes to the east of Greenwich and later to the west. In different time zones, clocks are generally set a whole number of hours before or after GMT.

Preparation

Copy the worksheets. Darken the room and set up the globe.

Main teaching activity

Ask the children about holiday trips abroad. Was there a time difference between their holiday destination and home? Can they explain the time differences between different countries around the world? Why must you put your watch forward when you go east to countries such as India, but put it back when you go west to countries such as the USA?

Use the globe and the torch to demonstrate the origin of time zones.

Explain that time zones are measured from Greenwich in London. Show that when it is noon (the Sun is overhead) in the UK, it is midnight on the opposite side of the globe. Demonstrate how the Earth rotates anticlockwise when viewed from above the North Pole, so we are all moving from west to east. When it is noon in the UK, places to the east have already passed through their noon, so it is 'afternoon', but places to the west have yet to reach noon, so it is still morning. The children should know that the Earth takes 24 hours for one complete rotation. Given that one rotation is 360°, can they calculate how many degrees the Earth rotates per hour? (360° ÷ 24 = 15°) Distribute the worksheets. Ask the children to find the time in the cities marked on the map when it is noon GMT.

Differentiation

Less able children should be able to read times directly from the time zone map.

Ask more able children to find the *time difference* between the various cities and GMT, and calculate times for various times in the UK. Discuss British Summer Time. What happens as you cross the International Date Line?

Plenary

As a class, work out what time it is in New York. Discuss why people suffer jet lag when they go on long journeys east or west. Do the children think they would cope better if their day was lengthened by travelling west, or shortened by travelling east? How would they feel being wide awake when everyone else was going to bed?

The answers are: London 12:00 noon, Paris 13:00, Berlin 13:00, Rome 13:00, Madrid 13:00, Lagos 13:00, Tokyo 21:00, New York 7:00, Los Angeles 4:00, Sydney 22:00, San Paulo 9:00, Moscow 15:00, Delhi 17:30, Peking 20:00, Auckland 00:00.

27 Plus VAT

Objectives

Numeracy
Find a simple percentage of small whole-number quantities.
Identify and use appropriate operations to solve problems, including calculating percentages such as VAT.

Literacy
To comment critically on the language, style and success of examples of non-fiction.

Resources

A collection of newspapers and magazines containing advertisements for a particular product type, for example computers; calculators; flip chart or board.

Vocabulary

percentage
decimal fraction
VAT

Background

Advertisers use a variety of techniques to promote their products. In advertisements for computers, the price *excluding* VAT is often highlighted and the VAT-inclusive price appears in much smaller type. In this lesson, children discuss this and similar tactics in advertising in the context of literacy work on the media. The activity links to work on VAT and percentage calculations in numeracy.

Preparation

Make a collection of printed media. Mark a selection of advertisements of similar products for discussion.

Main teaching activity

Introduce the lesson with a general discussion of advertising. What is the purpose of advertising – is it to convey information or to persuade you to buy the product? What do you look at when studying advertisements for computers in magazines? What attracts your attention? What language do the advertisers use? From the consumer's point of view, what are the features of a good advertisement?

Proceed to study computer advertisements. Does the price include or exclude VAT? What is VAT? (Value Added Tax is collected by the government to pay for services such as schools and hospitals. VAT is added to the price of most things you buy, for example a CD. Essentials like food are not taxed. Some organisations, such as schools, do not have to pay VAT.) Develop a discussion of VAT as a national tax that consumers pay on their purchases. Why might advertisers choose to highlight their prices excluding VAT, when it has to be paid? How is VAT calculated?

Develop the lesson by explaining that VAT is calculated as a percentage of the basic price. Demonstrate that if VAT was 10%, for example, and you purchased a computer costing £500 then the VAT would be 0.1 × £500 = £50. The total price would be £550. Solve a number of similar problems for various prices and VAT rates of 10%, 20% and 15%. Demonstrate that, for these different percentages, the multiplying decimal fractions are 0.1, 0.2 and 0.15 respectively.

Finally, state that the current VAT rate as fixed by the government is 17.5%, to calculate the VAT on £500 you must multiply by 0.175. For the computer example, 0.175 × £500 = £87.50; the total price is £587.50. Alternatively, add 10%, 5% (half of 10%) and 2.5% (half of 5%) to the price: 17.5% of £500 = £50 + £25 + £12.50 = £87.50. Write a table of prices similar to this one on the board. Ask the children to work in pairs or small groups to calculate the prices including VAT.

price excluding VAT	VAT @ 17.5%	total price including VAT
£100.00	£17.50	£117.50
£200.00		
£400.00		
£500.00		
£1000.00		
£1500.00		

Differentiation

Less able children should complete the basic VAT calculations.

More able children can search the media provided for computer advertisements. Can they find advertisements that highlight the ex-VAT price, or state that prices include VAT? If the price is not a multiple of hundreds, they could round it up and calculate the VAT mentally.

Plenary

Complete the price table as a class, filling in the VAT and total price columns. Conclude the lesson with some rapid percentage calculations, for example 10% of £85.

28 Making conversions

Objectives

Numeracy
Use, read and write standard metric units.
Know imperial units (mile, pint, gallon, pound, ounce).
Know rough equivalents of pounds and kilograms, ounces and grams, miles and kilometres, litres and pints or gallons.
Solve a problem by representing data on a line graph.

History
To study changes that have taken place since 1930.
Links to QCA History Unit 13: How has life in Britain changed since 1948?

Resources

Squared paper, pencils, rulers, calculators; flip chart or board.

Vocabulary

about the same as
table
line graph
metric unit
imperial unit
calculate
convert

Background

In the 1940s, imperial units were used throughout Britain. Journeys were measured in miles, petrol was sold in gallons, food in pounds and ounces, and milk and beer in pints. Metrication began in the UK in the 1970s, along with the introduction of decimal coins, but imperial units are still used in certain contexts: pint bottles of milk, distances measured in miles, bathroom scales weighing in stones and pounds. (Background information is at www.metric.org.uk)

To compare and feel comfortable with both systems, children should know the rough equivalents of metric and imperial units. More exact conversions can be made with conversion charts in the form of line graphs. These comparisons can be introduced as a study of twentieth-century social history.

Preparation

Set out resources for group work.

Main teaching activity

Introduce the lesson with a discussion of imperial units set in a historical context. For example, if you are working on the 1940s, discuss rationing – what units were used to measure petrol, food and other rationed items during wartime? How do these units relate to the metric units we use today? Draw a conversion table on the board. Explain that it shows that to convert a measurement in kilograms to a measurement in pounds we must multiply by 2.2. If we

want to convert a measurement in pounds to one in kilograms, we must multiply by 0.45. To save making calculations every time, we could prepare a conversion chart similar to the one below. This is a line graph with pounds on one axis and kilograms on the other. To plot the graph we must first prepare a table.

Demonstrate how to complete the table with the help of a calculator, and then plot the data on a graph. Proceed to use the graph to make some conversions.

Set the children to work in pairs or groups to plot their own conversion charts for different measures.

metric quantity	imperial quantity
1kg	2.2lb
0.45kg	1lb
1g	$^1/_{28}$oz
28g	1oz
1km	$^5/_8$ mile
1.6km	1 mile
1 litre	1¾pt
0.57 litres	1pt
1 litre	0.22gal
4.5 litres	1gal

kg	lb
1	2.2
2	4.4
3	6.6
4	8.8
5	11
6	13.2
7	15.4
8	17.6
9	19.8
10	22

Differentiation

Less able children could reproduce the lb to kg conversion chart to develop their practical graph-plotting skills.

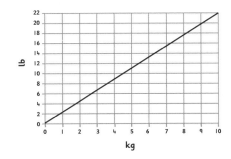

More able children can produce conversions from miles to kilometres, grams to ounces, pints to litres and gallons.

Plenary

Ask selected children to show their charts to the rest of the class and demonstrate how they are used to convert one measure to another. In a follow-up history lesson, children could be asked to research ration quantities, and convert them to metric units.

Linked to
H i s t o r y

29 How have things changed?

Objectives

Numeracy
To solve a problem by representing, extracting and interpreting data in tables and graphs, including those generated by computer.

History
To learn how to find out about events, people and changes from an appropriate range of sources of information, including ICT-based sources.
To investigate how an aspect of the local area has changed over a long period of time.
Could be linked to QCA History Units 12: How did life change in our locality in Victorian times? and 13: How has life in Britain changed since 1948?

Resources

Access to the Internet; flip chart or board.

Vocabulary

data
database
graph
chart
table
change
survey
investigate

Background

Two key historical topics studied during Key Stage 2 are the Victorians and the 1940s. How have things changed nationally and locally since these periods? A wealth of historical data is available on the Internet that children can search to investigate changes during the past 50–150 years. The website of the UK genealogical society – www.genuki.org.uk – includes extensive information on communities of all sizes, including some census data. For example, census information gives the population of Cambridgeshire as follows:

Children can search for similar data for their county or locality and use it to plot graphs showing changes over time. A particularly useful website is www.eh.net/ehresources/howmuch/ This site presents a calculator that can be used to compare changes in the purchasing power of money. For example, it shows that £1 in 1891 had the same purchasing power as £61.54 in 2001; £1 in 1948 was equivalent to £22.08 in 2001.

year	population
1891	276 156
1901	282 336
1911	301 239
1921	307 502
1931	327 745
1939	345 592
1951	389 477
1961	434 915
1971	503 785
1981	573 200
1991	643 439

Preparation

Prepare for the lesson by locating a selection of websites providing historical data relevant to the history topic the class is researching. The two websites noted in the Background section are good starting points.

Main teaching activity

Introduce the lesson with a discussion of changes that have taken place since the Victorian era or the 1940s. How have children's lives changed? How has the value of money changed? How has the population of the country changed? How has people's health and diet changed? How have jobs and wages changed?

Develop the lesson by setting the children to work in small groups on an Internet research task. For example, to find how the population of their village or town has changed during the past 100 years, to find how average earnings have changed, or to research the change in the value of money.

Differentiation

Less able children should be set a specific question, for example: *What was the population of London in 1891, 1951 and 2001?* Direct them to an appropriate website.

More able children can be set more open-ended investigations, for example to discover as much as they can about changes in their village during the past 100 years, presenting their findings as charts and graphs. They could start at www.genuki.org.uk and progress from there, following links and using search engines.

Plenary

Ask groups to report their findings. What data have they managed to locate? Have they plotted any charts or graphs? What do they show? As a follow-up activity you could arrange a visit from a local historian to talk about changes in the locality.

30 Box challenge

Objectives

Numeracy
Make shapes with increasing accuracy.
Calculate the surface area of a cuboid.
Design and technology
Undertake focused practical tasks that develop a range of techniques, skills, processes and knowledge.
Could also build on QCA Art and Design Unit 5B: Containers.

Resources

A4 sheets of thin card, scissors, rulers, pencils, glue, dry sand, a measuring cylinder; a selection of card boxes to disassemble.

Vocabulary

cuboid
box
net
capacity
area
face
edge

Background

In this lesson, children are challenged to make an open box from a single sheet of card. The box must be folded and glued from a single net drawn on the card sheet supplied. No additional pieces of card are allowed. A prize could be awarded for the box with the greatest capacity.

Preparation

If possible, print 1cm squares on the card sheets to aid children's setting out and area calculations. Set out the craft materials in preparation for group work.

Main teaching activity

Introduce the lesson with a discussion of the manufacture of cardboard boxes. Take some boxes apart to show how they are folded from a single sheet. Discuss the shape of boxes. What is meant by the surface area of a box? Explain how the surface area can be calculated, and that it is a measure of the amount of card used. What is meant by the capacity of a box? This is the amount of space or volume the box surrounds. Discuss

the capacity of different-shaped boxes. Which shape has the greatest capacity for a given amount of cardboard – wide and shallow, tall and narrow, or cubic? (For an open cuboid box, the greatest capacity is obtained with a square base, and height equal to half the breadth, but do not expect children to predict this result!)

Explain that the children's task is to draw a net on the card sheet provided and fold it into an open box. Their goal is to use as much of the card as possible to produce a box with the greatest possible capacity. Sketch some possible nets on the board.

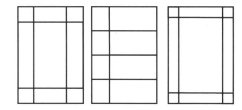

Set the children to work in groups on the box-making activity. Show them how to measure the capacity of their completed boxes by filling them with sand and pouring the sand into a measuring cylinder. Explain how to calculate the surface area of a box by measuring its edges and calculating the area of its faces.

Differentiation

Less able children should concentrate on drawing a net, cutting it out and folding it into a box, then making the capacity and area measurements.

More able children should make several boxes of different shapes and measure and compare their areas and capacities.

Plenary

Conclude the activity by asking children to report their findings. What is the largest capacity box they have produced from the A4 sheet? Which box has made best use of the available materials? Make a display of the children's boxes, sequencing them by capacity.

31 Traffic trouble

Objectives

Numeracy
Express simple fractions as percentages.
Use a fraction as an 'operator' to find fractions of numbers or quantities.
Begin to convert a fraction to a decimal using division.
Solve a problem by interpreting data in tables.

Geography
To investigate an environmental issue, for example increasing traffic congestion.
Builds on QCA Geography Units 12: Should the high street be closed to traffic? and 20: Local traffic – an environmental issue.

Resources

A copy of photocopiable page 162 for each child, calculators.

Vocabulary

fraction
percentage
operator
survey
proportion

Background

We are all familiar with traffic jams and overcrowded trains. Traffic congestion could be eased if more people took the train or bus, but how many more trains and buses would be needed? It is not possible to ask every commuter how they travel into a large city on a given day. However, the numbers can be estimated accurately by making a survey in which data for a representative sample is collected. The proportions of different transport modes for the sample can then be assumed to apply to the population as a whole. Totals are determined by 'multiplying up'. In this lesson, children use their calculation skills to interpret a hypothetical transport survey and answer associated questions. The activity forms the basis for a discussion of local transport issues. It could be followed up with a local transport survey, or opinion polls in other subjects using the same sampling technique. For example, in PSHE children could survey opinions on a variety of topical issues such as school uniforms, bullying, fox hunting or pocket money.

Preparation

Copy and distribute the worksheets with the calculators.

Main teaching activity

Introduce the lesson with a discussion of the children's transport to school. Ask them to consider how their parents travel to work. How far do they travel? Do they use the car, train or bus? Do they complain about traffic jams and delays? What are the transport issues in the locality of the school? Consider transport policy – how could more people be persuaded to use public transport, to cycle or to share cars?

Set the children to work in pairs or small groups on the worksheet activity. Discuss making a survey of a representative sample as outlined in the Background notes. The children complete the table by calculating the percentage of commuters in the sample using different forms of transport, then calculate totals by multiplying up. Remind them of the links between fractions and percentages, and the use of fractions as operators. For example, if 50 people from 200 travel by train, then the fraction is $^{50}/_{200} = {}^{25}/_{100} = 0.25 = 25\% = {}^{1}/_{4}$.
25% of 10 000 = 0.25 × 10 000 = 2500.

Differentiation

Less able children should concentrate on the basic calculation task.

Challenge more able children to list suggestions to encourage more people to cycle and use the bus. Can they find out if the local council are implementing any of their suggestions? Suggest looking at the local council's transport policy on the Internet.

Plenary

Review the worksheet calculations as a class. Talk through the children's transport policy suggestions. Discuss local transport issues and plan your own survey. The answers are:

transport	fraction	percentage	number
car	$^{200}/_{500} = {}^{2}/_{5}$	40%	0.4 × 20 000 = 8000
bus	$^{125}/_{500} = {}^{1}/_{4}$	25%	0.25 × 20 000 = 5000
train	$^{50}/_{500} = {}^{1}/_{10}$	10%	0.1 × 20 000 = 2000
bicycle	$^{20}/_{500} = {}^{1}/_{25}$	4%	0.04 × 20 000 = 800
motorcycle	$^{25}/_{500} = {}^{1}/_{20}$	5%	0.05 × 20 000 = 1000
walk	$^{80}/_{500} = {}^{4}/_{25}$	16%	0.16 × 20 000 = 3200
TOTAL		100%	20 000

Linked to
Geography

32 Holiday choice

Objectives

Numeracy
Identify and use appropriate operations to solve 'real-life' problems involving money, using one or more steps.
Solve a problem by extracting and interpreting data in tables.

Geography
To study a range of places and environments in different parts of the world.

Links to QCA Geography Unit 18: Connecting ourselves to the world.

Resources

A selection of brochures for popular holiday destinations; a copy of photocopiable page 163 for each child; calculators and pens; wall maps of the UK, Europe and the world.

Vocabulary

cost
table
most expensive
least expensive
value
total
discount
currency

Background

Selecting a holiday from a brochure is an exercise in applied mathematics. Weather charts, tables of hotel facilities, car hire alternatives and departure timetables must be interpreted. Once the basic costs are identified for a 7- or 14-night stay, extras such as a sea view, insurance and airport taxes must be added. There may even be a discount for early booking! In this lesson, children discuss holiday destinations and make cost calculations to inform their choices.

Preparation

Visit a travel agent to collect some holiday brochures. Copy and distribute the worksheets.

Main teaching activity

Introduce the lesson with a discussion of holiday destinations the children have visited. (Treat this issue sensitively – some children never go on holiday.) Locate popular destinations on the maps, for example Blackpool, North Wales, the south coast of England, mainland Spain, the Spanish holiday islands, the Greek islands, Florida. Discuss the climate, activities and accommodation at the alternative destinations. Show the children the holiday brochures. Look at the tables and compare some of the prices at different times of year and for different forms of accommodation.

Set the children to work in pairs or small groups on the worksheet activity. They should interpret the tables of information for the holiday village to answer the questions at the bottom of the page. Suggest that the children write down a list of costs for their holiday, for example as below, then use a calculator to find the total.

Two adults hiring a chalet for two weeks in August	2×290	= £580
Bike hire	2×20	= £40
Sea view	2×20	= £40
Insurance	4×15	= £60
Total		£720

Differentiation

Help less able children make the basic holiday cost calculations required for questions 1 and 2.

Challenge more able children to choose and cost a holiday from the brochures you have provided. Specify a date on which they are to take their holiday.

Plenary

Review the answers to the worksheet questions as a class. Discuss the holiday choices and cost calculations the children have made using the brochures.

The answers are:
1. £280
2. £760
3. £711

Linked to
Literacy
History

33 Number words

Background

Many mathematical terms have their origin in Latin and Greek, as do so many other words in the English language. The Latin and Greek names for the numbers 1 to 10 are listed in the table below, along with prefixes and examples of words derived from these roots. In this lesson, children use dictionaries to research the origin and meaning of words with a number connection, for example unicorn, bicycle, triangle, quartet, heptathlon and decade. The activity links to work on prefixes, spelling and word origins in literacy.

number? Can the children think of words that use the same or similar prefixes or word parts to make a number link?

Develop the lesson by discussing the Greek and Latin origins of number-based prefixes. Write the table opposite on the board and add a selection of words from the children to the final column.

Explain that the children's task for the lesson is to use the dictionaries provided to find further examples of words with number parts indicated by a prefix. Suggest that they find at least one word for each number 1 to 10. They should write down the word, highlight its number prefix and write a definition of the word.

English	Greek	Latin	prefix	example
one	hen	unus	uni-	unicorn, unit
two	di	bi	bi-	bicycle, binary
three	tria	tres	tri-	triangle, triplet
four	tetra	quattuor	tetra-, qua-	quadrangle, tetrapod
five	penta	quinque	penta-, quin-	pentangle, quintet
six	hex	sex	hex-, sex-	hexagon, sextuplets
seven	hepta	septem	hept-, sept-	heptathlon
eight	octo	octo	octo-	octopus
nine	ennea	novem/nones	non-	nonagon
ten	deca	decem	dec-	decimal, decade

Preparation

Set out dictionaries in preparation for group research.

Main teaching activity

Introduce the lesson by writing the words *unicorn, bicycle, triangle, quartet, heptathlon* and *decade* on the board. Ask the class to spot a connection between each of the words and a number. Which part of the word specifies the

Differentiation

Less able children should use a standard dictionary to research their words and definitions. Show them how to search for words beginning *uni-* and identify those in which uni represents 'single' or 'one'.

More able children can use an etymological dictionary to help research the origins of the words they find. Challenge them to find words with a specific mathematical meaning, for example *unit, binary, triangle, quarter, pentomino…*

Plenary

Compile a list of words the children have discovered on the board. Ask for definitions of the words and explanations of their origins (etymology). Make a class display based on the children's writing.

34 Mathematical crosswords

Background

Solving and compiling word puzzles and crosswords develops knowledge of word spellings and meanings. Crosswords can also be devised to include mathematical problems. In this lesson, children discuss different types of crosswords and tackle puzzles with mathematical themes. More able children are challenged to create mathematical crosswords of their own.

Preparation
Copy and set out the worksheets with the other resources. Make a selection of crosswords with different styles of question for discussion.

Main teaching activity
Introduce the lesson with a discussion of crosswords. Show some examples and discuss the style of questions. Simple or 'quick' crosswords generally have straightforward clues that give dictionary-style definitions of the words required, for example *Shape with six sides (7)* = 'hexagon'. Cryptic crosswords are much harder. The clues in a cryptic crossword are word puzzles or riddles, for example *Valentine with saccharine centre (10)* = 'sweetheart'. Discuss how crosswords are set out and numbered, identifying the 'across' or horizontal clues, and the 'down' or vertical clues.

Set the children to work in pairs or small groups to solve the word puzzles on the worksheet. Puzzle 1 is a straightforward wordsearch, with 12 shape words to find. Puzzle 2 is more cryptic, giving mathematical clues that must be solved to find the words.

Differentiation
Less able children should concentrate on solving the first crossword.

More able children can tackle the more challenging crossword. When they have completed it successfully, challenge them to create similar crosswords of their own.

Plenary
Review the crossword answers with the whole class, discussing the word definitions and mental calculations required where necessary. The answers are:
1. rhombus, trapezium, cube, cone, kite, heptagon, sphere, cylinder, pyramid, square, disc, circle
2.

¹s	e	v	²e	n			³t	
u			v			⁶s	i	x
⁴m	⁵o	d	e				n	
	c		⁷n	i	⁸n	e		
	t				e			
⁹r	o	w			¹⁰t	e	n	

35 Heads or tails?

Background

Deciding who starts a game by tossing a coin and calling 'heads' or 'tails' exploits the random nature of coin tossing to make a fair choice. The probability of a head is equal to the probability of a tail. Since there are just two equally likely outcomes, the probability of either is '1 in 2', '50:50' or 'evens'. We assign events that are certain to happen the probability 1 and events that are certain not to happen the probability 0. The probability of an event that has an equal chance of happening or not, such as tossing a head, is $1/2 = 0.5$.

The most likely outcome of a repeated coin-tossing test is $1/2$ heads and $1/2$ tails. However, there is a good chance that the fractions will not be exactly $1/2$. With six tosses it would not be surprising to obtain twice as many heads as tails (4H, 2T), but as the number of tosses increases, the fractions of heads and tails will get closer and closer to $1/2$.

In this lesson, children conduct coin-tossing tests to check probability theory. They use their ICT skills to record, display and interpret their results.

Preparation

Set out coins, paper and pencils for practical work. Set up the computer running spreadsheet software.

Main teaching activity

Introduce the lesson by tossing a coin and asking the children to call 'heads' or 'tails'. Remind them of the vocabulary of probability and chance. Draw a probability line like the one below on the board. Where on the line is the probability of obtaining a head or a tail when tossing a fair coin?

probability

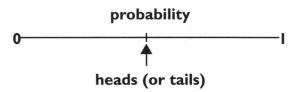

heads (or tails)

Ask the children to predict the most likely number of heads when tossing a coin 10, 20, 30, 100... times. Make sure that they understand that there is a chance that in a particular trial the outcome will differ from the most probable outcome.

Set the children to work in pairs or small groups to toss a coin 20 times. Each group should count up the number of heads and tails obtained. Record the numbers obtained on a frequency table similar to the one on the right. Set the children to translate the frequency table into a bar chart, using the facilities of a spreadsheet program.

result of tossing coin 20 times	number of times observed
0 H, 20 T	0
1 H, 19 T	0
2 H, 18 T	0
3 H, 17 T	0
4 H, 18 T	0
5 H, 15 T	1
6 H, 14 T	0
7 H, 13 T	1
8 H, 12 T	4
9 H, 11 T	5
10 H, 10 T	7
11 H, 9 T	5
12 H, 8 T	3
13 H, 7 T	2
14 H, 6 T	1
15 H, 5 T	0
16 H, 4 T	0
17 H, 3 T	0
18 H, 2 T	0
19 H, 1 T	1
20 H, 0 T	0

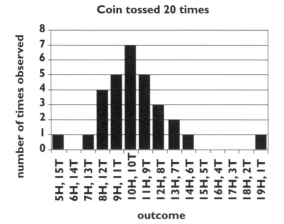

Coin tossed 20 times

Differentiation

Less able children should concentrate on the basic single-coin-tossing exercise to contribute to the class frequency table and bar chart.

Challenge more able children to extend the activity to explore the possible outcomes when tossing two coins together. The four possible outcomes are illustrated below. Each has a probability of $^1/_4$.

(H)(H)   (H)(T)   (T)(H)   (T)(T)

Plenary

Interpret the class bar chart together. What was the most frequent outcome for tossing a coin 20 times? Combine all the class data to find the total numbers of heads and tails tossed. Calculate an overall ratio of heads to tails. In the sample data given here:
total number of heads = 309
total number of tails = 291
ratio of heads to tails = $^{309}/_{291}$ = 1.06

36 Assessment 2

Objectives

The assessment activities in this book are designed to introduce Key Stage 2 children to SAT-style questions. They are set in cross-curricular contexts based on the preceding term's lessons. The questions in Assessment 2 test the children's progress in: recognising and extending number sequences; solving problems involving money and measures; working with and ordering fractions, decimals and percentages.

Resources

A copy of photocopiable page 165 for each child; advertisements for computers or similar products with prices of different models.

Preparation

Make copies of the assessment sheet. If you feel that the sheet is too 'busy', the three activities could be separated and enlarged on individual sheets.

Lesson introduction

Begin the assessment lesson by reviewing the relevant cross-curricular topics covered during the term. Remind the children of some of the projects and investigations they have undertaken, and ask them to recall and recount their work. Emphasise the mathematical content, for example: *Do you remember how we compared the value for money of different crisp brands and packages?*

Main assessment activity

Distribute the worksheets and ask the children to work on them individually. Guide the whole class through the questions one at

a time, reading the text with them, and prompting them to work out and fill in their answers. Try to make the whole activity enjoyable!

Practical activity

Ask the children to identify the price of a particular model of computer from the advertisements you have provided. What is the price excluding VAT? What is the price including VAT?

Plenary

Review the answers to the questions as a class. Collect the completed question sheets to use as an aid to judging individual children's progress, and to include in your records. The answers are:

1. 8, 10, 12; multiples of 2 or even numbers
16, 25, 36; square numbers
11, 13; prime numbers

2.

product description	price per litre	rank
value Cola	60p	1
US brand Cola	90p	3=
kid's bottle pack	£1	5
single can	90p	3=
six-pack	80p	2

3. 0.1, $^1/_8$, 20%, 0.3, $^1/_3$, 50%, $^3/_5$, 75%, $^5/_6$, $^7/_8$

Linked to
I C T

37 Fraction sequence

Background

Fractions, decimal fractions and percentages are alternative representations of parts of a whole, for example, $1/4 = 0.25 = 25\%$. Children will be familiar with representing fractions and percentages visually, for example as shaded squares on a grid, a slice of a pie or the position of a needle on a petrol gauge.

$\frac{1}{4}$ **25%**   **0.25**

On the computer, a 'progress' bar shows the fraction of a process completed and the amount still to go. A similar bar is used in TV broadcasts to represent statistics such as percentage possession during a football match. In this lesson, children use the graphics facilities of computer software to explore different visual representations of fractions. They produce cards for a fraction and percentage matching and sequencing game.

Preparation

Set up the computers running your preferred design/graphics software. Ensure that you can use it confidently to draw and colour squares, rectangles, segments of circles and other shapes to represent fractions.

Main teaching activity

Introduce the lesson by reminding the children of the different ways in which fractional quantities can be written. Reproduce the following table on the board, asking the children to help to fill in the columns. Develop the lesson by discussing how fractions are represented visually in different circumstances, for example by 'progress' bars during computer operations, by percentage bars showing football statistics, by a needle on a car fuel gauge, by countdown clocks on quiz shows or as slices of pie on pie charts. Sketch examples on the board.

$\frac{1}{2}$	0.5	50%
$\frac{1}{4}$		
$\frac{1}{3}$		
$\frac{3}{4}$		
$\frac{1}{5}$		
$\frac{3}{5}$		
$\frac{1}{10}$		
$\frac{9}{10}$		
$\frac{4}{5}$		
$\frac{2}{3}$		
$\frac{7}{10}$		

Explain that the children's task is to use the computer to design visual representations of the fractions you have listed in the table. They should be printed on thin card and cut into playing cards to make a fraction-sequencing game. They should also include cards giving text versions of each fraction or percentage.

Differentiation

Help less able children to produce and shade square grids to represent fractions.

Challenge more able children to devise a variety of representations, including partially shaded pie charts, time bars and gauges.

Plenary

Look at the different fraction representations the children have produced. Are they clear? Can the children identify all the fractions and percentages shown? Conclude by shuffling fraction cards in packs and asking children to play games in groups in which they must sequence and/or match the fractions as they turn the cards over one at a time.

38 Equal fractions

Objectives

Numeracy
Recognise relationships between fractions.
Reduce a fraction to its simplest form by cancelling common factors.
Know imperial units.

History
To study changes since Victorian times and the 1930s.
Could link to QCA History Units 11: What was it like for children living in Victorian Britain? and 13: How has life in Britain changed since 1948?

Resources

Old school rulers; flip chart or board; a copy of photocopiable page 166 for each child.

Vocabulary

equivalent
reduce to
cancel
half, quarter, eighth
third, sixth, ninth, twelfth

Background

Old school books reveal that both Victorian and 1940s children spent far more of their maths lessons working with fractions than children do today. This was because of the role of fractions in the non-decimal measurement systems then in use (and also because they had no electronic calculators). An old school ruler graduated in feet, inches and fractions of an inch demonstrates the importance of a good grasp of fractions to deal with measurements such as $1^5/_{16}$ inch or $2^{31}/_{32}$ inch.

An old wooden ruler is a good starting point to introduce relationships between fractions and the process of reducing a fraction to its simplest form by cancelling.

Preparation
Copy and distribute the worksheets.

Main teaching activity
Introduce the lesson by distributing the old rulers and examining the inch scales with the children. Remind the children about the history of imperial units and that children in the Victorian era/1940s would have made measurements with these rulers. Discuss how the inches are divided into various fractions, for example identify an inch that is divided into $1/_2$s, $1/_4$s and $1/_8$s. Discuss the relationship between these fractions ($1/_4$ is half of $1/_2$, $1/_8$ is half of $1/_4$).

Develop the lesson by writing a list of fractions based on these ruler divisions on the board. For example:
$3/_4$, $2/_8$, $6/_8$, $2/_4$, $5/_8$

Can any of the fractions be reduced to a simpler form? Explain the process of identifying and cancelling common factors in the numerator and denominator. Demonstrate with some examples.

Set the children to work in pairs on the first set problems on the worksheet. They could use their rulers to confirm practically for example, that $6/_8 = 3/_4$.

The second set of problems is based on $1/_3$rds and related fractions. Identify an inch divided into $1/_{12}$ths ($1/_4 \times 1/_3$) and discuss the related fractions of $1/_9$ths ($1/_3 \times 1/_3$), $1/_6$ths ($1/_2 \times 1/_3$) and $1/_3$rds. Set the children to complete the second set of problems on the sheet.

Differentiation
Less able children should concentrate on the first set of problems.

The most able could identify $1/_{16}$ths and $1/_{32}$nds on the ruler and complete the final set of problems.

Plenary
Review the answers to the worksheet problems as a class. Conclude the lesson with some quick-fire 'cancelling' problems, for example $2/_4 = ?$, $6/_8 = ?$, $4/_{12} = ?$, $3/_9 = ?$
The answers are:
1. $1/_4$, $1/_2$, $3/_4$, 1, $1/_8$, $1/_4$, $3/_8$, $1/_2$, $5/_8$, $3/_4$, $7/_8$, 1
2. $1/_3$, $1/_2$, $2/_3$, $5/_6$, 1, $2/_9$, $1/_3$, $4/_9$, $5/_9$, $2/_3$, $7/_9$, $1/_6$, $1/_4$, $1/_3$, $5/_{12}$, $1/_2$, $7/_{12}$, $2/_3$, $3/_4$, $5/_6$, $11/_{12}$
3. $1/_8$, $1/_4$, $3/_8$, $1/_2$, $5/_8$, $3/_4$, $7/_8$, $1/_8$, $3/_{16}$, $1/_4$, $6/_{16}$, $1/_2$, $5/_8$, $3/_4$, $7/_8$

39 Finding factors

Background

In Lesson 21, children were introduced to prime numbers and used Eratosthenes' sieve to identify prime numbers to 100. Numbers greater than 1 that are not prime are called compound numbers. All compound numbers can be built up from prime numbers by multiplication, for example $4 = 2 \times 2$, $6 = 2 \times 3$, $8 = 2 \times 2 \times 2$, $9 = 3 \times 3$, $10 = 2 \times 5$, $12 = 2 \times 2 \times 3$ and so on. The primes that are multiplied to produce a compound number are called the *prime factors* of that number. The process of finding the prime factors is called *factorising* the number. The ability to find factors is an important skill when working with fractions and in later work with algebra. In this lesson, children review and develop their work on prime numbers and practise factorising numbers to 100.

Preparation

Set up the 100-square grid.

Main teaching activity

Introduce the lesson by reminding the children of their previous work on prime numbers. Use the 100-square grid to recap the process of identifying primes with Eratosthenes' sieve. Continue by discussing the numbers that have been crossed out on the grid during the process. Explain that these compound numbers can all be made by multiplying prime numbers together.

Start listing compound numbers and their prime factors on the board:
$4 = 2 \times 2$
$6 = 2 \times 3$
$8 = 2 \times 2 \times 2$

$9 = 3 \times 3$
$10 = 2 \times 5$
$12 = 2 \times 2 \times 3$
$14 =$
$15 =$
$16 =$

Ask children to continue the list, finding the prime factors by trial and error.

Develop the lesson by introducing a systematic method for reducing a number to its prime factors. Write down the number. Test in sequence to see if it is divisible by 2, 3, 5 or another prime number. Write it as the product of the smallest prime number by which it is divisible and a second factor. Is the second factor a prime number? If it is, the prime factors have been found. If not, test in sequence again to see if it is divisible by 2, 3, 5 or another prime number. Write the original number as the product of two primes and a third factor. Is the third factor a prime number? Repeat the process until the original number has been reduced to a product of primes as illustrated below.

15 3×5	The prime factors of 15 are 3, 5
36 2×18 $2 \times 2 \times 9$ $2 \times 2 \times 3 \times 3$	The prime factors of 36 are 2, 2, 3, 3
95 5×19	The prime factors of 95 are 5, 19
50 2×25 $2 \times 5 \times 5$	The prime factors of 50 are 2, 5, 5

Set the children to use this method to find the prime factors of all the numbers to 100.

Differentiation

Less able children could find and list the prime factors of all the numbers to 20, then progress to 50.

More able children can find the prime factors of the numbers to 100 and beyond.

Plenary

Use the children's results to write the prime factors of all numbers to 100 beneath each number on the grid. Display the completed prime factors grid in the classroom.

Linked to
History

40 Changing families

Objectives

Numeracy
To find the mode.
Begin to find the median and mean of a set of data.

History
To study changes since Victorian times.
Links to QCA History Units 11: What was it like for children living in Victorian Britain? and 12: How did life change in our locality in Victorian times?

Resources

Flip chart or board; a copy of photocopiable page 167 for each child.

Vocabulary

mean
median
mode
data
average

Background

The average number of family members in a household has declined since Victorian times. Parents have fewer children, and it is less common for extended families (more than two generations) to live together in the same house. In this lesson, children compare modern and Victorian patterns of living. They make a survey of the household numbers for children in the class and compare them with Victorian households. They use different forms of average – the mode, median and mean – for making comparisons between the data sets, and discuss their relative merits. Be sensitive to the variety of family patterns that may be represented in your class, particularly in an ethnically diverse class.

Preparation

Copy and distribute the worksheets.

Main teaching activity

Introduce the lesson with a discussion of how family life has changed between the Victorian era and the present day. How are houses different? How is transport different? How are school and work different? How are families different? Explain that the children are going to compare the number of people living in Victorian homes with the numbers they share their homes with today.

In the first part of the lesson, make a quick survey of the household numbers for the children in the class. Who lives in a house with 2, 3, 4, 5… people altogether? List the numbers on the board in numerical order, as in the example below:
2, 2, 2, 2, 2, 2, 2, 3, 3, 3, 3, 3, 4, 4, 4, 4, 4, 4, 5, 5, 5, 5, 6, 6, 7, 8

Develop the lesson by discussing alternative ways of finding an average or typical value from the data set. The mode is the most common number (2), the median is the middle number when all the data is written in sequence (4), the mean is the sum of the numbers divided by the number of numbers (3.85). The mode has the advantage of giving us the most common household size, but as in this case, it may give a false impression of a typical household (somewhere between 3 and 5). The median gives a better impression of a middle or typical value. The mean is a more accurate calculation of the middle value than the median but it is not necessarily a whole number. This can seem odd when dealing with people!

Set the children to complete the worksheet.

Differentiation

Less able children should find the mode and median of the data.

More able children should also calculate the mean value.

Plenary

Compare the children's calculations of the mean, median and mode of the Victorian household data with the class data. Discuss reasons for the changes that have taken place since Victorian times, particularly child mortality. Whether you mention changes in family planning and contraception will depend on your school's sex education policy and the maturity of your class. The answers are: mode 7, median 6, mean 6.5.

Linked to
Geography

41 Where are you?

Objectives

Numeracy
Read and plot coordinates in all four quadrants.
Geography
To use and draw maps and plans at a range of scales.

Resources

A copy of photocopiable page 168 for each child; a selection of maps with reference grids, for example Ordnance Survey maps; flip chart or board.

Vocabulary

coordinates
x-axis, *y*-axis
quadrant

Background

Coordinates and grids play a key role in graph plotting, mapping and navigation. Locations are defined by giving a pair of coordinates with respect to two perpendicular number lines or axes that cross at the origin. The origin is the reference point from which distances along the axes are measured. Children should already be familiar with plotting pairs of positive coordinates in the quadrant above and to the right of the origin. In this lesson, they extend their understanding of coordinates to include locations in the other three quadrants, as illustrated below. The activity is set in the context of mapping an imaginary prehistoric site.

how coordinates can be used to locate a point on a map.

Develop the lesson by explaining that in some applications coordinates can be negative as well as positive. Draw a grid on the board similar to the illustration below with the origin at the centre. Discuss the signs of the coordinates in the four quadrants. Explain that by using this system, coordinates of any point can be given, not just points above and to the right of the origin.

Show the children the worksheet. Explain that it is an imaginary prehistoric site similar to Stonehenge, mapped by archaeologists. The site is roughly circular, so they have decided to locate the origin of their map at the centre. The children's task is to answer the questions by reading and plotting coordinates.

Differentiation

Less able children should concentrate on the first two questions, in which they are required to read coordinates.

More able children can tackle the questions in which they plot points at specified coordinates and identify the shape they define.

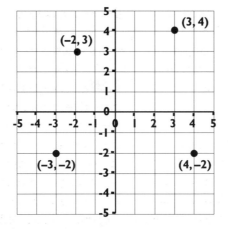

Preparation

Copy and distribute the worksheets.

Main teaching activity

Introduce the lesson by reminding the children of the importance of grids in mapping. Use the maps to demonstrate the

Plenary

Review the answers to the worksheet problems as a class. Conclude the lesson with some quick-fire coordinate questions based on the map grid: *What is located at (–5, 2)?* The answers are:
1. a (3, 2), b (3, –2), c (–3, –2), d (–3, 2)
2. e (0, 4), f (4, 0), g (0, –4), h (–4, 0)
3. an isosceles triangle

Linked to
Art & Design

42 Animated shapes

Objectives

Numeracy
Recognise where a shape will be after two translations.
Recognise where a shape will be after rotation through 90° about one of its vertices.

Art and design
Work on their own and with others in projects in two dimensions at different scales.
Use a range of materials and processes.
Links to QCA Art and Design Unit 6A: People in action.

Resources

Multiple copies of photocopiable page 169 (the flick books work most effectively if the sheet is copied onto thin card. Each book is made with at least five copies of the four grids arranged in sequence to give a minimum of 20 pages); felt-tipped pens, rulers, bulldog clips, scissors; flip chart or board.

Vocabulary

translation
rotation
90°
clockwise
anticlockwise
horizontal
vertical
diagonal
bigger
smaller

Background

An animation is a sequence of still images of shapes and figures in changing positions, shown rapidly one after the other to create the illusion of continuous motion. The principle of animation can be demonstrated with a flick book. In this lesson, children animate shapes, making them move in a straight line (translation), rotate and change size (enlargement or reduction). The activity links to work on space and movement in art and design. Some children may wish to develop the technique to produce animated figures.

Preparation

Copy and distribute the worksheets with the resources.

Main teaching activity

Introduce the lesson by discussing cartoon animations. Do the children know how they are created? Discuss the process as outlined in the 'Background' notes. Develop the topic by sketching a grid on the board and drawing a triangle as illustrated on grid 1 on the worksheet. Explain that you wish to create an animation of the triangle rotating around the ringed vertex. Where will the triangle be when it has turned by 90° clockwise? Ask the children to help you locate it as in grid 2. Where will the triangle be after further 90° rotations? Draw grids 3 and 4 with the children's help.

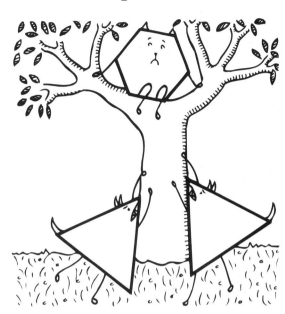

Show the children the worksheets. Explain that the task is to produce animations of moving shapes. They should cut out multiple copies of the frames, and stack them in sequence to make a simple flick book. The book can be held together at one end with a bulldog clip. Flick through the pages of the book to see the shape rotate.

Differentiation

Less able children should concentrate on making the rotating triangle animation.

Challenge more able children to use the blank ends of the grids to produce animations of shapes travelling in straight lines horizontally, vertically or diagonally. Can they animate a shape expanding from the centre of the frame? Children who are particularly interested in the topic may like to explore animation on the computer. Programs such as *Microsoft PowerPoint* enable pages to be displayed rapidly one after another to produce animated movement.

Plenary

Ask children to demonstrate the flick books they have produced. Is the animation smooth or jerky? How could it be made smoother? (By introducing frames showing the shape(s) at intermediate positions.)

43 Internet search

Objectives

Numeracy
To classify quadrilaterals, using criteria such as parallel sides, equal angles, equal sides.
To use mathematical vocabulary and language.

Literacy
To extend vocabulary through working with explanations linked to work from other subjects; reference texts, including ICT sources.

ICT
To work with others to explore a variety of information sources, for example searching the Internet for information.

Builds on QCA ICT Unit 5B: Analysing data and asking questions using complex searches.

Resources

Computers connected to the Internet; flip chart or board.

Vocabulary

quadrilateral
rhombus
parallelogram
trapezium

Background

Appropriate definitions of all the mathematical terms that children need for Key Stage 2, and examples of their use, are available on the Internet, but it can be a challenging task to locate them amongst all the other information that is there! In this lesson, children develop their ICT skills by researching mathematical topics on the World Wide Web. They investigate the 'hits' produced by different search engines when various combinations of key words are entered, then present a report on their findings. A topic with a specialised vocabulary, such as the properties of quadrilaterals, is a good starting point for this type of research activity.

Preparation

Prepare for the lesson by testing your preferred Internet search engines with various relevant key words/questions. The search engine *Google* (www.google.co.uk) for example, produced over 50 000 hits for the word *quadrilateral*. Fortunately, several of those in the top ten were relevant to Key Stage 2. When the search was refined by entering key words 'quadrilateral Key Stage 2 mathematics' the hits were reduced to 162, but fewer relevant to children appeared in the top ten. The search engine *Ask Jeeves*

(www.ask.co.uk) linked directly to a very useful site when the question *What is a quadrilateral?* was entered.

Main teaching activity

Introduce the lesson by listing some quadrilateral words on the board:
quadrilateral
parallelogram
rhombus
trapezium

Explain that the children's task during this lesson is to use the Internet to research the meanings of these words, and to write a brief report on their findings including diagrams and definitions.

Set the children to work in pairs or small groups at computers. Discuss the use of Internet search engines and strategies for searching productively for the information required. If children have not done so before, demonstrate how to copy text and diagrams from web pages for pasting and editing in their personal word-processed reports.

Differentiation

Less able children may need some guidance to locate appropriate websites. Show them how to enter an appropriate question in a search engine such as *Ask Jeeves*.

Challenge more able children to compare the results obtained with various search engines, key words and questions. What strategies can they use to refine their searches?

Plenary

Ask groups to report their findings. Have they located useful information on quadrilaterals? Which search strategy was most productive? Use printouts of children's reports to create a display.

Linked to

I C T

D & T

44 Making spinners

Objectives

Numeracy
Use the language associated with probability to discuss events, including those with equally likely outcomes.

ICT
To learn how to organise and reorganise text and tables.

To work with others to explore a variety of ICT tools.

Links to QCA ICT Unit 6B: Spreadsheet modelling.

Design and technology
To undertake focused practical tasks.

Resources

A copy of photocopiable page 170 for each child; card, glue, scissors, large headless matchsticks or similar; computers running spreadsheet software such as *Microsoft Excel* or *Textease*; flip chart or board; a demonstration spinner, based on the illustration below.

Vocabulary

probability
chance
trial
test
fair
equal chance
uncertain

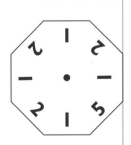

Background

Number spinners are an excellent starting point for introducing the mathematics of probability. A hexagonal spinner is equally likely to land on any one of its six edges. The probability of landing on each edge is thus 1 in 6 or $1/6$. If each edge is labelled with a different number, then the probability of a certain score is also $1/6$. For an octagonal spinner, the probability is $1/8$. If two or more edges have the same score, then the probability of that score is increased, for example for the spinner shown here, the probabilities of scoring 1, 2 or 5 are $4/8 (= 1/2)$, $3/8$ and $1/8$ respectively. These probabilities can be indicated on a probability line. Note that the total probability for any score $= 4/8 + 3/8 + 1/8 = 1$. This is a good check that probabilities have been calculated correctly.

In this lesson, children calculate probability values for scores on a variety of spinners, then use their design, technology and computer skills to make the spinners and test their predictions.

Preparation

Copy and distribute the worksheets with the craft materials. Set up the computers running spreadsheet software. Prepare a demonstration spinner.

Main teaching activity

Introduce the lesson with the demonstration spinner. Remind the children about probability and discuss the probability of the spinner landing on one edge, or of producing a specific score. Draw a probability line on the board and mark the probabilities of the different scores on the line.

Set the children to write the theoretical probability values in the tables on the worksheet.

Review their answers. Explain that they are now going to make the spinners and check their predictions. Set the children to cut out the spinners, back them with card and make spindles with matchsticks.

The children investigate their spinners, recording the scores in repeated trials in a frequency table. Data can be transferred to the computer, and bar charts of different scores plotted. (Also see Lesson 35.)

Differentiation

Ensure that less able children have understood how to predict probabilities for events with equally likely outcomes, and have filled in the tables correctly.

More able children can spend more time on the practical investigations and the interpretation of their results. They should appreciate that, by chance, their experimental probabilities may differ to some extent from their theoretical predictions, particularly if they have only made a small number of trials.

Plenary

Review the answers to the worksheet questions. Discuss the results of the practical tests. If time allows, combine class data to obtain results for a large number of trials. The answers are shown in the tables.

1st spinner	
score	probability
0	$\frac{1}{6}$
1	$\frac{1}{6}$
2	$\frac{1}{6}$
3	$\frac{1}{6}$
4	$\frac{1}{6}$
5	$\frac{1}{6}$

2nd spinner	
score	probability
1	$\frac{1}{2}$
2	$\frac{1}{3}$
3	$\frac{1}{6}$

3rd spinner	
score	probability
1	$\frac{1}{2}$
2	$\frac{3}{8}$
5	$\frac{1}{8}$

Linked to
H i s t o r y

45 Shapes and angles

Objectives

Numeracy
Recognise and estimate angles.
Use a protractor to measure acute and obtuse angles to the nearest degree.
Check that the sum of the angles of a triangle is 180°, for example by measuring and paper-tearing.

History
To study beliefs and achievements in ancient Greece.
Links to QCA History Unit 15: How do we use ancient Greek ideas today?

Resources

A copy of photocopiable page 171 for each child; protractors and pencils; a large demonstration protractor; flip chart or board; a large sheet of paper.

Vocabulary

angle
triangle
degree
protractor
acute
obtuse

Background

The Greek philosopher and mathematician Euclid discovered and taught the mathematics of angles, lines and triangles that we learn in schools today. (See also Year 5, Lesson 11 on page 23.) In this lesson, children use a protractor to measure the angles in triangles and other polygons. They identify acute and obtuse angles, confirm by measurement that the sum of angles of a triangle is 180°, and investigate the internal and external angles of polygons.

Preparation

Copy and distribute the worksheets with the pencils and protractors.

Main teaching activity

Introduce the lesson by reminding children about Euclid and his work. Explain that Euclid was a great mathematician who lived in ancient Greece. He developed the mathematics of geometry – lines, angles, triangles and other shapes. His discoveries are still very important today, for example in architecture, navigation, astronomy and many other branches of science and technology. In today's maths lessons, we learn the same ideas about angles and triangles taught by Euclid to his pupils more than 2000 years ago.

Develop the lesson by drawing a large triangle on a sheet of paper. Explain that the ancient Greeks discovered a rule (or

theorem) about the angles of a triangle. They found that when they measured the three angles and added them together they always obtained the same value. Can the children predict what this value is? Perform the paper-tearing demonstration of the angle sum of a triangle, as illustrated below. Introduce the protractor and remind the children how to use it to measure an angle in degrees. Measure the angles of triangles drawn on the board and calculate their angle sums.

Set the children to work in pairs or small groups on the worksheet activity. They should measure the angles of the triangles, label them as acute or obtuse, and confirm a total of 180° in each case.

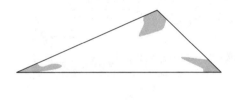

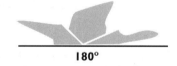

180°

Differentiation

Less able children should work on the first two examples, which involve internal angles of triangles only.

More able children can progress to the final example, which is a more open-ended investigation of the internal angles of other polygons.

Plenary

Review the children's answers to the worksheet problems. You could use the children's work and paper-tearing demonstration as part of a display about Euclid and other Greek thinkers. Conclude the lesson with some rapid mental calculations using addition and subtraction to find unknown angles in triangles.

Linked to
Art&Design

46 Viewpoints

Objectives

Numeracy
Visualise 3-D shapes from 2-D drawings.
Art and design
Be taught about visual elements including form and space.
Links to QCA Art and Design Unit 6C: A sense of place.

Resources

A copy of photocopiable page 172 for each child; plans and designs (for example, architect's drawings showing buildings from different viewpoints; cutaway drawings of models provided with plastic aircraft construction kits; art books containing reproductions of paintings with realistic and impossible viewpoints, such as works by Escher and Picasso).

Vocabulary

shape
cube
two-dimensional
three-dimensional
sketch
draw

Background

Visualising a 3-D structure from a 2-D drawing is a sophisticated mental skill. When we are familiar with the perspective clues provided by a good artist or draftsman we can mentally rotate a drawing of a shape to predict what it would look like from a different point of view. In this lesson, children compare the ways in which designers and artists incorporate 3-D information in their plans, drawings and paintings. They apply the visual vocabulary they learn to problems in which they interpret 2-D drawings of 3-D shapes shown from different viewpoints.

Preparation

Copy and distribute the worksheets.

Main teaching activity

Introduce the lesson by discussing the problem of drawing a 3-D object on a 2-D sheet of paper. Consider some alternatives approaches. Use plans and reproductions in art books to illustrate the key ideas. Architects, for example, illustrate the design of a house from three different viewpoints on the same plan. They show front, side and 'bird's eye' views of the building. Designers and artists who want to give a realistic impression of an object use

perspective. Parts of the object closer to the viewer appear larger and obscure parts behind. Lines that are parallel in reality, for example railway tracks, appear to converge to a vanishing point in the distance.

In the twentieth century, abstract artists realised that photographs could capture realistic images and so decided to concentrate on alternative approaches to art, often with multiple or impossible viewpoints in the same painting. For example, in many works by Picasso heads are painted in profile with both eyes visible. In a realistic profile we see only one eye.

Develop the lesson by showing the children the worksheet. Discuss how the drawings represent three-dimensional stacks of cubes. Explain that the children's task is to visualise and sketch the stacks from different points of view.

Differentiation

Less able children should concentrate on the basic task of interpreting and sketching the shape drawings given on the sheet.

Challenge more able children to make their own sketches of different 3-D shapes from alternative viewpoints.

Plenary

Review the worksheet answers as a class. Have the children sketched the alternative viewpoints suggested? Do the class agree that their sketches show the shapes as they would appear? The answers are:

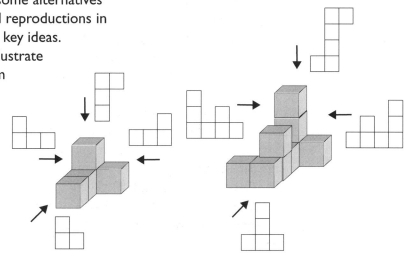

Linked to
S c i e n c e

47 Floating force

Objectives

Numeracy
Record readings from scales to a suitable degree of accuracy.
Science
To learn how to measure forces and identify the direction in which they act.
Links to QCA Science Unit 6E: Forces in action.

Resources

Small plastic lemonade bottles, string, dry sand, water buckets, force meters/newton meters (spring balances); paper and pencils; a plastic ball, a stone.

Vocabulary

measure
scale
difference
reading
table

Background

If you try to push a football under water, you can feel a force called *upthrust* pushing back. The upthrust is the force from the water as gravity tries to return the water to the space from which it was displaced by the ball. Objects that are light for their size float because the upthrust is sufficient to balance their weight. Objects that are heavy for their size sink because the upthrust is insufficient to balance their weight, even when they are totally submerged. Although a heavy object does not float, it is still lighter in water as a result of upthrust. In this lesson, the children measure the weight of objects in and out of water.

Preparation

Assemble the resources and set them out in preparation for practical work.

Main teaching activity

Discuss the forces involved in floating and sinking. The force of gravity pulls a ball towards the Earth. When it is floating on water there must be an opposite force balancing the force of gravity. This is the force from the water, which is called the upthrust. Demonstrate how you can feel the upthrust increase as you try to push a ball under water in a bucket.

Consider an object that sinks, such as a stone. The upward force from the water is not sufficient to balance its weight, so it sinks to the bottom. But is there still an upthrust? Is the stone's apparent weight affected when it is submerged? How do the children predict that the measured weight of an object will

change as it is lowered into water?

Set the children to work in small groups to investigate floating and sinking forces. They should fill small plastic lemonade bottles with sand to act as weights, then suspend the bottles from force meters with string. The weight of the sand-filled bottle should be recorded in newtons. The bottle can then be lowered into water and the new weight recorded. Explain that the upthrust is equal to the difference between the object's weight in air and its weight in water.

Differentiation

Less able children should make the basic measurement for a sand-filled bottle.

Challenge more able children to investigate how the weight in water and the upthrust change as sand is taken out of the bottle to decrease its weight in air. They should record their results in a table like this one.

weight of bottle and sand in air	weight of bottle and sand in water
10N	7.5N
8N	5.5N
6N	3.5N
4N	1.5N
2.5N	0N (just floats)

Plenary

Discuss the children's results as a class. Did the upthrust change when sand was removed from the bottle? What was the weight of the bottle and the upthrust when it just began to float? Suggest that the children weigh a bottle filled with water. How does its weight compare with the weight of a sand bottle that just floats? (The two weights are equal.)

Linked to
Geography

48 Fraction pies

Objectives

Numeracy
Use a fraction as an 'operator' to find fractions.
Express simple fractions as percentages.
Recognise and estimate angles.
Solve a problem by representing and extracting data from pie charts.
Geography
To analyse evidence and draw conclusions.
Could build on QCA Geography Unit 12: Should the high street be closed to traffic?

Resources

A copy of photocopiable page 173 for each child; protractors, calculators; flip chart or board.

Vocabulary

pie chart
angle
fraction
percentage

Transport to school

car 10%   cycle 25%
walk 40%   bus 25%

Background

A pie chart is a way of displaying data that enables percentages or fractions in different groups to be compared with each other and with the whole. A pie chart representing transport to school, for example, shows that $^2/_5$ walk, $^1/_4$ come by bus, $^1/_4$ cycle, and the remaining ($^1/_{10}$) come by car. As children become skilled at estimating angles as fractions or percentages of a circle, these comparisons can be made visually without any need for calculation. However, this is a skill that needs some practice. In this lesson, children interpret and construct pie charts using data from a transport survey and a census. They can apply the technique to represent data from surveys in other areas of the curriculum.

Preparation

Copy and distribute the worksheets with protractors and calculators.

Main teaching activity

Introduce the lesson by reviewing the children's knowledge of the links between fractions and percentages. With the children's help, compile the following list on the board:

$^1/_2 = 50\%$ $^1/_3 = 33\ 1/3\%$ $^1/_4 = 25\%$
$^1/_5 = 20\%$ $^2/_3 = 66\ 2/3\%$ $^3/_4 = 75\%$
$^1/_{10} = 10\%$ $^3/_{10} = 30\%$ and so on.

Develop the lesson by drawing a circle and dividing it into pie slices (segments). Label the angles of the slices and review the

children's knowledge of the connection between fractions of a circle and angles. Use the fractions as operators to multiply 360° to find the corresponding angles.

$^1/_2 \times 360° = 180°$ $^1/_3 \times 360° = 120°$
$^1/_4 \times 360° = 90°$ $^1/_5 \times 360° = 72°$
and so on.

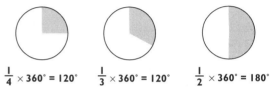

$\frac{1}{4} \times 360° = 120°$ $\frac{1}{3} \times 360° = 120°$ $\frac{1}{2} \times 360° = 180°$

Use the first problem on the worksheet to introduce the concept of a pie chart. Make the link between the angle or size of a slice of the pie and the fraction of a whole.

Set the children to work in pairs or small groups to answer the worksheet problems.

Differentiation

Less able children should solve problems 1 and 2, in which they must interpret existing pie charts.

More able children can proceed to problem 3, in which they must represent the data in the table with a pie chart. They should use their protractors to make sure they have drawn the angles of the slices correctly.

Plenary

Review the answers to the worksheet problems as a class. Conclude the lesson with some quick-fire fraction/percentage of a circle calculations, for example: *What angle is 25% of a circle?* The answers are:
1. car: 2, cycle: 5, bus: 5, walk: 8
2. panda: 20%, dolphin: 25%, giraffe: 5%, elephant: 40%, polar bear: 10%.

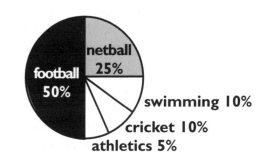

football 50%   netball 25%   swimming 10%   cricket 10%   athletics 5%

Linked to
L i t e r a c y

49 Lucky draw

Objectives

Numeracy
Use the language associated with probability to discuss events, including those with equally likely outcomes.
English
To take part in group discussion, considering alternatives and reaching agreement.

Resources

Sets of eight numbered table tennis balls (or similar) in bags; pencils and paper.

Vocabulary

fair
equally likely
certain
uncertain
chance

Background

Pulling numbered balls from a bag is the standard method for selecting teams to play each other in a sports tournament. It is a fair process because the selection is random – at the outset any team has an equal chance of being drawn against any other team. However, as the draw proceeds the probabilities change. For example, if there are eight teams in the draw, each team has a probability of $1/8$ of being the first out of the bag. The remaining teams then each have a probability of $1/7$ of being drawn to play that team. By the time the draw is down to the last two teams they know they are certain to play each other, but that they have a 50-50 probability of being drawn first and playing at home, or second and playing away.

In this lesson, children develop their understanding of probability by playing a ball-from-bag drawing game in groups. They must agree predictions before the balls are drawn to maximise the points they score.

Preparation

Number the balls and place them in bags ready for team games.

Main teaching activity

Introduce the lesson with a discussion of the probabilities associated with drawing numbered balls from a bag as outlined in the 'Background' notes. Show the children a bag containing eight numbered balls. Ask them to predict the probability of drawing any one number ($1/8$), an even number ($1/2$), a multiple of 4 ($2/8 = 1/4$) or a triangular number ($3/8$) from the bag.

Draw a number and ask how the probability has changed for the next ball to be drawn. For example, if the first ball drawn is 2, the probability of an even number next becomes $3/7$, since there are 3 even numbers in the 7 numbers left.

Set the children to play a game in teams of three or four. Two teams play against each other. One team makes predictions about the next number to the drawn, the other team draws the balls. The predictions allowed are *even number, odd number, prime number, square number*. If the prediction is correct, the team scores a point. If it is not correct, the point goes to the other side. After the last ball is drawn, the points are totalled to find the winner. The teams then swap roles.

The teams should discuss and agree their predictions at each stage as the game proceeds. They may need to make jottings to calculate probabilities. The best strategy is to make the prediction with the maximum probability.

Differentiation

Less able children could restrict their predictions to *even number* or *odd number*.

More able children could develop the game with a greater range of allowed predictions and/or more numbers in the bag.

Plenary

Conclude the lesson with a discussion of the best strategy for winning the game. Is the best strategy always a winning strategy?

50 Assessment 3

Objectives

The assessment activities in this book are designed to introduce Key Stage 2 children to SAT-style questions. They are set in cross-curricular contexts based on the preceding term's lessons. The questions in Assessment 3 test the children's progress in: recognising where a shape will be after rotation by 90° about one of its vertices; plotting coordinates in all four quadrants; interpreting pie charts.

Resources

A copy of photocopiable page 174 for each child; a force meter, a weight (sand-filled bottle or similar), a water bowl.

Preparation

Make copies of the assessment sheet. If you feel that the sheet is too 'busy', the three activities could be separated and enlarged on individual sheets.

Lesson introduction

Begin the assessment lesson by reviewing the relevant cross-curricular topics covered during the term. Remind the children of some of the projects and investigations they have undertaken, and ask them to recall and recount their work. Emphasise the mathematical content, for example: *Do you remember how we displayed the results of our traffic survey as a pie chart?*

Main assessment activity

Distribute the worksheets and ask the children to work on them individually. Guide the whole class through the questions one at a time, reading the text with them, and prompting them to work out and fill in their answers. Try to make the whole activity enjoyable!

Practical activity

Ask the children to predict how the weight of a sand-filled bottle will appear to change as it is lowered into water. Ask them to make and record two readings to check their prediction.

Plenary

Review the answers to the questions as a class. Collect the completed question sheets to use as an aid to judging individual children's progress, and to include in your records. The answers are:

1.

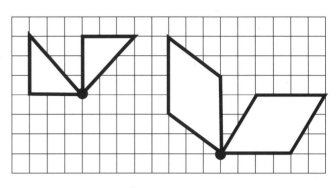

2.

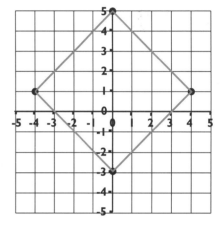

A square

3. red: 12, blue: 9, pink: 1, purple: 2, yellow: 6, green: 6

Hot and cold

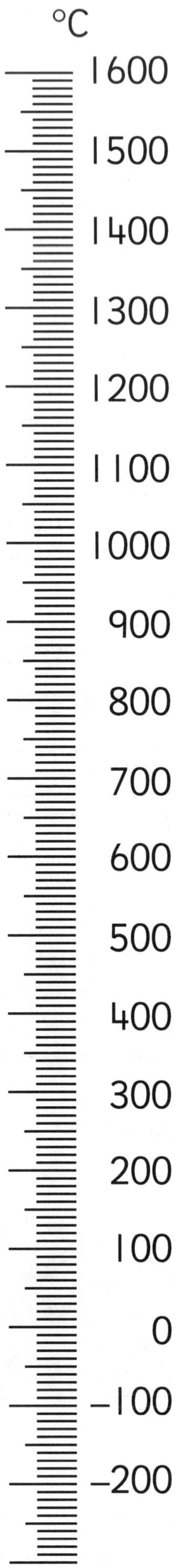

°C

substance	melting temperature/°C
water	0
gold	1064
oxygen	−219
mercury	−39
iron	1540
lead	328

1600
1500
1400
1300
1200
1100
1000

1. Write the substances in order of melting temperature, lowest first.

900

1. _____   4. _____

800

2. _____   5. _____

700

3. _____   6. _____

600

2. Mark the melting temperatures on the scale on the left.

500

3. Calculate the difference between:

400

the melting temperatures of gold and iron

300

_____

200

the melting temperatures of lead and gold

100

_____

0

the melting temperatures of mercury and lead

−100

_____

−200

the melting temperatures of oxygen and mercury

_____

Food pyramids

● Fill in the missing numbers in these food pyramids.

food pyramid	how many does I consume?	multiply up	total in pyramid
fox		I	I fox
frog	I fox eats 100 frogs		frogs
worm	I frog eats 100 worms		worms
leaf	I worm eats 10 leaves		leaves

food pyramid	how many does I consume?	multiply up	total in pyramid
polar bear		I	I polar bear
seal	I polar bear eats 20 seals		seals
large fish	I seal eats 2000 large fish		large fish
small fish	I large fish eats 200		small fish

Can you explain why polar bears and foxes are less common than worms and small fish?

_____

_____

Victorian sums

● Can you do Victorian arithmetic?

Multiplication

1. 234×23

2. 516×17

3. 856×42

4. 731×29

5. 629×67

6. 3451×26

7. 6791×53

8. 5413×126

9. 983×432

10. 5671×373

Division

1. $256 \div 8$

2. $435 \div 12$

3. $561 \div 15$

4. $781 \div 11$

5. $392 \div 18$

6. $4523 \div 20$

7. $5632 \div 16$

8. $7943 \div 25$

9. $9881 \div 13$

10. $8673 \div 19$

● Find the cost of:

1. 3 tons of hay at £24 a ton.

2. 6 cows at £64 each.

3. 13 houses at £564 each.

4. 1 piano, when 6 pianos cost £1500.

5. 1 ship, when 5 ships cost £12 000.

6. 3 yokes of oxen, when 2 yokes cost £450.

7. 15 lots of land, when 8 lots cost £1200.

8. 72 rods of fence, when 10 rods cost £350.

9. 17 dozen chairs, when 8 dozen cost £128.

10. 85 reams of paper, when 6 reams cost £350.

Colour fractions

● Make colour wheels. Colour them using the percentages in the table. What colour do you see when the wheel spins?

colour %	colour seen when spun
R 50% G 50% B 0%	
R 50% G 0% B 50%	
R 0% G 50% B 50%	
R 25% G 75% B 0%	

● Test your own colour percentages.

It's all done with mirrors

- Place two mirrors on the lines.
- Look at the triangle and circle in the mirrors.
- How many reflections can you see?

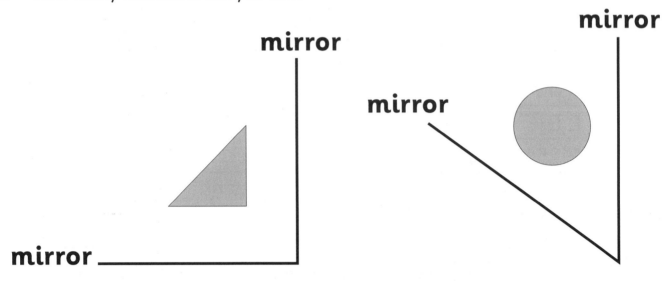

- Draw the reflections of the shapes in the mirrors on the grids.

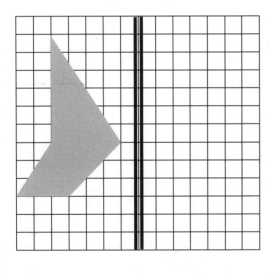
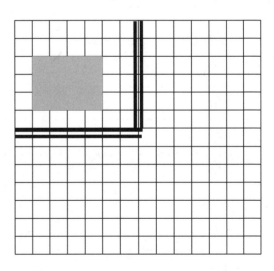

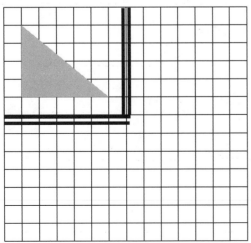
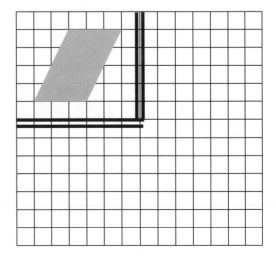

Distance club

● Shane and Sophie belong to a distance club. They keep a record of the distance they walk or run every day.

date	Shane distance in km	Sophie distance in km
1 May	2.0	1.5
2 May	3.0	3.0
3 May	2.5	3.5
4 May	1.0	2.0
5 May	0.0	4.0
6 May	0.0	1.0
7 May	4.5	2.5
8 May	5.0	2.5
9 May	2.5	2.0
10 May	1.0	5.0
11 May	1.0	4.0
12 May	1.5	1.5
13 May	3.0	2.0
14 May	3.5	2.0
15 May	2.0	3.5
16 May	1.5	1.5
Total		

1. Calculate the total distances
Shane and Sophie have covered. _____

2. On what date did Shane receive his 25km certificate? _____

3. On what date did Sophie receive her 25km certificate? _____

4. What is the average distance that
Shane and Sophie cover each day? _____

Building fences

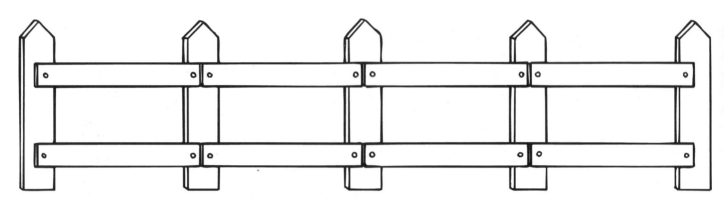

1. Complete this table.

length of fence in metres	number of posts	number of bars	number of nails
1	2	2	4
2	3		
3			
4			
5			

2. Explain in words how to calculate the number of posts, bars and nails for any length of fence.

_____

_____

_____

_____

3. Can you write formulae for the quantities for *n* metres of fence?

length of fence in metres	number of posts	number of bars	number of nails
n			

Discount fares

● Bus and train companies offer discounts on standard fares. Complete these fare tables.

London return, full fare £100

fare type	discount	saving	fare
Standard	–	–	£100
Young person	50%	£50	£50
OAP	25%	£25	
Weekend	10%		
Early booking	20%		
Last minute	75%		
Family rail card	40%		

Paris return, full fare £200

fare type	discount	saving	fare
Standard	–	–	£200
Young person	50%	£100	
OAP	25%	£25	
Weekend	10%		
Early booking	20%		
Last minute	75%		
Family rail card	40%		

Birmingham return, full fare £80

fare type	discount	saving	fare
Standard	–	–	£80
Young person	50%		
OAP	25%		
Weekend	10%		
Early booking	20%		
Last minute	75%		
Family rail card	40%		

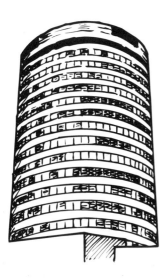

Name

1. The table shows the temperature in four cities on the same day.

°C
40
30
20
10
0
−10
−20

city	temperature in °C
London	5
Moscow	−12
Rome	17
Sydney	35

Mark the temperatures on the scale.

Find the temperature difference between:

Rome and Sydney | Moscow and London

°C | °C

2. Fill in the discount prices on these labels.

Full price £20

Discount 25%

Discount price
£

Full price £8

Discount 20%

Discount price
£

Full price £12

Discount 33%

Discount price
£

Full price £15

Discount 50%

Discount price
£

3. Some children counted the dandelions in a 1 square metre quadrat thrown to random locations on the school field.
Their results for 15 trials were:

2, 4, 3, 4, 4, 0, 1, 2, 3, 2, 2, 3, 5, 1, 0

Find the mode, median and mean for the number of dandelions per square metre.
The field is a rectangle 100m × 50m.
Estimate the total number of dandelions on the field.

Goal average

1. Which team has the best goal average?

team	goals scored	games played	goal average
Rovers	24	12	
United	36	18	
Town	10	10	
City	27	9	
Albion	30	15	
Wanderers	25	10	

2. Which player has the best scoring percentage?

player	goals scored	games played	% scoring record
Smith	16	32	$\frac{16}{32}$ = 50%
Jones	15	20	
Evans	12	30	
Taylor	12	36	
Driver	12	40	
Cooper	9	36	

■SCHOLASTIC

Ideal shapes 1

● Cut out or copy these nets. Fold and glue to make Platonic solids.

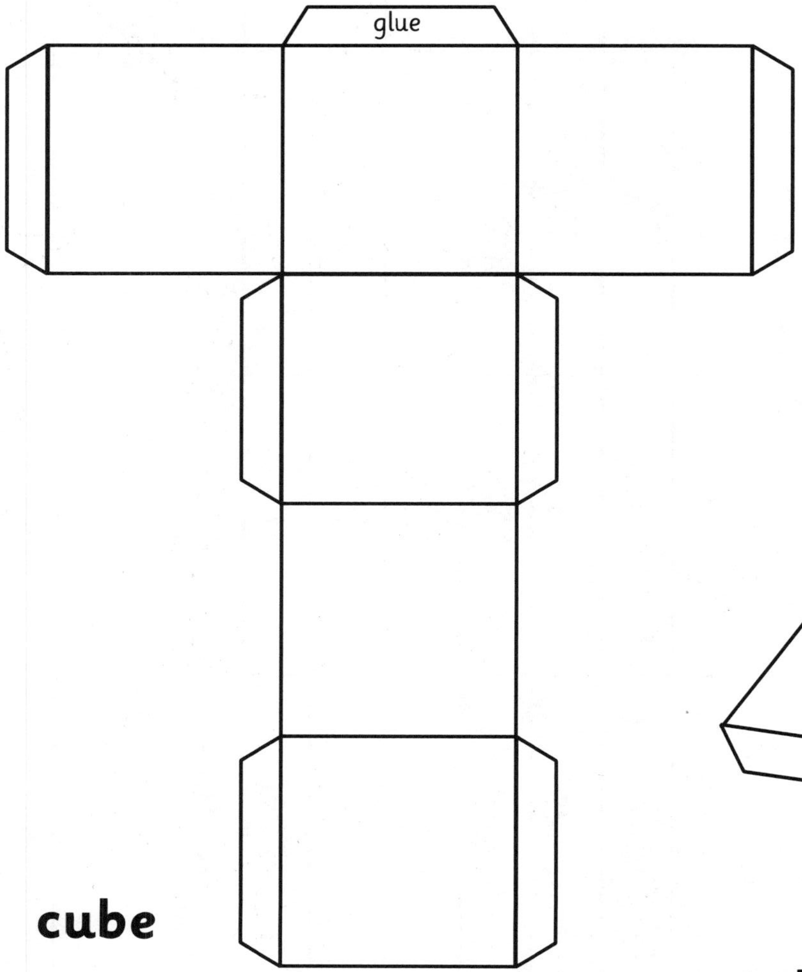

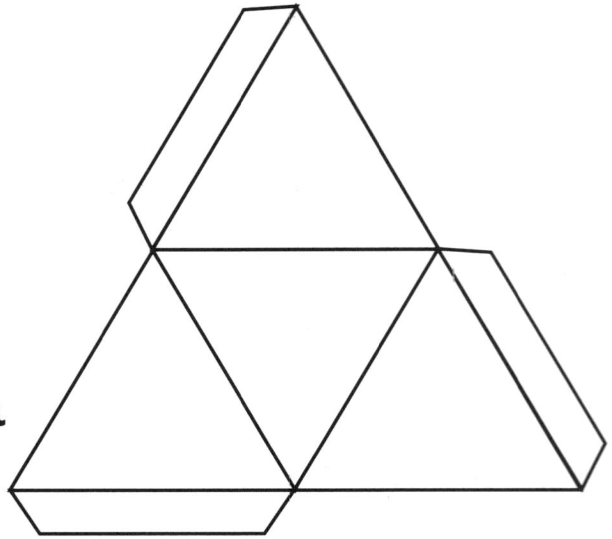

tetrahedron

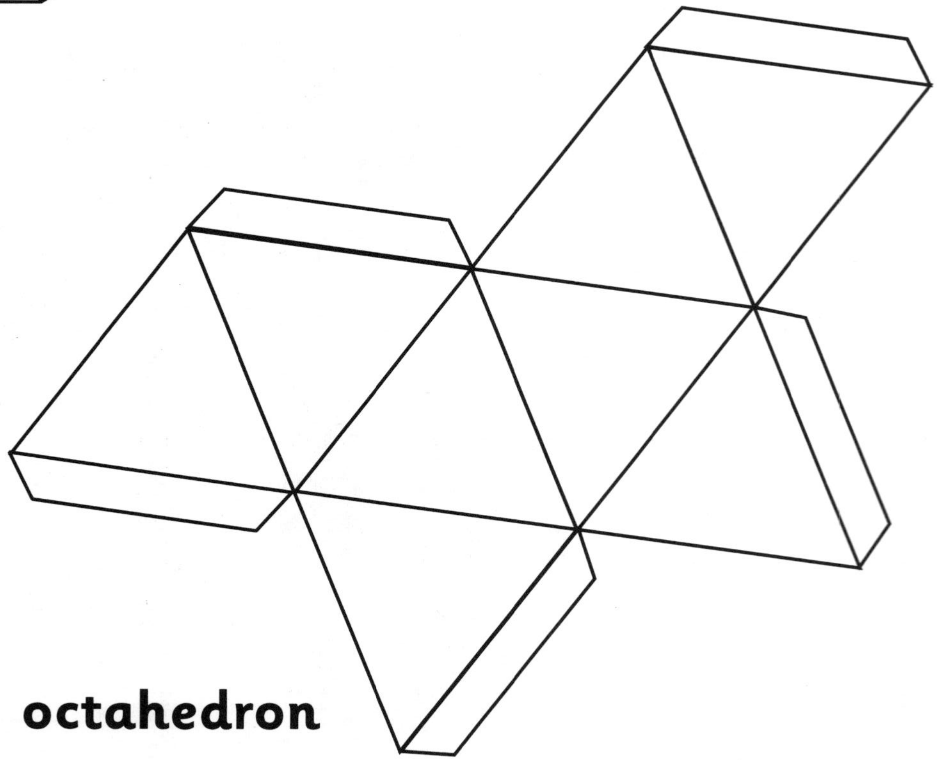

octahedron

glue

cube

Ideal shapes 2

● Cut out or copy these nets. Fold and glue to make Platonic solids.

icosahedron

glue

dodecahedron

◢ SCHOLASTIC

DIY

● The floor tiles chosen for the kitchen and the lounge are different colours.

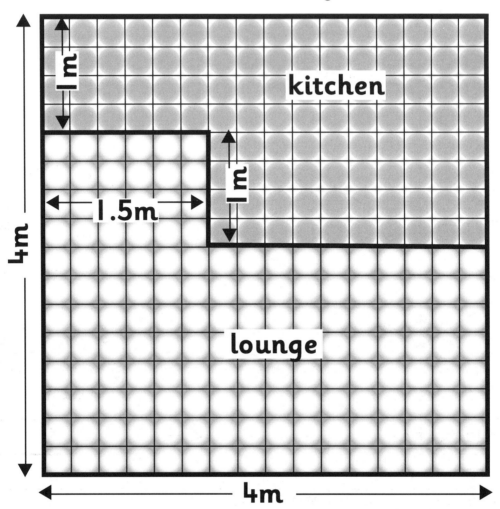

1. Calculate the floor areas of the kitchen and lounge in square metres.

_____

2. Floor tiles come in packs. Each pack covers 1.25 square metres. How many packs are needed for the lounge? How many packs are needed for the kitchen?

_____

3. Calculate the perimeter of the kitchen and the perimeter of the lounge.

_____

4. Skirting board comes in 4m lengths. How many lengths are needed altogether?

_____

Best buys

- Which is the best buy? Fill in the gaps in the tables.
- Rank the products by value: 1 = best buy, 5 = most expensive.

Potatoes

product description	quantity	price	price per kg	rank
new potatoes	1kg	£1.20		
baking potatoes	2kg	£1.80		
washed potatoes	5kg	£4		
small sack	10kg	£7.50		
large sack	20kg	£12		

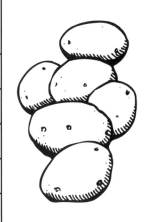

Crisps

product description	quantity	price	price per kg	rank
small packet	30g	45p		
large packet	60g	72p		
family pack	200g	£2		
multi-pack	8 × 30g	£3.36		
pan fried	50g	£1		

Lemonade

product description	quantity	price	price per litre	rank
value lemonade	2 litre bottle	98p		
deluxe lemonade	1 litre bottle	£1.05		
kid's bottle pack	8 × 250ml	£1.60		
single can	500ml	45p		
six-pack	6 × 500ml	£2.40		

Mountain maths

Which route will you take to climb Snowdon?

●   Complete the table to decide.

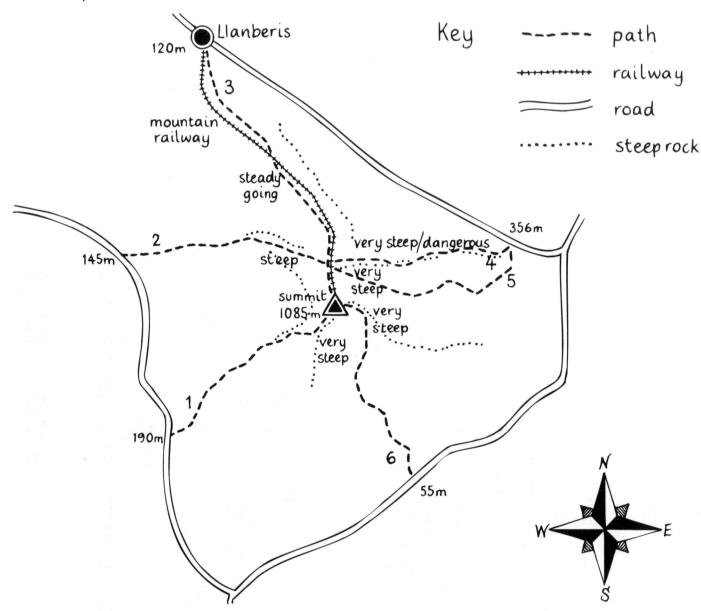

path	name	start height	height gained	description
1.	Rhd-Ddu path	190m	895m	very steep
2.	Ranger path			
3.	Llanberis path			
4.	Crib Goch			
5.	Pyg track			
6.	Watkin path			

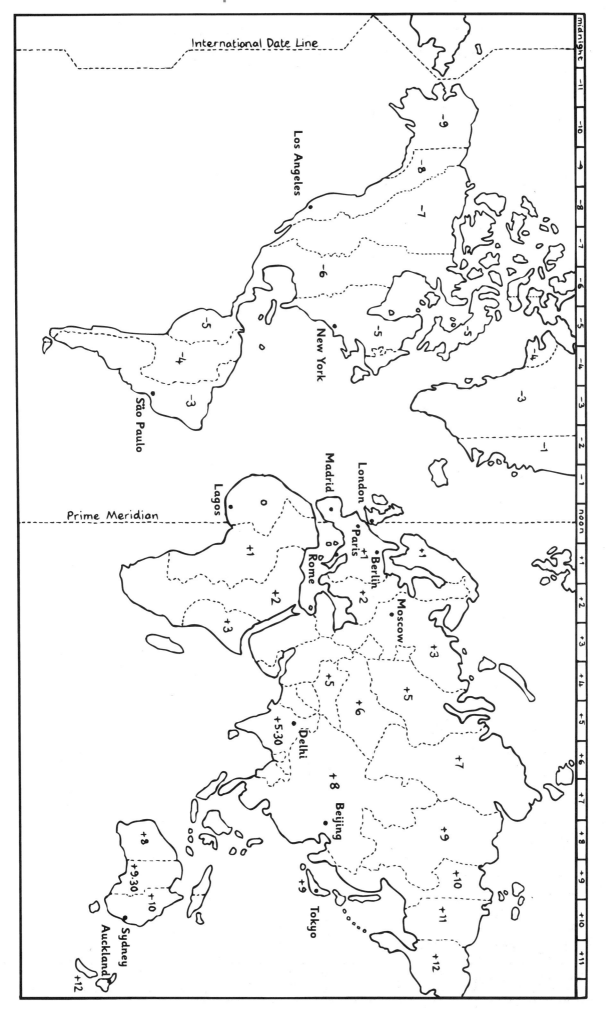

Time zones

Traffic trouble

A sample of 500 people were asked how they travelled to work in a city.
This table gives the result of the survey.

1. Complete the table.

transport	number	fraction	percentage
car	200	$200 \div 500 = \frac{2}{5}$	40%
bus	125		
train	50		
bicycle	20		
motorcycle	25		
walk	80		
Total	500		

2. Altogether 20 000 people travel to work in the city each day.
How many travel using the different modes of transport?
Use the results of the survey to complete this table.

transport	%	number
car	40%	$0.4 \times 20\ 000 = 8000$
bus		
train		
bicycle		
motorcycle		
walk		
Total		

Holiday choice

Sunny Holiday Village
Prices per person in £

month	caravan		chalet		hotel	
	7nts	14nts	7nts	14nts	7nts	14nts
May	90	40	120	190	150	240
June	100	180	130	230	160	280
July	110	200	140	250	170	300
August	130	240	160	290	190	340
September	110	200	140	250	170	300
October	90	140	120	190	150	240

Extras
Sea view £20 per booking per week.
Bike hire £10 per person per week.
Insurance £15 per person per week.

Discounts
Children under 14 half-price.
Early booking 10%.

● Calculate the costs of these holidays:

1. Two adults staying in a chalet with a sea view for 1 week in June.

2. Two adults and two children under 14 staying in a caravan in September for 2 weeks. Two bikes for 2 weeks. Insurance for all 4.

3. Two adults and three children staying in the hotel for 1 week in August. Sea view, 3 bikes, insurance for all 5, early booking discount.

Mathematical crosswords

1. There are 12 shape words hidden in this grid. How many can you find?

s	d	a	r	h	o	m	b	u	s
t	r	a	p	e	z	i	u	m	q
e	r	k	u	p	i	s	c	j	u
r	t	i	y	t	g	p	y	p	a
c	g	t	a	a	j	h	l	y	r
o	i	e	f	g	c	e	i	r	e
n	h	r	d	o	l	r	n	a	d
e	j	s	c	n	v	e	d	m	i
k	o	v	a	l	n	m	e	i	s
c	u	b	e	b	e	s	r	d	c

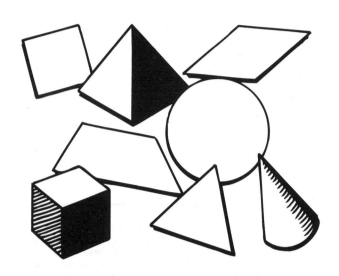

2. Can you solve this crossword puzzle?

Across

1. Next prime number after 5 (5)
4. Most common member of a set of data (4)
6. Third triangular number (3)
7. Three squared (4)
9. Horizontal line of cells on a grid (3)
10. The decimal number (3)

Down

1. The result of adding (3)
2. A number divisible by 2 (4)
3. Has length but no width (4)
5. Greek eight (4)
8. 2-D plan for a 3-D shape (3)

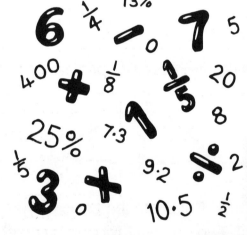

Name

1. Continue these number sequences.
Explain what is special about the numbers in each sequence.

2	4	6			

This is the sequence of _____

1	4	9			

This is the sequence of _____

2	3	5	7		

This is the sequence of _____

2. Find the price per litre of cola. Which is the best buy?

product description	quantity	price	price per litre	rank
value Cola	2 litre bottle	£1.20		
US brand Cola	1.5 litre bottle	£1.35		
kid's bottle pack	10 × 250ml	£2.50		
single can	500ml	45p		
six-pack	6 × 500ml	£2.40		

3. Arrange these simple fractions, decimals and percentages in size order – smallest first.

$$\frac{1}{8} , 20\%, \frac{3}{5}, 75\%, 0.1, \frac{7}{8}, 0.3, \frac{1}{3}, 50\%, \frac{5}{6}$$

Equal fractions

● Write these fractions in their simplest form.
(If the fraction cannot be made any simpler then just repeat it.)

1.

$\frac{1}{4}$ = ☐ $\frac{1}{8}$ = ☐ $\frac{5}{8}$ = ☐

$\frac{2}{4}$ = ☐ $\frac{2}{8}$ = ☐ $\frac{6}{8}$ = ☐

$\frac{3}{4}$ = ☐ $\frac{3}{8}$ = ☐ $\frac{7}{8}$ = ☐

$\frac{4}{4}$ = ☐ $\frac{4}{8}$ = ☐ $\frac{8}{8}$ = ☐

2.

$\frac{2}{6}$ = ☐ $\frac{6}{6}$ = ☐ $\frac{5}{9}$ = ☐ $\frac{3}{12}$ = ☐ $\frac{7}{12}$ = ☐

$\frac{3}{6}$ = ☐ $\frac{2}{9}$ = ☐ $\frac{6}{9}$ = ☐ $\frac{4}{12}$ = ☐ $\frac{8}{12}$ = ☐

$\frac{4}{6}$ = ☐ $\frac{3}{9}$ = ☐ $\frac{7}{9}$ = ☐ $\frac{5}{12}$ = ☐ $\frac{9}{12}$ = ☐

$\frac{5}{6}$ = ☐ $\frac{4}{9}$ = ☐ $\frac{2}{12}$ = ☐ $\frac{6}{12}$ = ☐ $\frac{10}{12}$ = ☐

3.

$\frac{2}{16}$ = ☐ $\frac{10}{16}$ = ☐ $\frac{6}{32}$ = ☐ $\frac{20}{32}$ = ☐

$\frac{4}{16}$ = ☐ $\frac{12}{16}$ = ☐ $\frac{8}{32}$ = ☐ $\frac{24}{32}$ = ☐

$\frac{6}{16}$ = ☐ $\frac{14}{16}$ = ☐ $\frac{12}{32}$ = ☐ $\frac{28}{32}$ = ☐

$\frac{8}{16}$ = ☐ $\frac{4}{32}$ = ☐ $\frac{16}{32}$ = ☐

Changing families

Census data tells us the number of adults and children living in different households in 1891.

head of household	number of adults and children in household	
A Akeroyd	4	
G Allen	5	
F Barrie	8	
C Berry	6	
D Bridgeman	7	
M Brookes	4	
F Cliff	5	
D Coats	9	
R Evans	8	
T Evans	7	
C Grieves	7	
B Harris	5	
L Heard	6	
K Jarvis	11	
B Jones	3	
G Jones	4	
R Jones	7	
S Lee	12	
C North	6	
D Pike	5	
M Rainer	7	

1. Use the spare column in the table to write the numbers in sequence.

2. Find the mode, median and mean numbers of people for the households listed.

3. How do these numbers compare with household numbers today?

Where are you?

● This is an archaeologist's map of a prehistoric site.

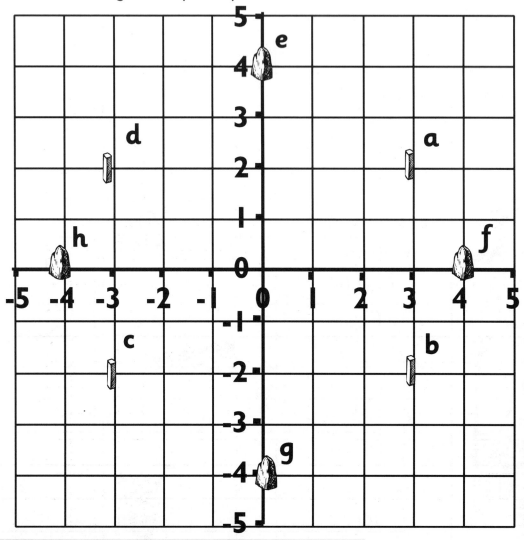

Key Standing stone | Post-hole

1. What are the coordinates of the post-holes? _____

_____

2. What are the coordinates of the standing stones? _____

_____

3. Fallen stones are discovered at (–2,–3), (2,–3) and (0,3).
Plot their positions on the grid.

What shape do they mark out? _____

Animated shapes

- Cut out copies of these grids to make a flick book.
- Can you make the triangle spin around the ring?

1.

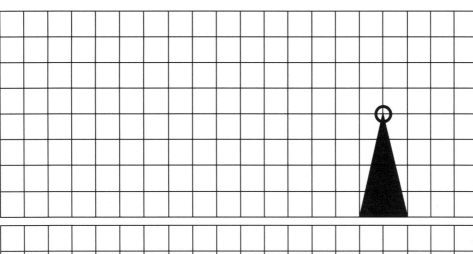

2.

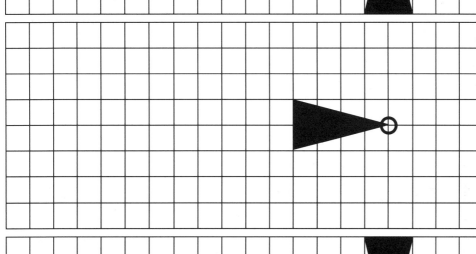

3.

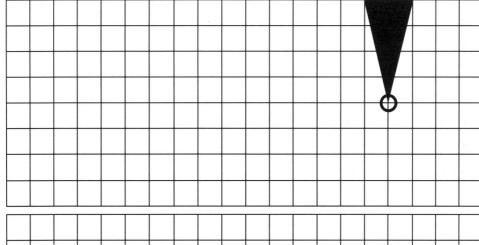

4.

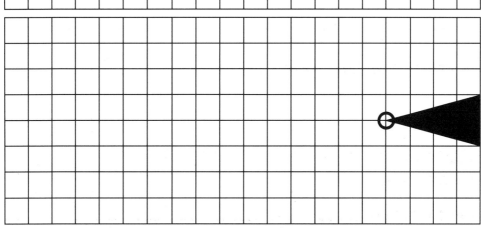

■ S C H O L A S T I C

Making spinners

- Complete the probability tables for these spinners.
- Then make and test them.

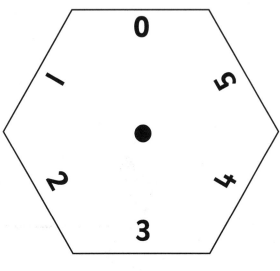

score	probability
0	
1	$\frac{1}{6}$
2	
3	
4	
5	

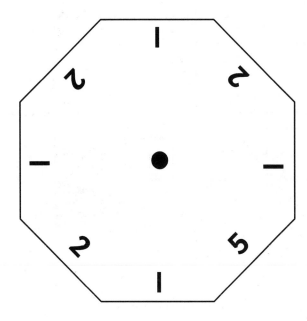

score	probability
1	
2	
3	

score	probability
1	
2	
5	

Shapes and angles

1. Label the angles in these triangles:

| acute = a | obtuse = o | right angle = r |

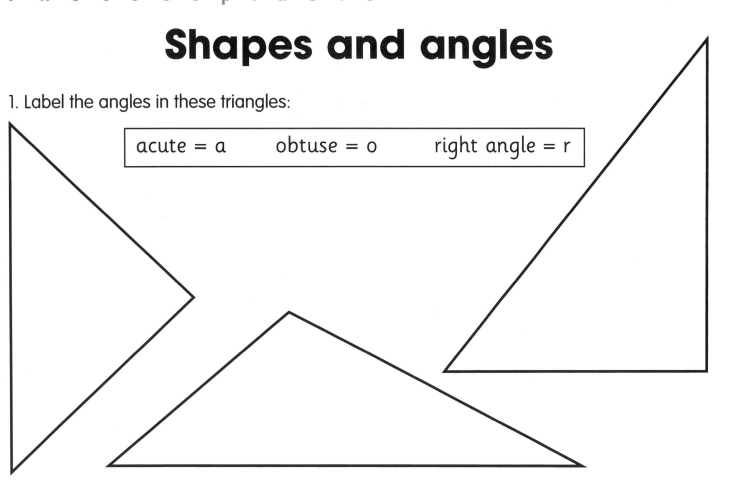

2. Measure the angles. Check that the angles in a triangle always add to 180°.

3. Investigate the sum of the angles in other polygons.
Draw some polygons of your own.

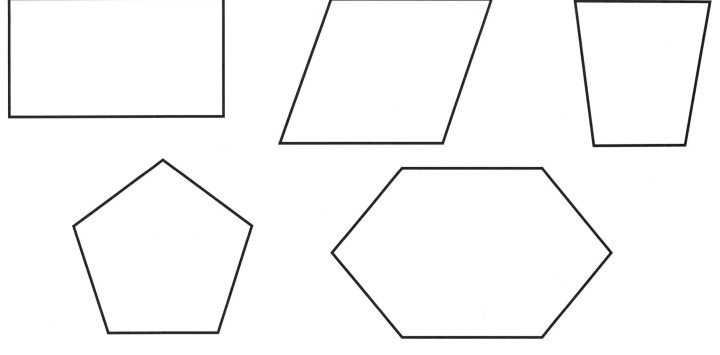

Viewpoints

● Sketch these shapes as they would appear from the viewpoints shown by the arrows. One sketch has been drawn for you.

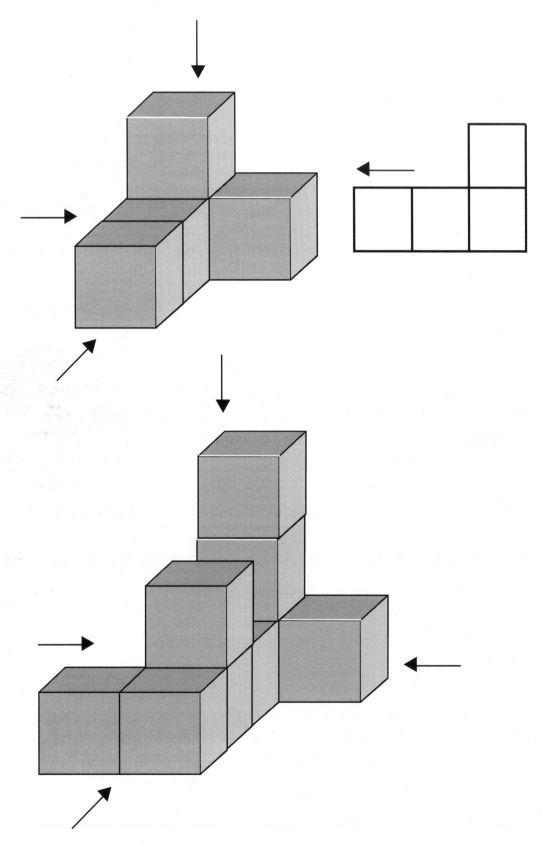

Fraction pies

1. This pie chart shows the results of a school transport survey. Twenty children were surveyed altogether. How many use each of the different forms of transport?

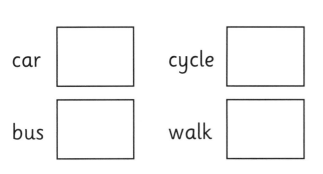

car [ ]   cycle [ ]

bus [ ]   walk [ ]

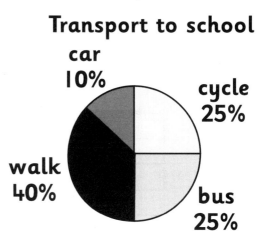

Transport to school

car 10%
cycle 25%
bus 25%
walk 40%

2. This pie chart shows the results of a favourite animal survey. Estimate the percentages choosing the different animals.

panda [ ]   dolphin [ ]

giraffe [ ]   elephant [ ]

polar bear [ ]

Favourite animals

panda
dolphin
giraffe
polar bear
elephant

3. This table gives the results of a survey of favourite sports for 100 children. Display the results on a pie chart.

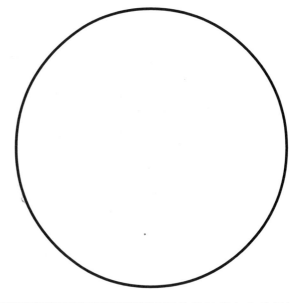

favourite sport	number
athletics	5
netball	25
football	50
swimming	10
cricket	10

Name

1. Rotate the triangle 90° clockwise around the marked vertex.
Rotate the parallelogram 90° anticlockwise around the marked vertex.

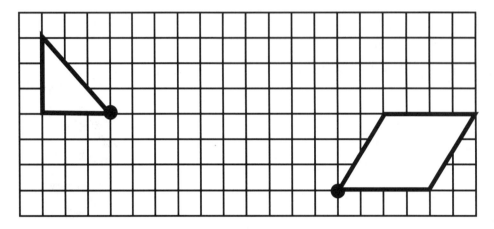

2. Plot points at these coordinates on the grid.

(–4,1) (0,5) (4,1) (0,–3)

Name the shape marked out.

_____

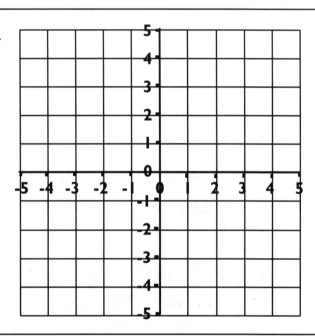

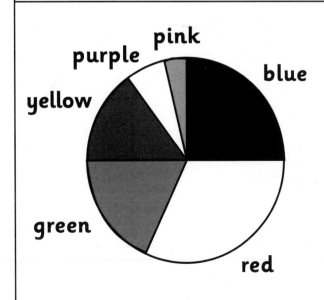

3. This pie chart shows the results of a favourite colour survey. 36 children took part. Estimate the numbers choosing each colour.

red

blue

pink

purple

yellow

green

Numeracy index

Cross-curricular index